Gardening the Mediterranean Way

Gardening the Mediterranean Way

Practical Solutions for Summer-dry Climates

Heidi Gildemeister

With 207 colour illustrations

Thames & Hudson

Contents

Becoming a Mediterranean Gardener   14

A Garden in Harmony with Its Surroundings   38

Mediterranean Dream Gardens
Choosing Your Personal Eden

56

Shade and light, together with the sound of dripping water, evoke a Mediterranean ambience.

Foreword

Shortly after the publication of her first book, *Mediterranean Gardening: A Waterwise Approach*, Heidi Gildemeister was invited to be a keynote speaker at the first *Pacific Horticulture* symposium, "Gardening Under Mediterranean Skies," held in San Francisco in 1998. It was clear that Heidi was serious about her research on mediterranean gardening, and her presentation provided inspiration and practical information for Californians coming to terms with decreasing water resources. A visit to her wonderful garden in the western Mediterranean a year later merely confirmed that here was a gardener who truly understood the opportunities, as well as the constraints of gardening in a winter-wet/summer-dry mediterranean climate.

The appeal of the mediterranean climate cannot be denied. The year-round, outdoor lifestyle is the envy of those in much of the colder parts of the world, and the architecture of the Mediterranean region reflects that penchant for outdoor living. The cuisine, based on garden-fresh fruits and vegetables and locally produced oils and wines, is a model for a healthy and satisfying diet. The colors of the Mediterranean are drawn from nature yet punctuated with a boldness that stands up to the intensely sunny skies. The plants—in the wild and in the garden—add textures, appealing colors, and, particularly, fragrances so characteristic of a mediterranean flora.

With the increasing recognition of the delights inherent in the Mediterranean lifestyle and the expanding populations in regions of the world that enjoy a mediterranean climate (California and parts of Chile, South Africa, and Australia), the paucity of books serving the gardener in those regions becomes apparent. We do have magnificent picture books about the architecture, the cuisine, the gardens, and the colors of the Mediterranean, and we have a few books about the plants commonly grown in mediterranean-climate gardens, including the thorough treatment provided in Heidi's *Mediterranean Gardening: A Waterwise Approach*. Yet few writers have told us how to create a garden that is in harmony with this distinctive and often challenging climate—and none so thoroughly as Heidi has here.

Gardening the Mediterranean Way (a complement to Heidi's earlier book) provides us with the process, the tools, and the techniques for designing, planting, and establishing a garden responsive to the climate. Examples are illustrated from all of the mediterranean-climate regions of the world, and models are set forth for gardeners everywhere, even in regions where only a likeness of a mediterranean-climate garden can be created. Among the twenty gardens presented are those serving a variety of purposes, fitting into a range of natural and human-made settings, and suiting everyone, from the lazy gardener to the enthusiastic plant collector.

In an early issue of *Pacific Horticulture*, the late botanist Mildred Mathias urged her fellow gardeners in California to become as adapted to the climate as the native plants have over the millennia of their evolution. The same could be recommended for gardeners throughout the world's mediterranean-climate regions. Let us learn to garden according to the season, to plant with respect for the limited water resources, and to embrace the annual summer dormancy—perhaps by relaxing in the cool shade of a vine-covered pergola and reading a good book, such as Heidi Gildemeister's brilliant, informative, and enabling *Gardening the Mediterranean Way*.

Richard G Turner Jr.
Editor, *Pacific Horticulture*

Introduction

The moment I finished the text for this book, I promised myself that I would write the preface that very afternoon. But a cheerful garden under the bluest of autumn skies was begging for my attention. As I succumbed, I felt like a student who goes to the fair instead of poring over books, but then it occurred to me (don't we all find excuses?) that it is the garden that teaches me what "gardening" is all about. What new experience would this afternoon bring? Returning to the house before dark, I passed the Algerian iris (*I. unguicularis* 'Alba') with its faintly scented flowers, like lilies of the valley. I looked for information about its scent and found no mention of it anywhere; scent is seldom mentioned in the books, although to me it seems a significant aspect of gardening. I hope that this book will bring out for its readers some (even if only a few) of the really important things in a garden, such as how to connect our dreams with the natural world around us.

When, in the 1970s, my husband and I settled on an island in the western Mediterranean, living conditions there were much as they had been in the nineteenth century—and even long before that, as customs on islands tend to change slowly. When the heat of the day ceased, I could still see olive oil being pressed by the light of a flickering oil lamp as the press was turned by a blindfolded donkey. Even today, the shepherd ties parsley from the orchard with a blade of grass; waste is certainly a modern invention. I am grateful for these experiences and hope to have brought a whiff of the ancient Mediterranean traditions into this book.

Under summer-dry Mediterranean conditions, it was impossible to plant what I longed for—the tropical paradise of the South American garden I had left behind. Although English-style gardens were still fashionable, our scarce water supply induced me to create my Eden with what was available and what

grew wild. A four-hectare (ten-acre) natural, water-saving Mediterranean garden evolved, and the seasons that rule plant life became my teacher. I got to know the available plants more intimately and learned about their likes and dislikes, as one does with a friend. A friendship enduring over time differs from that of a recent acquaintance, and I cherish those plants that have proved their worth over the years.

"Why stop," I thought, "at the borders of the Mediterranean Basin if there is so much to be explored beyond?" My countless trips to many different regions as then-president of the Mediterranean Garden Society gave me the opportunity to explore the five mediterranean-climate zones in the world and the fascinating range of their plants. I made enjoyable and valuable contacts with gardeners in these areas, and they made me realize that we share not only a similar climate but also the same concerns, and that we can learn much from each other.

Until a well-known California garden journal published my article "My Mediterranean Garden" in 1997, the concept of "Mediterranean" was believed to apply exclusively to the Mediterranean Basin. Californian gardeners, I was told, felt that they gardened in a "summer-dry climate," but this definition did not take into account their mild winter and the rain it brings. Couldn't the phrase "summer-dry climate" apply equally to a desert climate with chillier nights and colder winters than those of a mediterranean climate? Once it was realized that the mild, humid winters of the mediterranean climate bring ready-made help to water-stressed gardens, I knew that gardeners in all mediterranean-climate regions would take advantage of a climate that does the watering for them. And today, these water-wise mediterranean gardens are fashionable.

In my first book, *Mediterranean Gardening: A Water-wise Approach* (see Bibliography), I discussed water-saving practices and included a thousand drought-tolerant plants from mediterranean-climate regions. Once the book had appeared in its sixth language, I was encouraged to write about designing Mediterranean gardens. Plants and landscaping with them have always been the focus of my gardening efforts, and they are the basis for the twenty garden projects that make up the present volume. Conservation has also been much on my mind, and equally important is the achieving of harmony, which is for me a sure way to happiness. May it work likewise for my readers.

How to Use This Book. Most gardeners will quite likely skip the first two chapters and plunge directly into the text to select their favorite kind of garden. But one day you will want to know how plants are influenced by the climate or what exactly is the meaning of "invasive," and that is when you will go back to Chapter 1.

Few of us are disciplined plant buyers. Who, after all, is not tempted by the colorful spring display at the nursery? We load the trunk of our car and, once we get home, we impatiently adorn the bare ground. When autumn is over and the brilliant display has drained away, we feel that something is missing. What was our intention? What have we done to enhance the glorious view for which the agent made us pay a higher price? And did those cheerful flowers really conceal the ghastly buildings that are creeping up on us on the horizon? We wonder and slowly turn back the pages to Chapter 2.

Gardeners who live under a Mediterranean sky and work in harmony with their surroundings make a valuable investment in the living green mantle of Earth which sustains all life by providing shelter, food, and even the very air we breathe. Gardening the mediterranean way exploits the benefits of a mediterranean climate by taking advantage of water-conserving plants that withstand the long, hot summers. When planted in autumn, they become established over winter, watered by the beneficial winter rains. In the summer that follows,

many are able to manage on their own, helped by sharp drainage and ample mulch, while a few may still need weekly water to survive the hottest summer months. The wide range of drought-tolerant plants encourages us to choose the right one for each site. A novice gardener is thus saved from the desperate wail, "Everything I plant dies!"

The inspirational garden projects of all styles and sizes described in this book will suit all readers and the surroundings they encounter when setting out. Most projects not only offer the design and plant choices for a given site, but also its challenges, such as pollution in a city garden or erosion and frost in a hill garden, so I have included methods for tackling these problems.

You will note that, in keeping with current garden-writing practice, the word "Mediterranean" when capitalized refers to the Mediterranean Basin or Sea and the areas around it. When the word is not capitalized, "mediterranean" refers to a type of climate, the vegetation, and gardens responding to that climate, wherever they might be.

What Is a Mediterranean Garden? For that matter, what is an Australian mediterranean garden? Setting aside fashion and style, the answer is that mediterranean gardens are those ruled by the climate for which mild, humid winters and long, hot, and dry summers set a clear parameter. No untimely watering will awaken a summer-dormant garden that lives with the mediterranean climate.

Many American gardens adhere to the Zone ratings devised by the United States Department of Agriculture, in order to determine what is considered suitably hardy for their area. According to these ratings, I would appear to garden in zone 10, which means an annual minimum temperature of 30 to 40° Fahrenheit (-1 to +4° Celsius). Yet the wind-exposed lie of our land has little winter sun, and with the same minimum temperature but a warmer exposure, I could have grown a much wider range of plants. Since I am not inclined to yield to limitations,

The natural countryside, once it has been cleaned up, can be of great beauty. In the foreground is *Euphorbia dendroides* in its summer-dormant state.

I have always tried out whatever I felt could thrive, and I am prepared to accept the losses that may occur. I have also made startling discoveries along the way. Many plants that were said to require wintering under glass did well in the open when planted in the garden's warmest spot. What can be grown in your garden depends much on the conditions you can offer the plants—the quality of the soil and its depth, drainage, wind protection, and whether they were carefully planted. However, as a general guideline, most plants in this book can tolerate a short-lived frost. So that this book can be used in both the Northern and the Southern Hemispheres, the text refers to seasons, not to months.

Plant Lists. The plants for each garden project are compiled in a list at the end of each proposal. Drought-tolerant plants from the Mediterranean Basin are at the forefront; these are the plants that gardeners from other mediterranean-climate regions want to know about. Species that are particularly sturdy and useful are mentioned in several of the garden proposals. Additionally, the other four mediterranean-climate regions in the world have thousands of plants, many of which are included in this book; you will undoubtedly be aware of others that are not listed here. My intention was to provide a generous fare, yet there is no end to the information that would be useful to gardeners in different areas. This is why we cherish our botanical library, whatever its size, or turn to various Web sites (see Addresses,

A rock rose (*Cistus ladanifer*)

the book all those plants native to a mediterranean-climate region that are potentially invasive in other regions. The result was disappointing: too many plants can turn invasive *somewhere* around the world if they only find the right location, and flagging them all would have been more confusing than helpful. Keep in mind that most plants can be managed successfully with a bit of attention, so that we do not have to forego the pleasure of growing them. However, the potentially invasive plants have been listed, separately for each continent, in Chapter 1 (page 33). Familiarize yourself with them, use the lists freely, and you will soon get a feel for the baddies.

Common Plant Names vary from one region to another, while botanical (scientific) names are like a lingua franca that can be understood by all. Is it really more difficult to remember *Bauhinia* than Pride of de Kaap? Many botanical names are quite easy to memorize; to overcome the initial barrier, why not begin with these? To please all readers, botanical names are preceded throughout by their common names as long as these are in general usage (and are known to me). Are you looking for the botanical name of that rengarenga you want to buy? You will find the common names listed alphabetically in the index, followed by the botanical names (in this case *Arthropodium*). Do you want to know more about rengarenga? Look up *Arthropodium* and you will find the page where it is mentioned.

A Cautionary Note. Mediterranean gardeners realize that books written for northern gardens apply only partially to mediterranean conditions but can be useful if appropriate adjustments are made. Northern gardens endure long, cold winters and frozen ground (in contrast to frost in the Mediterranean, which, if it does occur, is normally short-lived). In summer, the higher air humidity in the North contrasts sharply with month-long mediterranean drought and dry air. Rain is not necessarily more abundant than in the Mediterranean Basin but is usually better distributed

page 207). If we cannot access them ourselves, a friend or family member may be able to get us the information we need.

Invasiveness. A potential downside of bringing together plants from similar ecological habitats is invasiveness. My initial idea was to flag throughout

throughout the year. In addition, hours of sunshine in Washington or London, for instance, are fewer and less stressful than mediterranean averages, and even if northern regions experience drought, solar radiation is less intense than under mediterranean skies, which are closer to the equator.

Because of these conditions, gardeners using this book should take note of the following:

• In the warmer mediterranean climate, many plants listed as deciduous remain evergreen (which influences your choice of plants).

• Flowering happens earlier. The lilac (*Syringa microphylla* 'Superba'), for instance, flowers in the winter.

• Mediterranean regions require that exposure recommendations be adjusted. For example, a plant that requires full sun in colder climates may require dappled shade in the mediterranean climate, and a recommended south-facing wall could be fatal for tender plants if they are exposed to mediterranean heat.

• In mediterranean regions, bulb-lifting (appropriate where frost lasts) is detrimental. Mediterranean bulbs start new growth with the first autumn rains; they build up foliage over winter and many flower as early as late winter while others wait until spring.

• Verify carefully whenever summer irrigation is recommended. Many drought-tolerant mediterranean plants are intolerant of summer water and decline if exposed to yearly summer irrigation (for example, mastic, or *Pistacia lentiscus*). Fungal disease often occurs where summer water is applied (see Saving an Oak Woodland, page 102).

• Verify the recommended plant choice. Many species, such as tall thistles, often used in northern gardens, are considered serious weeds in mediterranean regions.

• Mediterranean vegetation tolerates more cold than is generally assumed. This is particularly true if these plants have excellent drainage, good aeration, generous mulch, and a site that suits them.

These preliminary thoughts, which will be discussed in greater detail in the pages that follow, are offered here to tempt and inspire all gardeners blessed with a mediterranean climate into exploring the possibilities of this very special environment. So let's get started!

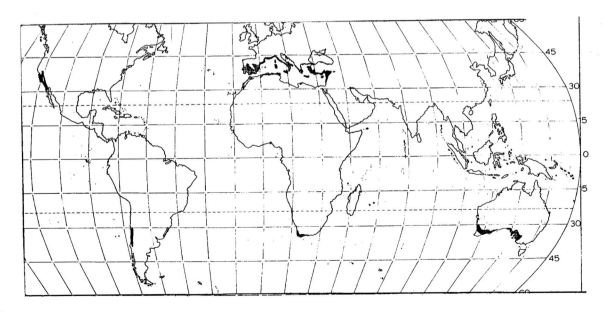

World map showing mediterranean-climate regions (from Di Castri, *Ecosystems of the World*)

Becoming a
Mediterranean Gardener

An almond tree (*Prunus dulcis*) in spring

Gardens have been made in the Mediterranean area for thousands of years, and in this first chapter we will learn about gardens ranging from Roman pleasure grounds to nineteenth-century examples. In all eras, Mediterranean gardens have been dependent upon—and suited to—the mediterranean climate, which will be described below in detail, along with the regions of the world where it prevails. Native plants and endemic plants will be noted, as well as the ways in which these plants are adapted to the climate. The first part of this chapter ends with a discussion of plant conservation and of the dangers posed by invasive species.

Next we will analyze the practical tools at the disposal of the Mediterranean gardener—not forks and spades, but rather the use of shade and of winter rains, and how to choose plants that will provide year-round interest and beauty—important points to be borne in mind when creating a water-wise garden. This section ends with a short questionnaire to help gardeners understand the conditions that prevail in their own gardens.

Going Back in Time

Lawrence Durrell, who spent his youth on the Greek islands and his old age in Provence, sees the olive as the synthesis of what it means to be Mediterranean. "The whole Mediterranean—the philosophers, the sculptures, the gold beads, the bearded heroes, the ships, the moonlight, the wine, the palms—all of it seems to rise in the pungent taste of black olives between the teeth. A taste older than meat, older than wine. A taste as old as cold water" (from "Landscape with Olive Trees," *Prospero's Cell* [London, 1975]).

The Mediterranean Basin, inhabited for more than eight thousand years, has been a source of inspiration for generations of gardeners. If we go back in history, we can see that, by Greek and Roman times, gardens functioned as a central focus of human society. Stone, water, and formal lines played a major role in the Roman pleasure garden, which used columns, porches, and porticoes, together with statues and vases. Plants too were employed as building material, for the sake of their reflection in water, for instance, or to provide a perspective against formal walls created by rows of trees or shrubs.

The elaborate Tuscan villa built by Pliny the Younger at the foot of the Apennines served as a model for makers of the great Renaissance gardens in Europe. Pliny's garden offered both running water and cool shade. Water ran through the garden in pipes and reappeared as fountains, cascades, or jets to be caught in marble basins. Cold and hot baths were part of the house, which was extended by pergolas and porticos, by terraces and stairways, all liberally adorned with statues and vases. The garden was constructed on a symmetrical plan, divided by straight, shady paths and encircled by walls. Plant growth, carefully tended, was exuberant and often pruned into delightful shapes, although the choice of plant types was limited.

A collection of historic artifacts in a Greek courtyard

The Romans used the soil efficiently and only later on separated the pleasure garden from the utilitarian *hortus* devoted to fruits and vegetables. By the first century A.D., however, inspired by the Greeks, Romans filled their courtyards with formal paths, vases, frescoes, and water features and included plants for their decorative value, often in containers or clipped into ornamental shapes called topiary. The same approach was adopted along the southern coast of the Mediterranean Sea.

The Moorish garden, a descendant of the gardens of ancient Persia, reached its culmination in Spain in the thirteenth-century gardens of the Alhambra, in which stone, water, and formal walls created by rows of cypress or trimmed shrubs, often reflected in water, were given a primary role. These gardens featured cisterns, springs, pipes, and canal systems to catch, guide, and distribute the water. Water was in short supply, and what was available was managed with care; taxes were even imposed on the basis of the benefits obtained from its use. Moorish gardens with some of these features can still be found today in India and North Africa, as well as in southern Spain. These oasislike gardens were characterized by water to reflect heaven in an earthly paradise and by cool shade, scent, fruit, and bird-

The author's garden in Spain

tively limited range of plants—were the main elements.

After the discovery of the New World, plants from the four corners of the globe progressively enriched Mediterranean gardens. As early as 1576, Carolus Clusius of the Leiden Botanic Garden in the Netherlands first saw the statuesque *Agave attenuata*, a native of Mexico, in a Spanish monastery. Gardeners in Europe noted that succulents traveled well and often revived after having been left without soil for weeks, which made them ideal early introductions for European gardens.

During the second half of the nineteenth century, a growing awareness of the plant world's diversity forged a new trend. Formal lines, symmetry, and bedding no longer satisfied gardeners and a "natural" style evolved. This style was often introduced by gardeners trained in northern Europe who brought their experience and ideas to mediterranean regions. Its culmination could be seen in the creation of private gardens in Spain, France, Australia, California, and South Africa. These gardens relied on the wealth of the world's plants, together with native plants from the area in which the garden was located; all found a place in the new setting. Splendid examples, such as the Hanbury Gardens on the Italian Riviera, the Huntington Gardens in California, and Marimurta on the Costa Brava in Spain, have survived to this day.

Mediterranean gardens are still enriched by historic garden styles, but gardeners today feel a strong urge to do their own thing, and ecological concerns are now essential frames of reference. The garden world today is rich in historical references, in both design and style, and with the diversified use of plant material, it will to an increasing degree find expression in a self-sustaining and ecologically correct environment.

song—the essence of the paradise garden described in the Koran and in the book of Genesis.

The enclosed gardens of medieval Europe were created in walled feudal castles and in monasteries. Agriculture was of great importance to these self-sustaining institutions, especially the monasteries, where monks preserved the knowledge of horticulture and plant lore along with religious and classical texts. It was here that many of the medicinal and spice plants characteristic of the Mediterranean flora found their way into cultivation. Every monastery had its medicinal herb garden for tending the sick.

With the reawakening of man's curiosity about the natural world during the Renaissance, gardens were transformed into magnificent schemes of water, topiary, and elaborate decoration. In this age of relative wealth, gardens were labor-intensive and often reflected the power of their creators. These gardens tended to deteriorate when conditions changed. But they would eventually inspire a school of garden design in southern Europe and California, where stone, formal lines, and symmetry—and a rela-

What Is a Mediterranean Climate?

It is generally accepted that the mediterranean climate occurs in southern and southwestern Australia, central Chile, coastal California, the western cape of South Africa, and around the Mediterranean Basin (see map on page 13). The largest area with a mediterranean climate is the Mediterranean Basin, which has given the climate its name, although stretches of the Mediterranean coast (in Egypt, Libya, and part of Tunisia) are too dry to be thus classified. More than half of the total mediterranean-climate regions on earth occur on the Mediterranean Sea.

Mediterranean-climate regions are found, roughly speaking, between 31 and 40° latitude north and south of the equator, on the western side of the continents. Yet they can extend eastward for thousands of kilometers into arid regions if not arrested by mountains or confronted with moist climates, such as the summer rainfall that occurs in certain regions of Australia and South Africa. The most extended eastward penetration goes from the Mediterranean Basin up into western Pakistan and into some zones of Turkmenistan and Uzbekistan (the source of many of our cherished bulbous plants).

In contrast, the mediterranean areas of California and Chile are constricted toward the east by mountains close to the Pacific coast. This is not the case, however, for Australia and South Africa, where monsoon troughs may bring summer rainstorms. In fact, the mediterranean regions of both Australia and South Africa have important but unpredictable rainfall in summer, a factor that has a significant effect on their vegetation.

The seasonality of the mediterranean climate differs profoundly from that of latitudes to the north or south. Writers, especially those from the north, tend to rave about such attractive features of the climate as "one continuous summer," "an ever-blue sky," or "everlasting sun." But those who live near the Mediterranean Sea know that these descriptions are not really accurate.

Mastic (*Pistacia lentiscus*) is one of the most useful plants for a summer-dry garden. Its evergreen foliage thrives in midsummer when most other plants are not at their best.

In most mediterranean regions, climatic changes are pronounced. It is in the autumn—after summer drought and dormancy—that the yearly life cycle of plants starts anew, like the awakening in spring that follows winter dormancy in the north. As I write, in late autumn, the day is radiant and warm, and garden work is a joy. "Such a nice autumn," I say to the farmer, who replies, "Si, es el veranillo de San Martin" (Yes, it is the little summer of Saint Martin, November 11). This "little summer" is known to last just a few days, attesting to the variability of the mediterranean climate.

In winter, periods of rain alternate with warm, sunny days. We know that after three days of howling winds, during which one closes all windows, turns inward, and appreciates the solid walls of one's house, one can again expect mild, sunny days.

Later, the splendid spring display is brought to an abrupt end by hot, dry winds and rising temperatures, which cause seeds to ripen and disperse. When the glorified "continuous summer" arrives, it is painfully long, so that plants retire into dormancy, making us believe they are about to die. Indeed, **a long, hot, dry summer is required by most mediterranean bulbs if they are to go dormant and ripen in the dry ground.** But that summer must be preceded by a cool season (winter and spring) with soft rains that let bulbs grow and sprout, so that their juicy stems and shiny foliage can develop in a humid soil before their jubilant spring display. These contrasts are characteristic of the mediterranean climate.

The irregularity of the rainfall, which can vary

At the end of summer a leafless *Urginea maritima* pushes out of completely dry ground.

The rock rose (*Cistus ladanifer*) covers the ground under pine trees.

considerably from year to year, accentuates the severity of the mediterranean climate. Rain does not fall evenly. Generally speaking, you can register more rain in the north than in the south, more in the west than in the east of a continent. Nor does rain arrive yearly at the same time or within the same intervals. At Gibraltar, for instance, rain starts falling nearly half a season earlier than at the Dead Sea. In the Holy Land, no rain at all falls in summer but early rains may come in autumn—manna to the arid soil and parched riverbeds—though it is not until the winter rains that the basins fill.

This same variability is true for temperatures. In winter, the thermometer may fall to zero degrees Celsius and may even bring a short-lived frost (see A Garden in the Hills, page 138), yet these temperatures depend a lot on the location of your house. In a hill garden, the clouds will hang low over the mountains, but on the coast in a protected corner you may enjoy the cherished winter sun. Mediterranean gardeners are grateful for their mild winters—mild enough for garden work to be an ongoing activity.

Laurustinus (*Viburnum tinus*) adorns a sparse olive tree with its abundant winter bloom.

For the benefit of those gardeners who like statistics, the mediterranean climate can be characterized further. Although, in a nutshell, it can be called a "winter-wet and summer-dry climate," scientists define it by the following criteria:

• mild to warm or hot summers
• intensive solar radiation, especially in summer
• cool to cold winters
• concentration of rainfall in winter with occasional downpours
• high variability of precipitation from year to year
• frequent marine fog and high humidity along the western coast of the continents where a mediterranean climate typically occurs.

Keep in mind, however, that if there is no summer drought, a region with predominantly winter rainfall does not of itself qualify as a mediterranean climate.

Another widely accepted and easily remembered theory holds that only those regions where olive trees grow can be considered truly mediterranean. However, according to Oleg Polunin and Anthony Huxley, authors of *Flowers of the Mediterranean* (see Bibliography), "the main objections to using the olive as an indicator are that it is probably not a native of the Mediterranean Basin but is a cultivated plant of eastern origin. Others have suggested the holm oak as a truer wild indicator plant, but it has a markedly western distribution. However, wherever one sees the olive, holm oak, the kermes oak, or the Aleppo pine growing, and particularly where any two of these are growing together, one can be pretty certain that one is in a mediterranean climate."

Native Mediterranean Plants

"What are these native plants you are always raving about?" a nurseryman once asked me, to which I could have replied: "Native plants are those that grew in this area before the circum-navigation of continents started in the sixteenth century." Sailors to Australia, North and South America, and South Africa brought back unfamiliar plants and intro-duced them, usually by seed, to the lands from which they had set out on their explorations. Even as early as the thirteenth century, Marco Polo traveled from his native Venice across Asia and brought back exotic seeds and bulbs to the Mediterranean. Many fruit trees, such as cherry and peach, were also introduced to the Mediterranean in early times from North Africa and Asia Minor. (See the section on invasive plants, page 30.)

One might also ask this question: **"Which plants are exotics?"** Certainly these are not the same species for every gardener the world over. Large-leaved plants with glorious flowers might qualify as exotic in the north, such as those requiring abundant water and a well-heated conservatory, whereas an alpine flower or a northern pine might seem exotic in a southern climate. To find out for sure, I consulted a dictionary to find that "exotic" refers not only to animals and plants but also to people who originate in a foreign country, especially one in the tropics. "Exotic" also means "not native" and having a "strange or bizarre allure, beauty, or quality." "Native" or "auto-chthonous" plants, on the other hand, are indigenous inhabitants of a country, those that originate or occur naturally in an area; "endemic" species occur naturally in one locality only and nowhere else. For one plant, this can mean an island, for another not more than a small patch on a field.

A native Mediterranean plant is one that originates in areas around the Mediterranean Basin, although a native of Australia's mediterranean-climate zone, such as the grevillea, could equally be called a mediterranean native. In a case such as this, it is important to indicate *which* mediterranean-climate region is meant, for we are all a bit possessive about our plants, the plants from our own region, and would want them to be described correctly.

To find out which were the early native plants in the Mediterranean Basin, we look for sources in myth-ology, history, religious writings, travelogues, and works of art. In Greek mythology, we find oak connected

The spurge olive (*Cneorum tricoccon*) is an endemic Mediterranean plant whose shiny foliage, brilliant red fruits, and neat, rounded shape make it ideal for garden use.

with Zeus, myrtle with Aphrodite, the olive with Athena, and laurel (*Laurus nobilis*) with Apollo. Laurel also provided the wreaths bestowed on scholars and heroes. Dionysus and the grape form another well-known team. Many plants, such as the pomegranate (*Punica granatum*), are represented in very early pictorial imagery. The acanthus leaf, which appears on the capitals of all Corinthian columns, should certainly be considered a Mediterranean native, although many species were imported early on from the East, such as the almond (*Prunus dulcis*), which is today considered by most a Mediterranean native.

The Bible mentions plants used for carpentry (carob, cedar, cypress, mulberry, oak, pine, plane), for decoration (box, laurel, myrtle, olean-der), and for food (almond, apricot, date, grape, melon, olive, pistachio, many grains). Biblical vegetables were cucumber, garlic, leek, and onion. Spices and medicinal plants included caraway,

Erica multiflora, a Mediterranean native, here seen in the wild

coriander, and garlic. Hard as it is to believe, the olive was brought to the Mediterranean by outsiders: it was introduced before the grape but after the fig, although all three plants appear in the Talmud, the Bible, and the Koran. The olive and the olive tree enjoy a special place in Holy Scripture: olive oil is said "to honor God and man." The olive is not only a fruit but also a holy object that represents peace and joy. Olives have made their way into city statutes and national constitutions.

Regardless of which source we explore, we come across the same species again and again. These were plants that could tolerate harsh climatic conditions, such as summer drought and the poor, often rocky **soil** around the Mediterranean Basin. They lived with the seasons and thrived in a climate that suited

them. Nomads might gather a few plants or fruits from these plants, but no gardeners pampered them or helped them survive.

What makes these native plants so sturdy? Many mediterranean species retain most of their leaves through the mild winter, a strategy that permits them to continue photosynthesizing, i. e., preparing their food, throughout the year. These hard, ever-green—or sclerophyllous—leaves usually last for several years. Such fascinating adaptations, also called survival strategies, all have the common aim of conserving water within the plants in order for them to survive the many months of summer drought. Cushion shapes and com-pact growth that create a cool center within each plant are commonly seen. Water loss through leaf openings, the so-called stomata, is further pre-vented by silvery light-reflecting leaves, by a felt-like cover or also by leaf

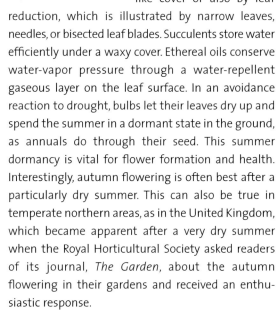

reduction, which is illustrated by narrow leaves, needles, or bisected leaf blades. Succulents store water efficiently under a waxy cover. Ethereal oils conserve water-vapor pressure through a water-repellent gaseous layer on the leaf surface. In an avoidance reaction to drought, bulbs let their leaves dry up and spend the summer in a dormant state in the ground, as annuals do through their seed. This summer dormancy is vital for flower formation and health. Interestingly, autumn flowering is often best after a particularly dry summer. This can also be true in temperate northern areas, as in the United Kingdom, which became apparent after a very dry summer when the Royal Horticultural Society asked readers of its journal, *The Garden*, about the autumn flowering in their gardens and received an enthu-siastic response.

Mediterranean plants worldwide adapt to the difficult climate not only above the ground but also below it, by displaying different types of roots. Mostly wide-branching and tightly interwoven with soil life, the roots of these plants are not only efficient at water uptake but they also anchor the plant to the ground. In a mutually beneficial relationship, soil-borne fungi, or mycorrhizae, help the roots absorb water and nutrients. Near the surface, secondary roots specialize in speedy water absorption during rapid downpours. **All parts of native mediterranean-climate plants are directed, in one way or another, toward water conservation.**

Among its native plants, the Mediterranean is especially rich in endemic plants unique to the region; these are seldom spectacular but often discreetly beautiful. Frequently threatened by extinction, these species occur in restricted areas, sometimes only in one isolated corner of an island or on an inaccessible cliff. The spurge olive (*Cneorum tricoccon*), for example, is endemic to the Balearic Islands with a small occurrence, although it occurs also in southern France, while *Rhamnus ludovici-salvatoris* is endemic to the island of Mallorca, where it was discovered in the late nineteenth century by Archduke Ludwig Salvator of Austria (hence its specific name), with an occurrence near Valencia in Spain. Both are tremendously garden-worthy evergreens, and seed is sometimes available.

Mediterranean gardens of today are often described either as a riot of color, with *Bougainvillea*, *Lantana*, and *Pelargonium* covering every inch of house and garden, or, in contrast, as a sparsely covered *maquis*-type landscape, its dry earth dotted with a few succulents and accented by several ill-placed rocks. But these are misleading pictures. The wide use of mediterranean natives suggests a third, and far more attractive, possibility. In all areas with a mediterra-nean climate, a rich flora has evolved that can be grown together with natives of the Mediterranean

Pride of Madeira (*Echium candicans*), seen here in the foreground, is an undemanding garden plant in all places where summers are hot and dry.

Basin. Each region has its own native plants, but all share an ability to thrive in mild, rainy winters and to endure long, dry summers. The water-saving characteristics of these plants and numerous other advantages have been praised at length. The beauty of their mostly evergreen foliage and their versatility enchant me every day. Choose from among the vast range of this exciting plant material that can tempt every gardener. Do not hesitate to use them all.

You may wonder why such gardens are preferable to the wild *maquis*, and the answer is that a garden created according to aesthetic and design principles is not merely an accidental assembly of plants but your very own creation. As in any other garden, you may group plants by texture, size, and color and observe ecologically correct plant associations. In your garden, it is your taste that determines their location. You choose the area where you need shade rather than simply accepting it where it occurs. You thus create (or restructure) an evergreen, drought-tolerant plant community, one that is harmonious, functional, and integrated into the surrounding countryside.

If native plants are used with the same tasteful creativity and imagination that underlie all successful gardens, they can have great appeal. "Natural-style" gardens using native plants are evolving and

Wormwood (*Artemisia arborescens*) reduces water loss with silvery light-reflecting foliage.

becoming more popular. *Veld & Flora*, the journal of the National Botanical Institute of South Africa at Kirstenbosch, features such a garden in each of its quarterly issues. The use of natives is logical, and many gardeners today are aware of their many virtues, but widespread acceptance is slow to come. Could it be that people are reluctant to pay for what they see growing in the wild and think of as worthless weeds from the fields?

Because of demand from their clients, mediterranean-climate nurseries are beginning to take up the challenge of offering native plants, displaying them in a separate area so that gardeners who are intent on saving both water and labor may become familiar with the wide range available: rosemary, whose color ranges from white to intense blue; all the scented lavender species; box and myrtle for topiary; miniature and fruit-bearing pomegranate; a wide range of rock roses for a riveting spring display; many thymes and salvias; and lately the edible and ornamental strawberry tree *Arbutus*.

Conservation of Mediterranean-Type Plants

*For of all the changes that man can make to the Earth,
none is more permanent than the extinction of a species.
From* Plants in Danger, What Do We Know?

The accelerating loss of plant species is alarming. Conservation is on everyone's mind these days, and the statistics are well known to all those who care. It is crucial that we match our needs and expectations with the fragile natural world that surrounds us and that we accept the conservation of nature as an important approach in modern gardening from which all mediterranean-climate regions will benefit. Gardens open to native plants, man-made complements to nature in balance with the region's character, are a means of handing on to future generations what we ourselves have received. As Burle Marx, the well known Brazilian master of design, proclaimed: "Preserve, protect and plant for posterity!"

In the vicinity of the Mediterranean Sea, an ancient center of human civilization, **landscapes were almost irreversibly damaged long ago**. As early as A.D. 1414, a decree from the senate of Venice prohibited the export of cypress trees from Crete, testifying to the advanced decimation of the cypress woods even then. The durable cypress wood was mainly used for shipbuilding, temple doors, and sarcophagi. It could also be a valuable part of a girl's dowry; a cypress tree planted at her birth later served as the mast of the young couple's boat. The cypress is also often found growing in cemeteries.

This spring show of native plants at the Kirstenbosch Botanical Garden near Cape Town, South Africa shows succulents and *Aloe ferox* x *Aloe arborescens* in front of Table Mountain.
Photograph J. Loedolff

At the center of the replanted Kaisariani forest lies a restored eleventh-century Byzantine monastery, resulting in a harmonious blend between nature and civilization.

Yew (*Taxus baccata*), another important forest tree, was also threatened, and nearly eliminated, many years ago, because of the beauty of its wood and its slow rate of growth. The very hard olive wood was used in mining. The Cornelian cherry (*Cornus mas*) was hard as horn, appropriate for darts in warfare and hunting, as well as for walking sticks. The wood of fir, pine, and juniper, like cypress, was used by the Greeks for building ships. When Xerxes lost his fleet of more than four thousand ships, a bridge was built for his army to proceed on foot, requiring—it is said—more than ten thousand tree trunks. Furthermore, fir and pine were not durable, so that ships made of them had to be replaced frequently. Funeral pyres, sometimes of Olympic size, also wasted a gigantic number of trees. Foundries, smelting furnaces, and pottery kilns devastated entire regions, and wood for fuel had to be brought by boat from far-away islands. Forest fires kindled by autumn winds were known to last for years. No wonder so few trees are left in the Mediterranean Basin.

A more recent threat is that facing the thousands of rare bulbs that are dug up every year. In fact, many species face extinction. When you buy bulbs, make sure that they do not come from wild stands. Bulbs sold out of the Netherlands, the largest bulb producer and exporter, must bear a label that identifies them either as "bulbs from wild source" or as "bulbs grown from cultivated stock." The term "nursery-grown" is insufficient, since it may refer to bulbs of wild origin. Any agricultural institution or university biology faculty, as well as Kew Gardens or the Royal Horticultural Society Garden at Wisley, can provide further information about the conservation of bulbs.

Before you assume that devastation has gone too far for recovery, take heart. Having gardened for the last twenty-five years in an abused landscape of bedrock with little overlying soil, I have seen that this is not so. The plant world of mediterranean natives is sturdy, and nature is only too eager to cover these rocks once more, if only we let her, quite apart from giving her a helping hand, such as putting in fences where animals roam. Native plants are particularly suited to provide the backbone of a garden; they are accommodating and fill most roles assigned to them; and using them in our gardens can help save them from extinction. If you collect seed in the wild, distribute some of it to your friends and leave at least two-thirds of what you find for the sake of natural propagation.

Another way in which you can help conserve native species is to protect plants threatened by overdevelopment. If you embark on construction work at your house, for instance, or if road work is undertaken near your home, make sure that existing vegetation is given protective fencing before it can be damaged by workers. If land clearing is inevitable, do not hesitate to transplant natives before they are uprooted by a bulldozer and then replant them appropriately afterward.

Barely two miles from the polluted center of Athens, on the western slopes of Mount Hymettus, lies the forest of Kaisariani. Together with its eleventh-century monastery, the mountain forms a harmonious blend of nature and civilization that has been designated one of the historical gardens of Europe by the European Union. After World War II, the Filodassiki Enosis Athinon (FEA) undertook the painstaking task of reforesting an area of 1,250 acres to transform the Kaisariani wasteland into a forest by planting more than three million trees (pine,

cypress, plane, poplar, carob, oak, fir, cedar, and almond). The seventeenth-century olive grove was restored and a collection of endangered Greek wild flowers was planted.

The International Union for Conservation of Nature and Natural Resources (IUCN), a network of governments, nongovernmental organizations, scientists, and other conservation experts, monitors the status of plants throughout the world. The coalition plans conservation actions and provides the assistance and advice necessary to achieve them. The IUCN Conservation Monitoring Center at 219c Huntingdon Road, Cambridge, England CB3 0DL, collects, interprets, and disseminates data as a basis for protection, and it produces the *Red Data Books*, a mesmerizing compilation of the threatened plants throughout the world. CITES, the Convention on International Trade in Endangered Species of Wild Fauna and Flora, protects endangered species from overexploitation and monitors their trade by means

From my garden diary

End of August 2003: Why did I ever bother to plant anything other than the drought-tolerant strawberry tree (*Arbutus*) and shiny myrtle (*Myrtus*) in billowing masses, lavender in every crevice on the rocky slopes of my garden, and the wide range of bulbous plants that delight us with their cheerful bloom and demand little more than "summer baking" in the ground? Such simple plantings would have been much easier to maintain than the countless plants we all want to try out and which, in our minds, we invest with magical qualities. After years, my garden still holds surprises, and it is thanks to this never-ending "trying out" that now I know which plants can be left to themselves, year after year, the ones that are content with the conditions my garden offers. Certainly, they need tidying up, refreshing their mulch layer, and also an occasional clipping to re-create their volumes. Yet that is little if we consider the advantages that go with their use: mainly, that worrying over the ever scarcer water supply is over. Had I known when I set out, I muse, what experience has taught me, my gardening life would have been easier. Still, exploring, experimenting are part of the fun.

In David Fross's garden in Arroyo Grande, California, *Eschscholzia californica* and *E. c.* 'Moonglow' are enhanced by grasses and sculpture.

Eschscholzia hybrids in the Fross garden

of a system of import/export permits. Seed banks such as those at Kew Gardens in England and at Kings Park Botanical Gardens in Perth, Australia, are among today's answers to the threat of plant extinction.

In most regions with a mediterranean-type climate, **native-plant societies actively protect their indigenous plants in the wild and also recommend their use in gardens**. In California, for instance, the garden suitability of the native flora has been widely studied. Exclusively dedicated to its preservation are the California Native Plant Society; the Regional Parks Botanic Garden at Tilden Park, Berkeley; the Santa Barbara Botanic Garden; and Rancho Santa Ana Botanic Garden (with an extensive seed bank of California species). The Leaning Pine Arboretum at the Environmental Horticulture Science Unit of the California Polytechnic State University campus at San Luis Obispo, has created a series of mediter-

The rare *Rhamnus ludovici-salvatoris* should be used more often in gardens. It makes dense rounded shrubs like box and is not invasive, although easily propagated by seed.

ranean display gardens with a wonderful array of mature mediterranean plantings developed and maintained by students. The admirable achievements of the Yerba Buena Nursery at Woodside (the oldest native-plant nursery in California) and of the Theodore Payne Foundation for Wild Flowers and Native Plants in Sun Valley, should be emphasized. The Tree of Life Nursery developed into the largest California native-plant nursery, and Native Sons Nursery in Arroyo Grande began in 1979 on one acre with the idea of producing the finest California native plants for landscape use. All are now significant players in both conservation and horticulture, fostering an awareness of the Californian climate and the ecological realities inherent in such an environment.

The arid south and southwest Australian garden scene is increasingly dominated by native plants. "Conservation through cultivation," the motto of the Australian Plant Society, has caught on. Using their unique, highly drought-tolerant flora, rich in

flowering trees, shrubs, and perennials (*Acacia*, *Anigozanthus*, *Eremophila*, *Grevillea*, *Hakea*, and *Melaleuca*), the society has largely succeeded in creating a new commitment toward conservation through waterwise gardening. Sanctuary gardens are devoted exclusively to native plants. The hundred-acre Canberra Botanical Garden features the plant world of the Australian heathland, with species running into the thousands.

The evergreen Chilean *matorral*, a treasure trove of drought-tolerant plants, is attracting increasing interest among horticulturists. Thanks to the Botanical Garden in Valparaiso, for instance, an ever-growing number of evergreen plants, many of them drought-tolerant, are being introduced to gardens in Chile and abroad.

Near Cape Town in South Africa, the Kirstenbosch National Botanical Garden features the native plants of South Africa. One may wander for hours through expertly landscaped areas bordered by virgin land, a wonderful way to get to know these plants intimately. In the same spirit, members of the Indigenous Bulb Association of South Africa (IBSA) rescue native bulbs, for example, on construction sites. Having saved them from extinction in this way, the group propagates the bulbs for distribution to members worldwide.

For full documentation, consult *Plant Conservation in the Mediterranean Area*, Geobotany 7 (1985), edited by C. Gomez-Campo, Dr. W. Junk Publishers, Dordrecht, and *Plants in Danger: What Do We Know?* (1986), published by the International Union for Conservation (www.iucn.org).

Invasive Plants

This ivy (*Hedera helix*) is about to destroy an arch that dates from Moorish times.

Most of the early introductions of exotic plants into mediterranean-climate regions took place in the Southern Hemisphere (Australia, the Cape of South Africa, and Chile). Along with humans, many plant invaders spread from one port to another via seeds that adhered to the fleeces of sheep or the hides of cattle. Others were released by botanical gardens, where they had been introduced for seed exchange or were to be studied for their potential as medicines, as dune stabilizers, garden ornamentals,

or animal fodder (for which many are still used). Most introductions have an interesting background, and I quote from the South African book *Plant Invaders*, edited by C. H. Stirton, "In an effort to develop an export industry in the form of tanning based on the bark of Port Jackson *Acacia saligna*, the South African government encouraged farmers to grow these by awarding prizes for the largest areas planted." Today, on the contrary, the prizes are given to those who do away with the very same plants. So-called hack groups devote their Saturdays to eliminating Port Jackson trees that have taken over entire riverbeds.

The major threat posed by plant invaders is that not only may they invade our gardens, but **they may also invade our fields, pastures, and forests, gradually crowding out native vegetation**. Introduced grasses have recently taken over entire areas of countryside on many continents. Whether you turn to Africa, Australia, California, or Chile, the story is the same, and at the moment, control is nearly impossible. Breeding natural enemies seems to have the best potential for the future. The so-called ornamental grasses have recently become a fad. Where once they were considered weeds and their decorative clumps were pulled out, they are now used to form harmonious, peaceful garden settings. It is not easy to determine in advance which ones will be invasive, but to be on the safe side, you may cut off the seed heads before they disperse their seed, even though it will eliminate one of their decorative features.

If I had excluded from this book all the plants that have become invasive somewhere around the world (i.e., in places where they found growing conditions that perfectly suited them), I would have had to omit many plants that in other regions are useful garden subjects, often the drought-tolerant ones. *Melaleuca armillaris*, for example, one of the

Australian paperbarks in the Myrtaceae family, has become a threat in coastal Florida where its seed can germinate in hot, humid sand. Yet in my drought-ridden garden, it is a graceful, undemanding survivor that stood up to a devastating hurricane in the winter of 2001, which felled most pine trees. Since plants are not equally invasive in all mediterranean regions, gardeners should familiarize themselves with the situation in their own area.

Some plants are location-specific, while others are less choosy and invade wherever they get the opportunity. And then there are the real "baddies"—certain alliums and oxalis in the Mediterranean Basin and many *Acacia*, *Lantana*, and *Nicotiana glauca* in South Africa. Yet just because a plant is invasive in South Africa does not mean that you have to exclude it from your garden on the shores of the Mediterranean, where they may not find the conditions that make them thrive elsewhere—for instance, a hot riverbank. By contrast, in extremely dry regions, such as the Succulent Karoo area in South Africa, where germination is difficult, invaders are in a significant minority.

"How do plants invade?" is a frequently asked question, to which there is a series of answers. Plants invade by one of the circumstances listed below or by any combination thereof:

• a high seed set (a high level of flowering, as with grasses)
• efficient seed dispersal by birds, water, or wind (difficult to control)
• a coincidence of seedling establishment and rainfall
• a disturbance of the soil seed bank, either manually or stimulated by fire
• a lack of competition from established plants, as after a fire
• fertilizer added through fire (ashes)
• a lack of natural enemies, which most invasive plants do not bring with them (a fact that has made them successful)
• a summer rainfall region, adjacent to the winter rainfall area, that facilitates the establishment of invaders (southern Australia and South Africa).

Methods of controlling invasive plants have their problems and pitfalls and, if not carefully chosen, do not necessarily eliminate the targeted plant. Remember that one of the characteristics of an invader is that it tends to defy removal. A chopped-down eucalyptus, for instance, resprouts from its bole, making several stems to replace the single one that was cut down.

Today's informed gardeners help to control plant invaders first by avoiding their introduction into the garden, and later by preventing their possible escape from it. They choose plants with care and periodically check on recent introductions into their gardens, replacing any plants about which they have doubts. Reliable advice on how to recognize plant invaders can be obtained from any government or university agricultural department or from knowledgeable garden friends. Most nurseries will provide guidance, if asked. Remember that the availability of plants does not always guarantee their lack of invasiveness.

Australia has a wide range of invasive trees, shrubs, annuals, and bulbous plants. Originally from South Africa's Cape Province, the attractive bulbous *Moraea collina* (formerly *Homeria c.*) has been found

Acanthus (*Acanthus mollis*) is a beautiful but invasive garden plant; it can, however, be easily controlled.

to poison livestock. Yet many of the plants that have had such devastating ecological effects in Australia over the past two hundred years were originally brought from mediterranean Europe.

California also has a high number of introduced species that have become naturalized, among them many grasses (Gramineae), but the Asteraceae family takes the lead, closely followed by the Leguminosae. Blackberry (*Rubus sanctus*), Pampas grass (*Cortaderia*), and Scotch broom (*Cytisus scoparius*) are also prominent on the list, accompanied by *Hypericum perfoliatum*, *Lantana camara*, and *Opuntia*. Salt marshes, dense forests (lack of light), and deserts (difficult germination because of lack of humidity) are less prone to invasion.

The Cape Province of South Africa is particularly vulnerable to plant invaders, and invasiveness is taken seriously there. Garden owners are now obliged to eliminate invasive plants (even if they are not invasive in their own gardens!), and nurseries are no longer allowed to sell what are termed "invasive aliens." Acacias, hakeas, mesquite (*Prosopis glandulosa*), Victorian box (*Pittosporum undulatum*), and other thicket-forming woody plants are estimated to have invaded nearly 3,500 square miles. Farmland is threatened by St. John's wort (*Hypericum perforatum*), which is poisonous to livestock, and the vicious spines of the jointed cactus (*Opuntia aurantiaca*), together with all other opuntias, render grazing land useless once they get out of hand. The maritime pine (*Pinus pinaster*), originally introduced from the Mediterranean Basin for forestation, has taken over whole areas of countryside to the exclusion of all native plants. Invaders are often adapted to fire and drought. The long list of invaders also includes the stinkbean (*Albizia lophantha*), *Eucalyptus*, and *Leptospermum laevigatum* from

The Aleppo pine (*Pinus halepensis*), prickly pear (*Opuntia ficus-indica*), and golden Cape sorrel (*Oxalis pes-caprae*) have taken over stony ground near the sea, creating a charming sight.

Australia, *Lantana camara*, the wild tobacco (*Nicotiana glauca*) and *Sesbania punicea* from tropical America, *Nerium oleander* from Morocco, and *Populus x canescens* from the Republic of Georgia and Iran.

The Spanish settled in Chile in the middle of the sixteenth century, some two hundred years earlier than in California. Plant introductions happened inadvertently, via the hay carried to feed livestock during the ocean voyage from Spain to Chile. Plants introduced to this mediterranean climate zone comprise a wide range of annual herbs from Europe, most of them found in rangelands. Other introductions, such as 2.5 million acres planted with *Pinus radiata* from North America, endanger Chile's deciduous native forests of *Nothofagus*.

Although the Mediterranean Basin is less prone to invaders, the area has its own invasive plants, such as the stately asphodel, which has overrun many a field. Thistles, appreciated as garden plants in northern climes, are also prominent invaders. Many alliums (*A. triquetrum*), *Acanthus*, and valerian (*Centranthus*) may be beautiful but are not always easy to dislodge, and climbing ivy (*Hedera*) and honeysuckle (*Lonicera*) can take a firm hold. With time, broom (*Cytisus scoparius*), Spanish gorse (*Genista hispanica*), Spanish broom (*Spartium junceum*), and gorse (*Ulex europaeus*), all from the Leguminosae family, will invade a sunny hillside, turning it into gold. Other invaders include introduced shrubs and trees such as the suckering tree of heaven (*Ailanthus altissima*), black locust (*Robinia pseudoacacia*), and *Wigandia* from the American tropics. *Albizia lophantha* and wild tobacco (*Nicotiana glauca*) seed with ease. From South Africa come the bulbous *Ornithogalum longibracteatum* and Cape sorrel (*Oxalis pes-caprae*).

If all this does not satisfy your curiosity, *Biogeography of Mediterranean Invasions* edited by R. Groves and F. di Castri, provides the historical background of plant invasions, mentions the role played by animals, and lists hundreds of well-indexed plant names.

Invasive Plants

Plant Invaders in Australia
Chrysanthemoides monilifera
Euphorbia
Medicago
Moraea collina (formerly *Homeria c.*)
Oenothera
Opuntia ficus-indica
Oxalis
Rubus
Solanum
Trifolium

Plant Invaders in California
Acanthus mollis
Ailanthus altissima
Alstroemeria sp.
Aptenia cordifolia
Asphodelus fistulosus
Carpobrotus edulis
Chrysanthemum coronarium
Cortaderia
Cotoneaster sp.
Cytisus scoparius
Delairea odorata
Eucalyptus globulus
Euphorbia dendroides
Hypericum calycinum
Hypericum perfoliatum
Lampranthus aureus, L. spectabilis
Lantana camara
Limonium perezii
Lobularia maritima
Mesembryanthemum crystallinum
Myoporum laetum
Oenothera speciosa
Opuntia ficus-indica
Oxalis sp.
Ricinus communis
Robinia pseudoacacia
Schinus molle, S. terebinthifolius
Spartium junceum
Tamarix sp.
Tropaeolum majus
Ulex europaeus
Vinca sp.
Washingtonia robusta

Plant Invaders at the Cape of South Africa
Acacia cyclops
Acacia melanoxylon
Acacia saligna, Port Jackson
Albizia lophantha, stinkbean
Eucalyptus
Hakea
Hypericum perforatum
Lantana camara
Leptospermum laevigatum
Nerium oleander
Nicotiana glauca
Opuntia aurantiaca
Pinus pinaster
Pittosporum undulatum
Populus x canescens
Prosopis glandulosa
Quercus robur
Sesbania punicea

Plant Invaders in Chile
Mostly annual grasses
Pinus radiata
Rubus ulmifolius
See *Biogeography of Mediterranean Invasions.*

Plant Invaders in the Mediterranean Basin
Acanthus
Ailanthus altissima
Albizia lophantha
Allium triquetrum
Arctotheca calendula
Centranthus
Cytisus scoparius
Genista hispanica
Hedera helix
Lonicera etrusca
Nicotiana glauca
Ornithogalum longibracteatum
Oxalis pes-caprae
Robinia pseudoacacia
Spartium junceum
Tamarix aphylla
Ulex europaeus
Wigandia

Surviving Summer Drought

In such rocky terrain, we should use only the most drought-tolerant plants. Here cypress, lavender, and rosemary (*Rosmarinus officinalis*) have been used generously. Their foliage enjoys resting on the dry bed.

A sound knowledge of the mediterranean climate is one of the most important tools in helping your garden survive a hot, dry summer. If you plan to establish a garden in a mediterranean climate region, bear in mind that you will certainly have to face certain unfavorable conditions. You have already resisted the temptation to transplant a northern-climate garden or a tropical paradise to the Mediterranean, but now you will find yourself facing summer drought, strong solar radiation, and dwindling water resources, to say nothing of erosion, howling winds, devastating fires, and accumulating waste. Most of these problems are manmade. I see them as challenges to test our resourcefulness and our imagination.

On the other hand, many opportunities present themselves to the mediterranean gardener. **Your best "tool" is the mediterranean winter rain**. In fact, winter rain does the watering for you! During the mild, often sunny winters, rain will water the garden so that the plants can drink their fill and prepare themselves for the long, dry summer ahead. Even permeable bedrock can store water, safe from evaporation, thus contributing to the water supply available to trees.

The wise gardener will exploit the benefits of a mediterranean climate and adopt a waterwise approach to gardening. With a careful selection of plants, a waterwise garden can produce a yearlong green cover and cheerful flowers. But where water is lacking, it will be easier for plants (and the gardener) to survive a summer drought

• if copious winter rains allow plants to fill up with water so that they do not face summer drought in an already water-stressed condition

Native plants survive summer drought in a dormant state. Under these olive trees, silvery-gray lavender, summer-dormant spurge (*Euphorbia dendroides*), and the green foliage of rock roses (*Cistus*) create a softly colored carpet.

• if the garden has been planted with windbreaks
• if the ground is shaded by a moving, dappled, or intermittent tree shade during the hottest noon and afternoon hours
• if well-grown specimens of drought-tolerant plants have been used
• if the plants are suited to their site
• if water-saving practices have been implemented (excellent drainage, generous mulch, appropriate root runs)
• if the roots are kept cool under rock, mulch, or neighboring plantings
• if planting was carried out with care, which may mean that the hole was watered *before* the planting took place, often the only chance to humidify the soil deep down

• if the plants have been grouped by their water needs (water-demanding ones near the house)
• if plants do not carry unnecessary weight, such as dead, weak, or sparsely foliaged branches
• if the lawn has been replaced by hardscapes (tiles, bricks, pavement, etc.) or by alternative planting

A plant's drought tolerance* will vary according to the growing conditions. Often more important than water is shade, mulch, and the time when the sun hits the plants. A cool root run beneath or between rocks may be better than a lavish bed layered with peat moss. Nursery-grown plants now tend to come in a peat mix, but peat is very difficult

* The words "drought-*tolerant*" and "drought-*resistant*" are not interchangeable terms. They have different meanings. A plant that *tolerates* drought (under favorable conditions and for a certain period) does not necessarily *resist* drought, when conditions become harsher, as in a long period of drought.

A Gardener's Questionnaire

is meant for those who are starting out or who intend to redo their garden. It focuses on the beginner, but we all occasionally like to be helped by an aide-mémoire.

What plants are found on your land?
Do you have trees, native shrubs, or only rock?
Which are the dominant native plants and which are the rarer ones?
Which ones do you like?

Once you are familiar with the plants on your own land, explore the immediate and wider neighborhood:
What grows in other gardens—and grows well?
What grows in abandoned gardens (testifying to their drought tolerance)?
Which plants are part of a nearby forest?
What can be found in nurseries? (Best to go well prepared and find a knowledgeable person to assist you).
Observe native and introduced plants as an indicator of the climate and soil on your site.

How about the soil?
What type of soil do you have (sand, loam)?
Do you have shallow soil over bedrock or, for instance, cracked soil?
Is your soil alkaline or acid?

Check on water
Do you have a spring, a well, or water from your municipality?
Do you have water at the height of summer when it is lacking everywhere?

Know your land
Sit at your future doorstep, watch the sun rise or set, listen to the sound of animals.
Do you have buildings on your land?
What is the lie of your land? Flat, undulating, steep?
Do you have a view?
Do neighboring houses encroach on you?
Is the noise from a nearby street overwhelming?
Is beauty around you?
Decide on what you like or want to disguise.
What type of landscaping suggests itself to you?

If you find a Mediterranean fan palm (*Chamaerops humilis*) on your land, you can always put it to good use.

to re-wet once it is dry and, what is more, the roots are reluctant to grow beyond peat into the new soil that you have prepared for them. It is best to check on new plants periodically until you get a feel for their water demands. Temporary shade, such as that given by a palm leaf tucked into the ground next to a plant, is often all it needs to alleviate stress.

Another important tool for the gardener is the **wide range of native mediterranean plants**, the ones that grow wild in the climate in which you are gardening. These tough and healthy drought-tolerant plants provide year-round cover and interest. Easy to cultivate and maintain, they adapt without problems to a garden that caters for their basic needs. Choose those plants you feel will adapt best to the conditions your garden can offer. If you know the environment in which a plant evolved in its native region, you can try to duplicate these conditions as well as your garden permits, matching each plant with a suitable site. Time invested in choosing planting sites with care is always well spent. Some plants have a wider tolerance range than others, and the ones you choose may even be more accommodating than you expected. Close observation will guide you.

When I look at my evergreen garden, I marvel how most plants manage to retain their foliage under difficult summer conditions. Quite a few do so without further ado, such as cedar, cypress, oak, olive, and pine, or buckthorn (*Rhamnus alaternus*), mock privet (*Phillyrea*) and mastic (*Pistacia lentiscus*)—the stalwarts. Plumbago (not invasive in Europe) even manages exuberant flowering. It is these tough ones we want to remember and use wisely when the time comes for planning and planting.

An **ecologically sound approach to gardening** is another means to guarantee success in a mediterranean garden. If you plant in early autumn in a well-chosen site, if you let well-mulched plants establish themselves over the winter and keep a watchful eye on them over the first summer, providing water and temporary shade, most will be well on their way. To be on the safe side, do this for a second year as well, after which they will proceed on their own. Once established, indigenous plants—watered by winter rain and mostly drought-tolerant in the summer—will liberate you from the chore of watering. However, excellent drainage is vital; the roots of many drought-tolerant plants rot easily and are not designed to withstand being waterlogged (at no time of the year and even less so during summer dormancy).

Native plants need a soil well furnished with vegetable matter, the so-called humus that contains many organisms that make soil nutrients available to plants. Humus increases the likelihood of a healthy soil life that will protect plants from pests and disease. You can supplement the humus content by adding well-decomposed compost, which results from all vegetable wastes and will ripen within months under favorable conditions. Well-rotted animal manure, an excellent fertilizer, can be replaced by commercial natural fertilizers that contain manure, horn, hooves, or algae. Well-planted and well-mulched plants will seldom need additional food, and health hazards will be few.

Remember that in large areas of southern Australia and South Africa, the soils are deficient in phosphorus, nitrogen, and micronutrients that have been leached out. Plants from these regions do not require added food.

Under a strong mediterranean sun, shade is vital, since it reduces transpiration from the leaves and evaporation from the soil. Shade comes in many guises and facilitates your garden life. Especially beneficial is the moving, dappled shade of trees that allows the sun to reach the plants for a few hours each day. Dark shade in a confined location, however, suits few plants.

Most mediterranean plants require good aeration around and within them, so be sure to give your plants the space they need to develop into healthy specimens. When they turn spindly, take them out; often they can be used elsewhere. Like any other garden plant, natives look best when well-kempt, which may involve shearing for compact growth and the removal of spent flowers.

In a small Australian garden, this subdivided square has been created to house all manner of drought-tolerant plants, which in winter find a dry bed on the colored gravel. The design is by Tim North.

A Garden in Harmony with Its Surroundings

Salt cedars or tamarisks thrive in coastal sand.

This chapter sets out some of the landscaping principles by which a beautiful and harmonious result may be achieved. Harmony is the key word, not only in the way one's garden relates to its surroundings but also in the way one's house fits the land on which it is built. The view from my garden extends beyond its boundaries, so I like what I call a "neighborly planting" approach, by which inhabitants on both sides of the fence can visually use elements in each other's gardens. Unity and simplicity will lead to better results than too much fussy contrasting detail, and a sense of scale and proportion in the planting is of paramount importance. I will also discuss the value of empty space in a garden, as well as the idea of "the picture and its frame" and the important role played by the use of color. Once the spirit of the place has been sensed, gardeners can create mood and atmosphere in their very own Eden.

A Garden Has Its Own Mind

A palm tree (*Phoenix canariensis*) dwarfs three white columns. Framing the distant hills, it creates a simple yet successful scene.

Working with nature has always been my guiding star. A natural balance makes the gardener feel at peace in a garden, rather than at war on a battlefield—pulling up and tearing down, turning over the soil, and spraying poisonous products. A natural garden also places fewer demands on the gardener, and it can be sustainable.

Robert Duffield, editor of *The West Australian Gardener*, writes: "I have come to believe that our English heritage has for 200 years inhibited the opportunities to adopt and adapt Mediterranean garden lifestyles to a climate ideal for them. For far too long we have been obsessed with expansive lawns and Northern Hemisphere plants. If I could have my life over, I would acquire a bush block, keep as many original trees as possible and sow it with West Australian wildflowers."

One learns new things in a garden all the time. After having lived with my garden for twenty-five years, I now accept the notion that the garden has its own mind—and that **it is often best to let the garden have its way**. When we start out, we are guided by preconceived ideas and visions. We change the soil, bring plants from faraway places, and add water. After a few years, we can see how the garden has responded, how it has reacted to this alien influence (ours). Many plants, for example, have faded away. "Did they not appreciate the location we gave them?" we ask ourselves. "Did we not offer what their roots required?" In the meantime, seedlings from plants that *do* like the conditions I have provided are establishing themselves in places of their own choosing, and I let them have their way. Nature has induced me to change my preconceived ideas and to adapt them to her wishes, to try to sense when all is right—even if only for the time being. Nature and I have a positive relationship, although at times I am not too sure whether she cares much about my vision of Eden.

We know little about nature's intentions, but all the same we can try to understand and accept them. For instance, it has always been clear to me that trees should not be cut down unless there is a good reason for doing so.* Clearing the view could be one of those reasons, as could eliminating a sick tree or one that interferes with other growth or the house itself. Oak, for example, takes precedence over the often invasive pines in my garden, and as soon as a pine tree interferes with an oak's spreading growth, it must go. Whatever the reason, however, give much thought to cutting down before you do so. We should always leave a few extra trees for an emergency. That

Many rock roses (*Cistus*) come up on their own and often complete an existing composition.

Without any effort on the gardener's part, a mock privet (*Phillyrea angustifolia*) has grown into a small tree; golden Spanish broom (*Spartium junceum*) and a pink rock rose (*Cistus*) have bloomed, and cypresses have self-seeded from a planted specimen.

way, when a storm creates havoc and fells a tree that the garden can't do without, you will have a substitute to fall back on. At the same time, I try to give young oak trees sufficient space so that in the future my garden will once again become an oak wood, as it was in times past.

*Note: in many areas, removing a tree requires a permit from the authorities.

What goes for trees is valid for all growth that comes up spontaneously. "Even the weeds?" I hear you exclaim. I keep some of these too, as long as they look right within the garden scheme and do not invade. Weeds can have a beneficial function, such as preventing the erosion of bare ground by spreading

out their leaves to hug the soil. For instance, a gray-leaved pink rock rose (*Cistus albidus*) seeds itself to a moderate extent in my garden and often finds just the right place to complement an existing picture. If too many seedlings come up, however, I have to edit. In other words, I must decide which ones can stay and eliminate the rest. I always pot up a few rock roses so that I will have an extra supply for any filling-in that might be required later on. Mock privet (*Phillyrea*) lends itself to creative shaping, or topiary, and I pot every single one that comes up in the "wrong" place. These plants will take off again if the transplanting is done at an early age. The same goes for wormwood (*Artemisia*), shrubby hare's ear (*Bupleurum*), and rue (*Ruta*), all of which are plants that self-sow with ease.

Now that every inch of my ten acres is covered with healthy growth, I realize that over the years much has come up on its own. Not everything had to be planted. I had the great good fortune to use what had been there when garden work began: the ancient oak and olive trees, the glossy evergreen foliage of the reliable mastic (*Pistacia lentiscus*) and noble myrtle shrubs, every single erica, and many delightful bulbs, such as cyclamen and snowflake (*Leucojum*), not to mention the rarer species.

A gardener's patience is often tried by the "in-between time," when one must wait for seedlings to grow, without being sure whether they will prosper. For some unfathomable reason, the seedlings we put most faith in often stall, while the unpromising waifs shoot up and form a good combination with two or three surrounding shrubs. No matter how much we plan, we can never be sure of the outcome, and it is wise to be flexible, to rearrange our thoughts and intentions, to regroup, reshape, and redesign the vision of our very own paradise.

A gnarled olive tree dominates this spectacular view, where the spurge (*Euphorbia dendroides*) has donned its dramatic summer attire.

A House That Lies Well in Its Land

Walls, steps, and shaped greenery help different levels of the surrounding terrain fit in with the design and location of the house. Design by Charles Shoup

The ancient Greeks set their temples harmoniously into the countryside. Floral motifs from their surroundings, such as the acanthus leaf (*Acanthus spinosus*), were often incorporated into their building elements, as in the capitals of Corinthian columns. Both Greeks and Romans included acanthus leaves in their gardens as well.

A house that lies well in its land is a pleasure to look at—for everyone, not just the owner. Yet more often than not, gardens are forgotten during the initial planning; they come as an afterthought, whereas house and garden ought to be a whole, each serving its distinct function, as the ancient Egyptians understood when they planned house and garden together. In addition, a house and its garden should not only blend into their immediate surroundings but should also be integrated into the overall landscape, if possible. Today, all around the Mediterranean, building activity is cutting up the countryside at an alarming pace. Houses are added to one another without any underlying thought, each proclaiming its individuality at an excessively high volume. Does this have to be so?

When you are at the planning stage in the construction of a house, **the surrounding topography may give guidance on how best to balance the house with its land.** Carefully adapted levels and identical or harmonizing colors and materials will link the house to the garden, and this will help avoid excessive diversity. The use of local stone, for example, will integrate your house into its surroundings. And why not draw on leftovers from house building for the garden? Brick, sandstone, slate, or composite tiles could very well be suitable for this purpose. If local sandstone frames the windows of your house, leftover slabs can be used to build garden steps. A beneficial side effect is that attractive moss will form readily on this quick-aging material.

Let your eyes wander away from your house. You will notice that they take in the neighboring roof (or a bleak wall), as well as shrubs and possibly a well-grown tree. Your eyes do not stop at the borders of your property but go beyond. There may be distant mountains or the sea; there is always the sky. Try to see the "beyond" as if it were part of your own garden.

This is what is called "borrowed landscape." If you have a breathtaking view, let all the elements in your garden come together to guide your eyes toward it, without distraction. Try looking at your house from outside the property, just to get an idea of the view from "beyond."

There are many ways to unite a garden to its surroundings. Building materials have already been mentioned, but a similar idea also applies to the plants we intend to use. **If you wish to create unity, find out which plants grow well in your neighborhood.** If many cypresses or palms grow near your garden, planting even a single cypress or palm inside your fence will give a wider scope to your garden (see drawing on page 46).

The notion of "borrowed color" follows the principle of "borrowed landscape." If you incorporate the colors of adjacent gardens into your own design, you will give more scope to your garden. A small garden will seem larger; a large one will gain in range. Depending on your neighbors' tastes, this may mean bringing faded shades to life or toning down strident ones (only the pale blue plumbago seems to calm the screaming purple of bougainvilleas). Even the paint on the house next door matters.

If you mean to **create harmony in color**, focus your attention not only on your immediate surroundings but also on the adjacent plots with their walls, plants, and flowers, on the burnt sienna of a near-

In a private urban setting, an artfully disguised lamp separates a garden from the street.

Wide steps with early-flowering iris (*Iris japonica*) negotiate a steep terrain.

A curving path molded into its terrain becomes an attractive as well as useful feature.

by ploughed field, on the countless green shades of neighboring woods, and the azure blue of the mediterranean sky. Picking up tints from the landscape around it (I purposely do not say "color" because the tints need not be exact) will solidly tie your garden to its surroundings. The colors you intend to use in your garden should *complement* (not necessarily match) those of the natural vegetation beyond. Integrate these shades into your scheme as if they were part of your own garden. Use them as a basic color palette.

The hills beyond my garden are covered with the cheerful yellow flowers of broom, and within the garden sweet-scented *Coronilla glauca* and *Euryops pectinatus* add more gold. Chosen to bloom simultaneously, they tie the garden into the landscape beyond.

Neighborly planting, a concept that evolves out of the notions of "borrowed landscape" and "borrowed color," is when you and your neighbors visually use the plant elements of each other's garden. Does the vegetation used by your neighbors appeal to you sufficiently for you to use the same (or a similar) one for your own garden? Do you find that your neighbors are inspired enough by your garden to borrow some of your ideas? If you cannot use identical materials or do not wish to do so, similar shapes, textures, or colors may prove attractive alternatives. If by good luck your taste coincides with that of your neighbors (or vice versa), the results can be most pleasing.

Tall grasses echo the color of the Californian hills, linking the garden to its surroundings.

The first step is to get together with your neighbors. Invite them over to see for themselves what their garden looks like from your side. They will undoubtedly appreciate the fact that their meager, luckless cypress hedge, for instance, is not really an asset for either of you. It is frequently said that our freedom ends where it limits the freedom of others. A tree wrongly positioned, wrong to the eye, and a house ascending skyward act as thieves, robbing us—or our neighbors—of the view. Creative neighborly relations mean that one tree can be planted on one side of the fence and the next on the other side, which involves the same amount of work and expense for both parties. Or a larger tree could find space where before only small ones could be fitted in.

Look for pleasant transitions, and also for a subtle transition from a more formal area to an informal one. Unless it is a decorative element, a fence is best not seen. In other words, if fencing cannot be hidden, make it worth looking at.

The Simple Methods Rule

Occasionally gardeners go to great expense to create diversity where simplicity would result in more beauty. An over-decorated garden lacks intent. Every one of its elements begs for attention, and this soon tires the visitor. By taking something away, one gives importance to the elements remaining in the garden, thereby creating a feeling of space and repose. Avoid more steps, building materials, or colors than necessary. If the house is a traditional farm structure, simple containers near a terrace or pool are preferable to over-decorated baroque vases. A large trough may find its place here, while the cupids will feel more at home in a cypress-surrounded city garden.

Plan the back area of the house as carefully as the front. The potting shed should not be an underprivileged spot. If it is well kept, it will give you pleasure while you are working there. As elsewhere, it is best to keep things from getting too complicated.

At the garden shop, I have been told, clients frequently look for the bizarre and are attracted by such anomalies as the virus-induced, tortuous growth of the cristata cacti. All of the red-streaked coleus sell out right away, leaving the beautiful, naturally green ones behind. It also seems that meager plantlets turn into an instant success once they have been transferred onto a bonsai dish—with a zero added to the price tag.

One evening, as I thanked my hostess for a lovely dinner, I gave her a compliment on her garden, which suits its surroundings to perfection. "Splendid mountains surround us," she answered, almost apologetically. "Too much diversity would distract from them."

This amusing nineteenth-century Mallorcan beach folly is best associated with sparse, salt-tolerant planting (*Tamarix*).

An old feeding trough planted with succulent *Aeonium* is all that is needed to adorn a paved space.

Controlling the Choice of Plants

An ever-expanding selection of plants invariably tempts gardeners to plant as many different species as possible, one of each if possible. We all find this hard to resist. Yet if we want to achieve a natural and easy look, **we should aim at repeating the plants we already use, those that do well with us**. Large expanses of identical or similar plants create a sense of unity and a feeling of space. In the past, mediterranean gardens were created with a restricted range of plant material, yet great beauty was achieved with what was available.

The view from my garden is harmonious and beautiful. All of the neighboring homeowners fence their gardens with an identical whitewashed low wall, which is high enough to keep animals from jumping into their gardens. In sunny spots, native pine and mastic are accompanied by rosemary, lavender, lantana, and oleander, with myrtle planted in the open shade of the pines. There is the occasional climber, a few palms, and aloe in large patches where soil is shallow. This quiet plant choice frames a dramatic view of the nearby sea and gives a restful feeling of

Even shapes can be borrowed in order to unite your garden with the surrounding land.

space. **An attractive appearance results from planting according to sound landscaping rules and from gentle grooming**, while the use of drought-tolerant plants permits easy, low-cost maintenance.

Contrast is the fashion today, but a unifying theme is often more satisfying. To this end, we associate plants for their similarity, plants that are not necessarily identical but similar. We consider their size and outline and the texture, shape, and color of their leaves, as we do with any plant choice. For instance, plants with needlelike leaves, such as the kapok bush (*Eriocephalus africanus*) or *Grevillea rosmarinifolia*, are

Marguerites (*Argyranthemum*) and African daisies (*Dimorphotheca, Osteospermum*) combine for a rich yet restrained display.

excellent companions for rosemary. Subtle harmony is achieved, more satisfactory than a conflicting contrast.

My garden, for example, is an open oak wood with a natural undergrowth of shrubs in rounded masses—spurge olive (*Cneorum tricoccon*), *Myrtus*, mastic (*Pistacia lentiscus*), and the rare *Rhamnus ludovici-salvatoris*. To fill in, I chose the similar volumes of the waterwise Mexican orange (*Choisya ternata*), rock rose (*Cistus*), *Hebe*, California holly (*Heteromeles arbutifolia*), fragrant olive (*Osmanthus*), tobira (*Pittosporum tobira* 'Nana'), India hawthorn (*Rhaphiolepis*), *Viburnum tinus*, and *V. suspensum*, whose volumes resemble those of the original plants and easily blend with them.

If the collector bug tempts you, one solution is to find a theme that unites your acquisitions. For example, collect a range of California lilacs (*Ceanothus*) or California fuchsias (*Epilobium*), or all the bulbs you can lay your hands on. I do not mean, however, that you should dot them about; plant in groupings. As always, good landscaping rules will guide you.

Perhaps you have some plants that stand out too much in the garden and give it a contrived look. These may have been a purchase you simply could not resist, although you knew perfectly well that you should have refrained; or perhaps they were a gift. Such plants can always be "concealed" in a location where they do not interfere with the general landscaping idea, but where they can be displayed to their best advantage. Plantings near the house are less likely to influence the overall aspect. Tall, strong-colored *Canna indica* is often difficult to place; it calls for attention and in a rural setting, for example, seems the wrong choice. Yet the canna may find its place in the courtyard, where it can hold its own together with other exotics.

A single palm tree accompanies the entrance to this Portuguese property, taking advantage of a carefully restored wall. Nothing more is needed.

The Power of Color

The color of flowers preoccupies every gardener, but too often one finds that the color of a climber, for instance, is in disharmony with the paint color of the house, or the color of the entrance door fights with the flower beds in front of it, or the containers clash with the paving of the terrace they are meant to adorn. I can think of gardens where green seems an outcast, where *Quercus rubra* 'Aurea' has been planted next to *Cedrus atlantica* 'Glauca', together with a red-leaved *Acer* and a silvery *Salix*, all accompanied by a few variegated plants. Contrast has been achieved to perfection—but for what purpose? As an alternative, consider subtle contrasts that complement each other or set each other off. Really, the rich palette of green and gray often seems better than an array of glaring colors that are used without any consideration for harmony. Color in itself is not always beautiful; it is what we do with it that creates beauty.

To achieve a true mediterranean look, **it is not necessary to splash contrasting colors around**. Green alone can achieve a restrained contrast that imparts a natural look. The foliage of mediterranean native plants is mostly evergreen, and I can find many greens in my garden—bluish-green lavender foliage, the dark, satiny green of mock privet (*Phillyrea*), or gray, silver, and even near-white artemisias. Look closely at the texture of the leaves. After the dried-up summer look, green comes back with the first rain in the form of fresh growth. (Flaming autumn colors play a minor role unless one gardens in a mountain region.)

Color-edged leaves can create illusions. White gives an illusion of coolness and light; white-edged leaves, for instance, bring light to a shady corner. Do not mix these with yellow-edged leaves, which would look muddy in this context.

Yellow means warmth, and golden daffodils bring sun to a gray morning. Yellow or yellow-bordered leaves can set off the wispy yellow flowers of the Cornelian cherry (*Cornus mas*), just as a yellow rose climbing into it would do. Pink *Iris germanica* flowers look wonderful near a pomegranate (*Punica granatum*), which is flushed with orange-tipped spring leaves. Each sets off the other's color and also complements it. This setting-off and complementing fulfill the great potential of color-edged leaves. A vast range of plant material with variegated leaves is at our disposal. Although variegation has its undeniable merits, it takes some thought to use it properly. Frequently employed to achieve contrast, variegated leaves tend to distract the eye and often blur the design.

The light is an important element in a mediterranean-type garden, where it brings the many greens to life. A noon breeze moves the leaves of an olive tree, making a myriad shiny sparkles stand out against a dark buckthorn (*Rhamnus*). Foliage reflects the sun; leaves catch the dew, small drops reflect the light in rainbow colors. The late afternoon light shines through the delicate petals of the *Oncocyclus* iris, making the rich colors glow like Gothic stained-glass windows. Light may be reflected on the paving of a dark, forgotten corner of the garden, where it creates a fascinating interplay of light and shade. Or you can create a semblance of light, imaginary light, by using white flowers or white-variegated foliage. See what happens when the wind moves the branches of the trees: the silvery underside of the foliage may show, the last rays of the sun may turn leaves to gold. All this can be part of your garden.

Moorish garden designers understood well the intricate play of light and shade. Galiana Palace, Toledo, Spain

ground cover of variegated y lightens a dark area, as a ingle shoot displays its leaves n a cypress trunk.

The drought-tolerant live-forever (*Hylotelephium*) provides just enough color to enliven this evergreen scene.

Scale and Proportion

The design of a mediterranean garden that is successful twelve months a year requires a well-chosen structural basis in which scale and proportion are significant elements. One must consider carefully the relationship between shade and light and between horizontal and vertical lines. It is also important to pay attention to the interaction between colors and to link them sensitively with their surroundings. **Your aim will be to achieve a successful balance of all the elements of the garden.** Such considerations, if added up and carefully carried out, may come close to excellence. But since we all want our gardens to be livable and to suit our lifestyle, we should not fret if all is not perfection.

A successful garden design includes empty spaces against which plant compositions can stand out. Empty spaces will anchor a view to the land and balance crowded garden areas. A whitewashed wall or a simple cypress hedge, like a pool, can fill the role of empty space. Along the same lines, a lawn—although ill suited to a waterwise garden, which would do better with paving or a field of lavender—can balance a busy picture and suggest tranquility. But the empty space can also mean the sea, the sky, or a large expanse of uncluttered, clean rock, whose simple lines contrast with more crowded areas. In a small garden, a terrace or the violet-covered ground beneath an umbrella-

One's expectation is heightened by several arches and, farther back, by the light framing a Greek goddess.

shape tree provide the empty space. In the same spirit, a successful composition of flower colors is best backed by a simple sea of green.

Although dividing a garden into compartments has its undeniable merits, such as providing wind protection, microclimates, or seclusion, you should know why you are dividing. Compartments can help to structure an ill-defined garden space, but they may require a succession of small spaces leading out into a wide-open expanse. Much can be achieved by changing the width of a path or of garden steps. Widening them imparts importance to an area, whereas narrowing a curving path will clarify its secondary role within the garden.

An additional interaction between garden elements is represented by "the picture and its frame." You may create a frame for a picture or, alternatively, compose a picture for an already existing frame. Depending on how well both are handled, they can either enhance or obliterate each other. For instance, when the newly risen moon casts a silvery path over tranquil waters, nothing manmade can equal this dramatic picture, which requires only that the garden setting provide a suitable frame. To achieve this, underline the scene with low shrubs or frame the space with a tree. It may take a year or longer to choose the appropriate plants, until, all of a sudden, the answer comes up—usually while one is looking for something else.

Several deciduous shrubs planted next to each other tend to create a confused outline of intertwining branches, and their siting requires care. A more satisfactory composition is that given by the arching branches of a single shrub, which stand out against a backdrop of solid green foliage or an ocher-washed wall. **A plant can improve the look of its neighbor or can visually wipe it out.** Ideally, each assists the other.

Consider the importance of the selected flower color and its mass in relation to the evergreen foliage that surrounds it. A small pink cushion will disappear in a vast sea of shiny green, while tall lilies in the same location might be a startling sight. Try anchoring the soaring foxgloves we all cherish to the side of a rock, but aim for the right proportion between the two. Likewise, three meager petunias would never do in open woodland, but three bulky ericas might be a delightful sight.

Gardening is painting, but it can also be sculpture, with plants introducing a third dimension. Gardeners know that plants are not static. If the significance of a single plant has changed, the picture is usually out of balance and the moment will come when we have to invent it anew. This may mean adjusting volumes and redefining shapes, shifting the ever-changing proportions. **The creation of a garden is an ongoing affair.** My hands will lower a plant here, define a shape there, or open up a passage. I step back, consider the outline of a shrub, take off just one more branch to get a better-defined vista, or lower the rosemary a tiny bit more to give importance to a plant behind it. A bit here and a bit there until the picture is right, in balance. Rearranging is continuous, strenuous, and fun.

I am sometimes asked if there is a moment during the year when our garden provides nothing to look

The carefully restored stonework, the solid mass of tall cypresses, and the wispy volume of a deciduous tree are perfectly proportioned.

at. And this makes me wonder whether a garden has to have something *all* the time. There will always be a point of interest if we are prepared to see it—the finely cut leaves of a bignonia silhouetted against a pale autumn sky, or large white clematis flowers shining against a dark trunk.

A Garden in Harmony with Its Surroundings

Although a mediterranean garden can have flowers in bloom throughout the year, it does not have to be designed for constant display. Expectation is important, too, as one awaits in joyful anticipation the opening of a bud or the ripening of fruits. It is as important to look forward to the first strawberries accompanied by jubilant birdsong as it is to eat them (the strawberries, not the birds!). A garden that has quiet phases (which does not have to mean dull) will be enjoyed all the more when the star performers come out. Contrast, then, means contrast in time, similar to that of foliage or color.

An artful Moorish window, divided by two slender columns, looks out over the garden. Notice the intricate design of the paving and the white marble water basin.

A gloriette stands out against the dramatic sky.

Creating Garden Atmosphere

Once you have sensed the spirit of your place, you can create moods. A range of elements can help you achieve whatever atmosphere you envisage. Your plants will be chosen accordingly, if you bear in mind that decorative effects always come last. Walls and hedges provide a protected feeling, and large expanses of a single plant or a wide open horizon give a feeling of tranquility. A tropical setting with exotic plants and colorful birds may simulate adventure or a mysterious paradise. Strong colors, such as flaming orange, fiery red, or intense yellow, can impart a feeling of warmth. On the other hand, the sensation of refreshing coolness in shade can be transmitted by a group of white flowers next to a small water feature and a dark cypress wall. When one sets out to create a desired atmosphere, intuition is often the best guide.

Harmony is subtle. Gardeners are often advised to plan for variety, but shouldn't one try instead to achieve *harmony*? Isn't tranquil peace what we seek in our troubled times? At the Huntington Gardens in California, one can read: "Japanese gardens are designed to induce a feeling of peace and tranquility, an effect enhanced by the sound of water, the wind in the trees, and the singing of birds." These words can apply to any garden—ours, too. Yet the Japanese are not the only ones to find peace in a garden. Certainly the Moors envisaged a tranquil reflection of paradise in their gardens where all the senses were catered to.

Time and again, I read in our guest book: "Thank you for a glimpse of paradise." If my garden is paradise, then paradise could mean birdsong, bees humming, the sound of sheep bells, plants keenly cared for, a few flowers, and quiet simplicity—a big, open sky, too. Or is paradise simply being at peace with oneself? Certainly it is not a question of size: I recall a handkerchief-size Moroccan *dar* (courtyard) where moving shade, divine scent, and peace prevailed.

"What is paradise?" I have often asked others. Recently a friend put *The Persian Garden, Echoes of Paradise* on our garden table. Would this book give me the answer? In a way it did. Paradise, I read, derives from the Persian *pairi-daeza*, meaning a walled space. Later the Greeks adapted the word to *paradeisos* in order to describe the gardens of the Persian Empire, and Greek translations of the Bible used it as a term for the Garden of Eden and for heaven.

The *paradeisos* offered the promise of divine order amid chaos. Outside its high walls, pitiless desert heat might brood, but within, everything was calm—a center for contemplation, for relief from the burning sun. One could pass through an airy, cool summer pavilion to see a cascading stream, flanked by shady walks and cypress avenues, where birds fluttered from tree to tree. The famous apple grew among the other fruits. Here there was little grass, but in patches of filtered sun flowers were scattered about—roses, anemones, bright blue muscaris, hyacinths, a minute iris, vibrant ranunculi, tulips (ancestors of the cultivated plants of the West), and fragrant jasmine—a paradise in an austere wilderness.

Note: Underground irrigation channels, known as *qanats*, depend on subterranean water at the foot of the mountains—the sacred water. (Khansari, 1998).

Mediterranean Dream Gardens
Choosing Your Personal Eden

Aloe arborescens in large patches brightens up a dark palm grove.

Our dreams are not necessarily realistic, nor do they always take material shape, but we can certainly try. It does not take long to jot down our observations and to make a few sketches to help us work out how we want to live and what we want to achieve. Once you have discovered your possibilities and your limits (the vital groundwork), you can begin the process of choosing your dream garden. The questionnaire on page 36 and the following descriptions of twenty different types of gardens that suit a mediterranean climate will certainly help in the process. These gardens, arranged after the Mediterranean Garden, in no particular order, offer practical and attractive solutions to any number of garden situations. As you leaf through the book, you will find many useful tips on how to achieve your dream and a wealth of ideas that will help you create your own place of delight.

The wide range of gardens described here is designed to tackle the general circumstances a mediterranean gardener is likely to encounter. The hot, dry summers and strong light, the devastating winds, destructive fires, and erosion are all analyzed. Saving water, that precious and endangered resource, is given prominence, but restoration and conservation are also addressed. There are also useful answers here for any gardener's personal situation. For example, if a lack of water is your garden's limiting factor, you will find advice on waterwise gardening methods.

This chapter will stimulate all of the senses with bewitching scent and eye-pleasing beauty, flavorsome foods, the caressing touch of feltlike leaves, and the sound of the wind, of water dripping from a faucet—or of silence.

We will explore the four seasons: autumn with its rich harvest in the Edible Garden, winter on the sunny terraces of the Garden in the Hills, a peaceful summer spent at your Coastal Garden. Do you want to enjoy an Olive Grove in spring, its trees underplanted with flowering bulbs, or harvest its olives in autumn in order to press them for oil, or delight in its idyllic setting throughout the year? The garden in Refreshing Shade, Delightful Scent is clearly at its best in summer, whereas Living with Animals requires the year-round presence of the owner. When do your containers have to be at their peak? Most of the gardens can be used year round, although a vacation home may require that you plan the flower display for a specific season.

The twenty successful gardens offered in this chapter—most of them water-conserving and sun-drenched— show a range of attractive and practical solutions. Whether you want to devote your days to the delights of a natural garden, or intend to rescue native mediterranean plants, or choose the Lazy Person's Dream Garden in order to save time, you will find a garden that responds to your

A find from an excavation is housed in a niche in this Greek garden, accompanied by a time-worn vase.

needs. The introductory notes list the themes dealt with in each project and provide references to other gardens—explore them all. Mix and match elements from the various projects to suit your own garden conditions.

Generous plant lists accompany each project, drawn up with a view to each garden's particular requirements. The lists make full use of the ample plant material from the rich flora of all the mediterranean areas of the world (southern Australia, California, central Chile, the Mediterranean Basin, and the Cape of South Africa). The native plants from the Mediterranean Basin have been given priority, however, so that gardeners from other regions can familiarize themselves with them. Easy, drought-tolerant, strong, and healthy, they virtually take care of themselves. They provide an evergreen plant cover to the mediterranean garden. The same plants will appear in several garden projects, which is testament to their versatility. But these plants are by no means the only ones that can be used under the circumstances described. They are meant as suggestions only, for gardeners to explore on their own, to replace them with plants from their own regions or with their favorites. With their attractive foliage and colorful blossoms, hundreds of plants are waiting to be discovered—and used!

The beautiful interplay of light and shade enhances this Greek garden. Design by Charles Shoup

The Mediterranean Garden
An Evergreen Eden

The perennial question of what exactly constitutes a native mediterranean garden finds a partial answer in the discussion in this section of a number of its characteristic features. These have evolved over time to meet specific practical needs. The Mediterranean Garden, an easygoing and self-sustained outdoor space, uses many attractive, yet little-known native Mediterranean plants. Here we will see how they may be used in the garden and how we can thereby contribute to their conservation. Many of the native plants that grow around the Mediterranean Basin make excellent garden subjects. An extensive list of them is given here, divided according to type and suitability for different sites. A word of caution: Many plants from the Mediterranean Basin self-seed with ease, such as those in the Leguminosae family (*Coronilla*, *Genista*, *Spartium*). Seedlings can be pulled out easily, and these plants seldom become a problem. But in Australia, California, and South Africa, they are prone to invasive behavior. For the convenience of gardeners in these regions, the most invasive plants are listed on page 33. Use with care or stay away from such lovely plants as valerian (*Centranthus*) and ivy (*Hedera helix*); both self-sow freely. And once it is in your garden, you will never get rid of Cape sorrel (*Oxalis pes-caprae*), an import from South Africa, although I cannot imagine a prettier sight than a field it has conquered.

A thriving Mediterranean garden possesses a solid backbone, with the house well anchored to its site. Such a garden displays a sense of scale, is well proportioned between color, volume, and texture, and uses a correct choice of plants. It befits its surroundings and is in harmony with the mediterranean climate. Carefully planted and—once established—easy to maintain, a native mediterranean garden will always repay the gardener's efforts.

The garden project in this section features the native plants indigenous to the Mediterranean Basin, and they have many qualities that can benefit gardeners from other mediterranean climate regions. Thanks to their sturdy constitution, their water-saving characteristics, and easy maintenance, native mediterranean plants are, of course, favorites. Their delightful scents—arresting aromas, heady perfumes, and the pungent odor of their disinfectant oils—make them irresistible. Their foliage is mostly small and compact, which predestines them to be sheared and clipped into the hedges and topiaries that are characteristic of

A woodland in the author's garden displays native plants from the Mediterranean Basin: ancient oak (*Quercus ilex*), white and pink rock roses (*Cistus*), and mastic (*Pistacia lentiscus*), cut into rounded shapes. Farther back is a small tree (*Phillyrea*). None is ever watered.

mediterranean gardens. Adapted to the climatic conditions of their native habitats, to the often steep and rocky terrain that falls down to the Mediterranean Sea, native mediterranean plants are not demanding. They make do with dry summers and poor soil low in nutrients. Yet they do need excellent drainage, ample mulch, and a great deal of light (although not all require direct sun). Their light requirements are easily understood if we consider that in mediterranean-climate regions the blue sky is seldom far away, even in winter. For more text on native plants, see Native Mediterranean Plants in Chapter 1 (page 21).

Note that these native plants are from only one mediterranean-climate region and that gardeners in other regions with a mediterranean climate will replace them with plants from their own regions. With time, for example, authentic Australian mediterranean gardens will evolve, using Australian building materials, Australian colors, and all the exciting plants from their mediterranean-climate regions. The same goes for California and South Africa. Less is known about the fifth mediterranean-climate region—Chile. Still, the plants are there, and I should love to know of a garden that is built around them. Boldo (*Peumus boldus*), for instance, has established itself well in my garden and now makes a pleasing dark-green mass not unlike laurustinus (*Viburnum tinus*).

Ingredients of the Native Mediterranean Garden

If we live in the Mediterranean Basin and intend to create a garden, how should we begin? It helps to remember that, in times past, the various elements that shaped such a garden nearly always emerged from necessity, often from the constraints that life around the Mediterranean Basin imposed on people. Daily food had to be wrenched from the hard, rocky, dry soil for which only limited water was available, and in early times the threat of famine was never far away. No wonder that food is ever-present in Mediterranean life. Such limitations and restrictions challenged the imagination of the Mediterranean peoples, who responded with great ingenuity and style.

❧ **A courtyard or patio** with attractive containers or any level ground on which one might sit outside seems the right place to start. Life in earlier days was fraught with countless dangers, to which artfully wrought iron gates and barred windows still bear witness. The enclosed walls of a courtyard whose roots go back to Roman and Moorish times gave protection and ensured a safe place for the family and animals. Spreading out into the countryside is our modern way of perceiving the garden that surrounds our house.

❧ **Shade.** Relief from the full sun has always been an urgent priority in the Mediterranean Basin. In summer, when the air is still during the hot midday hours, all life seems to cease. Shady pergolas and arbors, a cool *bosco*, even a lone tree, all provide welcome relief from the heat. If the shutters are closed in the early morning hours, the house remains cool—and not only for the sake of *siesta*. (Or you could hang a hammock between two conveniently spaced trees!) In the evening, people tend to move outdoors to catch the refreshing breeze. They gather on the plaza until the late-night hours to enjoy the renaissance of life.

Provide shade against the intense summer sun for your outdoor dining table during leisurely meals. Mediterranean people have always been gregarious, and tasty, rich food plays an important part in their

The often steep and rocky terrain tumbles down to the Mediterranean Sea.

lives. An outdoor kitchen is an integral part of each Mediterranean setting, and alfresco dining is enjoyed by everyone.

❧ **A pergola** provides shade for a cool walk much as trees do. It will also support vines that produce the grapes pressed for wine in the autumn. Homeowners in the mediterranea-climate regions of Australia and South Africa have recently been turning surplus land on their plots into vineyards, and home-grown wine has become the fashion of the day. Apart from grapevines, many flowering climbers can cover a pergola, or you can choose jasmine for its scent.

❧ **Decorative paving.** Lawns have never been a Mediterranean feature. Indeed, where would the water required to keep it green have come from? An attractive alternative to a lawn—and, incidentally, a way to keep one's feet dry during rainy winters—are stone slabs or decorative paving or pebbles assembled into an artistic design. To this day, the simplest courtyard can introduce a decorative element at little cost. Try a mosaic or simply use gravel. Add more gravel if you wish to create a tidy look or to provide a dry bed for the plants. Gravel also suppresses weeds and seals in moisture at the same time. Choose a color that complements in a pleasing way the shades of the garden and the house.

🌿 **Terraced land.** Terracing is seen everywhere around the Mediterranean Basin, often near the house. Steps and stairways reflect the steep terrain and connect the different levels of the garden. This practice evolved to keep the soil from being washed away and to create a favorable soil depth where fruit trees could be planted with vegetables beneath them. Terraced soil may also mean a raised bed that provides plants with all-important drainage or a leveled path that has the added advantage of guiding the water from a sudden downpour to a place where it will not deluge your plants but do good where it is needed.

🌿 **Evergreen plants** will give your garden an instant mediterranean look, a "southern" feel, for the leafless limbs of deciduous plants make one think of northern winters. Evergreens provide a well-furnished look and cover the ground throughout the year. Give priority to the reliable and hard-working mediterranean natives (see page 70). Most of these evergreens are veiled for weeks on end with colorful blossoms; they are healthy and dependable in a difficult climate and beautiful in an unassuming way. Give consideration also to foliage with a strong accent on the silvers and grays that are a prominent feature of the *maquis*, the shrub-covered Mediterranean landscape near the sea. Choose plants that do not make demands on time or water, such as the versatile strawberry tree (*Arbutus*), artemisias, ericas, laurel, myrtle, Jerusalem sage (*Phlomis*), every

juniper, lavender, mastic, rosemary, sage, and thyme. As in any garden, the final effect, the "picture," will depend on your imagination and landscaping skills and, of course, on the care given to the plants.

Do not be afraid to repeat your evergreen plants over and over. Remember that the original selection available to the Mediterranean gardener was limited and that today's potpourri had not yet taken over the region. Plants grown en masse were often thought of as building elements in the garden.

🌿 **Topiary.** The original palette of the Mediterranean garden was limited to the *maquis* shrubs, which were enhanced by being clipped into pleasing shapes. Lavender and myrtle, rosemary and santolina were plants from the wild *maquis* that gained a great deal of attraction with careful clipping and shearing. Cypress and myrtle were grown as fat cushions or as inventive topiary. The cushion shape, a clever protection against dehydration, is a typical feature of the Mediterranean plant world. Although most mediterranean plants are easily pruned, my first choice would be evergreen box (*Buxus balearica* and *B. sempervirens*). Mock privet (*Phillyrea angustifolia* or *P. media*) lends itself to shaping, and although buckthorn (*Rhamnus alaternus*) is really a tree, it gives particularly good results where a large, rounded, green volume is required.

🌿 The **cypress** is an integral part of the Tuscan landscape and appeared often in paintings by the early Florentine masters. Today cypress trees are threatened by health problems, but we would not want to do without their sky-soaring spires. You may substitute the rare Mediterranean *Tetraclinis* or introduce such conifers as *Callitris* from Australia, *Calocedrus* and *Chamaecyparis* from Asia and the United States, or *Widdringtonia* from South Africa, as all have a growth pattern similar to cypress.

🌿 **Elegant palms** and the wide range of sword-leaved plants (all of the latter were introduced to the Mediterranean Basin from elsewhere but have been used since the earliest times) give structure to the garden in the same way that cypresses do. They introduce focal points and can be used as a less labor-intensive substitute for clipped and shaped evergreens or topiary.

• **Reduced color palette.** The true Mediterranean garden has never been known for a riot of colors and the emphasis is largely on evergreen plants. Colorful exotics did not reach the Mediterranean until relatively recently; even if these plants had been available, certainly no Renaissance gardeners would have made use of them. Yet the distinct foliage and often graceful carriage of many evergreens and silvery gray plants brought great variety to a garden in which color was added by tiles and cheerful bulbs, which are such a characteristic feature of the Mediterranean lands. To this day, the all-important interplay of stirring light and shadow brings the limited palette of an evergreen garden to life and provides it with outstanding visual delight.

• **Fragrance.** Close your eyes and think of the enchantment that engulfs you when you step on thyme along a garden path. Imagine dried lavender flowers in your bureau drawers or in a potpourri in your drawing room. In the old days, lavender was swept into the corners of rooms in order to release its purifying fragrance. During the long, hot summers, aromatic scent lingers all day long in the *maquis* air. Did Napoleon not declare that, with his eyes closed, he would be able to recognize his native Corsica as he approached it? One can never plant enough lavender. It does well in the full sun among stones where no summer water can reach them. And, of course, an aromatic bouquet of herbs will enrich your cooking. The aromatic oils contained in the leaves of many Mediterranean natives have been extracted for medicinal uses for many centuries, while fields of cultivated flowers, such as carnations, jasmine, and violets helped to fuel the perfume industry. Richly scented flowers that release their bewitching perfume mostly at night will delight you during warm summer evenings. Plant them near your outdoor dining area or under a window or wherever their nightly scent will be noticed. For a

Nothing is as pleasurable as sitting out in summer under the moving shade of a palm tree.

choice of scented plants, see Refreshing Shade, Delightful Scent on page 110.

• **A small water feature.** Even a token basin or a tiny drip (using recirculated water) is a must in a mediterranean garden. In earlier times, the water supply—once the rains were over—was meager. Water was needed to grow food and was certainly not splashed about or used for such luxuries as flowers. Carefully guided in channels or rills or dripping from a tap, water served a purpose, mostly to water the vegetable garden and the orchard. For decorative purposes, however, size is irrelevant, and even the smallest water feature, with no purpose other than delight, gives a feeling of luxury and a vision of the earthly paradise.

• **Containers** have multiple purposes. In early times, when water was needed and used to grow food, containers were a way of confining the earth. They could be watered easily, and they eliminated any waste of soil or water. The lady of the house could keep a few treasures in containers, such as herbs for the kitchen, a small lemon tree, or undemanding bulbous plants from faraway lands. (Left to rest, the bulbs would do without water in summer.) Containers take all shapes—from a discarded tin or a half-broken oil jar to a terra-cotta pot or an elaborate, decorated vessel. Mediterranean peoples have a strong artistic bent, and to this day their creativity in the garden is still apparent. No wonder that Cretan terra-cotta vases and pots, *pithária*, are universally preferred to plastic vessels. In our day, decorative containers can involve a serious investment, and not all of them will be able to withstand freezing. If you do not want to invest in such luxuries, look for simple, well-chosen replicas. There is no limit to your inventiveness.

❧ **Decorative vases and statues** offer visual diversion in a mass of evergreen mediterranean foliage. These ornamental features, often seen today covered with moss, provided a large garden with a feeling of order and rhythm and a sense of place. Remember that today, too, simplicity and order should rule in the layout of a garden. If you choose, for example, an axial theme with an exciting vista, accented by such objects as vases or a column, you may demonstrate great inventiveness.

❧ **Columns.** There were once many Greek and Roman temples around the Mediterranean, and when they fell into disuse, the stone was often recycled. Look for a column to add interest to your garden. It does not have to be an archaeological find; in fact, you can even cheat by using a cleverly disguised concrete pipe. A single column will suffice, but a series of them may be the beginning of a handsome pergola.

❧ **Fruits and vegetables.** Growing food has always been of great importance in Mediterranean gardens, and if we want to create such a garden today, we can do nothing better than growing tomatoes on poles and beans on tall canes, ground-covering cucumber and

A roof supported by columns provides a fine shady spot for overlooking the garden in summer without stepping out into the glaring light.

melon, and fruits and nuts, such as figs, grapes, plums, and almonds. You may even be tempted by more exotic choices. If you remember to plant fruit trees today, well spaced out for a rich yield, you will be grateful for this decision when the time comes for harvesting. The Edible Garden on page 146 will inspire you with an endless selection of plants to choose from.

Before we start to explore the different types of plants available to us in an authentically native Mediterranean garden, I would like to offer two general—but very important—bits of advice.

❧ **Work with the seasons.** In spring, the mediterranean garden has its moment of glory with long-lasting flowers. Later, during the hottest summer months, the garden and the gardener go into a state of dormancy, reawakening to a jubilant autumn, which brings shorter and cooler days and the first autumn rains. Winter and its rain will bring water for the garden. Enjoy each season for the delights each of them offers you.

❧ **Be individual.** There is a certain similarity in all mediterranean gardens through the use of the same elements, but do not let this restrict your inventiveness. There is plenty of room for personal interpretation, just as the people of the Mediterranean have demonstrated for generations. There is ample opportunity for each garden to display its own personality. I would even say that individuality is one of the characteristic traits of the mediterranean garden. You have only to look at the style of each entry way as you approach a garden or a house.

Native Mediterranean Plants

In mediterranean regions, intense light bathes the rocks, the hills, and the ever-present sea, while sunlight flows through the leaves of the trees and creates shadows. Envision your garden as a series of rooms surrounding your house, with the blue mediterranean sky serving as their roof. Hard-leaved evergreen trees and shrubs will provide the frame and the walls for your garden.

Trees. Naturally growing trees should always be preserved as long as they are healthy and not over-crowded, in which case thinning may be required. Trees act as a windbreak, prevent erosion, and add to the richness of the vegetative cover. If you need to fill in with new trees, choose such evergreens as the Spanish chestnut (*Castanea sativa*), oak, cypress, and cedar. As a windbreak in sun or shade, plant the mediterranean buckthorn (*Rhamnus alaternus*), which can be grown either as a small tree or as a bulky, glossy-leaved green mass (you will have to pull out excess seedlings). Carob (*Ceratonia siliqua*) prefers a wind-protected site in full sun. Plant junipers of various sizes and shapes, depending on their requirements. Where planting space is limited, cypress trees will screen an undesirable view; *Tetraclinis* will give a similar visual effect and is apparently not affected by health hazards such as

the cypress often is today. For soils rich in silica, choose cork oak (*Quercus suber*), together with an underplanting similar to that used with maritime pine (*Pinus pinaster*). The Aleppo pine (*Pinus halepensis*) is a quickly growing pioneer plant that requires vigilant control before it gets out of hand.

Deciduous trees, such as the Judas tree (*Cercis siliquastrum*) are useful, since they let the sun through in winter. They also offer abundant early flowering and provide welcome shade in summer. They all need some space if they are to develop their visual potential, and dense stands will need thinning before the trees are fully grown.

Shrubs will provide shelter and screening, or they can frame an enthralling view. In full sun, accompany the trees with the rounded evergreen masses of the strawberry tree (*Arbutus unedo*) or with box (*Buxus*) and mastic (*Pistacia lentiscus*), or the tall laurustinus (*Viburnum tinus*). Oleanders (*Nerium oleander*) flower for many months. In spring, colorful and spiny *Calycotome* covers south-facing slopes with gold, but alas is weedy. Add more sunny splashes with *Coronilla* and broom (*Cytisus*, *Genista*, *Spartium*). Their sweet fragrance complements their cheerful blossoms. The chaste tree (*Vitex agnus-castus*) reaches out with white, pink, or blue flower spikes and is resistant to oak-root fungus. Near the sea, use feathery pink *Tamarix* to provide an accent; this plant not only tolerates but actually likes some salt. The deciduous pomegranate (*Punica granatum*) takes kindly to pruning and provides interest through-out the year. Its foliage is orange-rust in spring, apple-green in summer, and golden in autumn. A long period of blooming is followed by well-shaped, juicy fruit.

Note: Plant collectors will want to adopt two little-known endemic shrubs: spurge olive (*Cneorum tricoccon*) and *Rhamnus ludovici-salvatoris*. These extremely interesting plants are not demanding and are easily grown from seed.

This house sits firmly on its terraced site; with time the jasmine (*Jasminum polyanthum*) will cover the lower wall.

Large expanses of rounded lavender plants are a common sight in the south of France; here the lavender is being successfully used by a winery in California.

Fruits will enhance the many textures of leaves in the garden as the seasons progress. For a wide range of possibilities, consult The Edible Garden on page 146. A wild apple tree will delight everyone who passes by with its small, red-cheeked fruits. A wild fig (*Ficus carica*), with its tart fruit, may grow from a rock. Enjoy watching hazelnuts (*Corylus avellana*) and walnuts (*Juglans regia*) ripen, as well as pistachios (*Pistacia vera*), which are widely grown in Greece.

Thorns and spines. Don't avoid them. They are common features of indigenous Mediterranean plants; they help increase the photosynthetic area and reduce leaf space and thus transpiration. They also help the plant to scramble up a tree or wall to reach light and, of course, they help defend a plant against such aggressors as goats and other browsers. The firethorn (*Pyracantha coccinea*), which is particularly vicious, grows into a formidable hedge. *Chamaerops humilis*, the only widely growing mediterranean palm, is decorative from the moment it is planted but gains even more in beauty as it matures. It grows slowly, either single-stemmed or in bunches, and its fronds develop aggressive spines. Propagation, although slow, is easy from seed and volunteers often appear around older palms. The rare *Phoenix theophrasti* grows isolated on Crete; you can help save it from extinction by planting it in your garden. Beware of the formidable thorns of most yuccas; this plant is not a Mediterranean native but

This laurel shrub (*Laurus nobilis*) has been converted into a rounded standard.

together with any of the germanders (*Teucrium*). Caper (*Capparis spinosa*) will spring from a rocky wall. For gentian-blue flowers, try *Lithodora diffusa* or *L. rosmarinifolia*, together with golden *Euphorbia characias* and *E. myrsinites*.

By all means take advantage of the typical mediterranean cushion plants, which include *Alyssum*, *Aubrieta deltoidea*, snow-in-summer (*Cerastium tomentosum*), and everlasting flower (*Helichrysum*). Near the sea, in rocky or sandy soil, plant *Thymelaea hirsuta* and *T. tartonraira*, together with tamarisk. The closely related *Daphne gnidium*, with thick, hairless leaves and small white flowers, favors the bare *garrigue* terrain or woods. Succulents are rare in the Mediterranean Basin, but you can cover rocky spaces with the Canary Island aeoniums or sedums, both planted in small crevices.

was introduced so early on that I shall include it here. If you cut off a bit of the spiny tips, you will not damage its appearance.

Perennials. Where you have a north-facing site that gets no sun in winter, *Erica arborea* and *E. multiflora* will do well, as will many hypericums (*H. balearicum*), all hellebores (*Helleborus argutifolius*, *H. foetidus*, *H. lividus*, *H. orientalis*). Lovely peonies (*Paeonia broteroi*, *P. cambessedesii*, and *P. clusii*) grow where their long, cordlike roots can reach deep into the ground and are kept cool through the summer beneath rock or gravel.

For sunny spots, use the bear's breech (*Acanthus*), whose large leaves come out with the autumn rains, gray-leaved wormwood (*Artemisia absinthium*), *Senecio cineraria*, and many rock roses (*Cistus*). Particularly lovely are *Cistus ladanifer* with delicate, snow-white petals and wine-red blotches, the large-leaved *C. laurifolius*, or the closely related *Halimium*. Avoid the invasive *C. albidus* or pull out unwanted seedlings. Yellow Jerusalem sage (*Phlomis fruticosa*) needs pruning to keep it in shape; *P. italica*, which is pink, is smaller and more compact. Use these

Annuals and perennials. Blankets of the following plants will help protect the soil: columbine

Two terra-cotta lions guard the entrance to a nineteenth-century Spanish park.

(*Aquilegia*), *Ballota pseudodictamnus*, marigold (*Calendula*), silverbush (*Convolvulus cneorum*), baby's breath (*Gypsophila*), sea lavender (*Limonium*), sweet alyssum (*Lobularia maritima*), love-in-a-mist (*Nigella damascena*), butcher's broom (*Ruscus*), and periwinkle (*Vinca*). "Exclamation points" are: the spectacular *Echium*, giant fennel (*Ferula communis*), tree mallow (*Lavatera arborea*), felty mullein (*Verbascum*), and foxglove (*Digitalis dubia*).

Climbers. These are not prominent among mediterranean flora, but the grapevine (*Vitis vinifera*) will rapidly cover your pergola. (Remember to select a seedless variety.) Use honeysuckle (*Lonicera etrusca* and *L. implexa*) liberally for foliage, flowers, scent, and growth speed, but also for drought tolerance and easy maintenance. A yearly cutting-back will keep it within bounds. *Rosa sempervirens*, a Mediterranean native, will climb to lofty heights. In winter, the delicate *Clematis cirrhosa* holds on to a shrub, and its dainty white bells, sometimes greenish white or cream with red spots, are best appreciated when it is planted near a path. Summer-flowering *Clematis flammula* is a wonderful ground cover in places where it can't climb, but given a support, it can race up into a tree, where it looks like a foamy white curtain. To improve its look, prune liberally once the year's growth has died down. *Jasminum fruticans* is the only true Mediterranean species (the so-called Italian jasmine hails from Nepal). *Smilax aspera* flowers in autumn with a far-reaching scent; it is not as spectacular as South American or South African climbers, yet has a quiet beauty of its own. However, unless grown in a pot, it runs away to become a thorny pest, hard to eradicate.

Bulbous plants or geophytes (bulbs, corms, rhizomes, tubers; see Glossary) make up one of the richest groups of mediterranean plants. They give a splendid display of color in spring, whereas in summer they die down and become dormant. Geophytes planted at the end of the summer will begin to grow with the first autumn rains. Use them for large, natural-looking drifts. Many alliums thrive in both sun and shade. The well-known *Anemone*

These columns in the Parc Fontana Rosa in Menton, France, were designed in 1923 by Blasco Ibañez.

blanda grows wild under shrubs; *A. coronaria* displays large flowers in olive groves from Spain to Palestine. *Crocus* species flower over a period of many weeks. Begin with *C. sieberi* from Crete, followed by *C. goulimyi* from the former Yugoslavia. The large orange stigmas protruding from the petals of *C. sativus* produce the famous culinary saffron; to harvest your own, you have to plant thousands! In the wild, *Gladiolus communis*, *G. illyricus*, and *G. italicus*, which closely resemble one another, color the fields, but where they pop up, they may look spotty. To pull them together, I plant *Salvia officinalis*, whose flower color combines well with the gladioli.

In sunny sites, irises are everpresent. Look for the well-known *Iris germanica*, the Spanish *I. xiphium*, and the 'Oncos' from the eastern Mediterranean. *Leucojum aestivum* will naturalize. *Lilium candidum*, the heady-scented Madonna lily, is depicted in the earliest paintings of the Annunciation. Gentian-blue grape hyacinth (*Muscari*) is a vigorous grower. *Narcissus tazetta* flowers for months in winter, and countless other species do the same for weeks in spring (*N. bulbocodium*, *N. jonquilla*, and *N. papyraceus*). *Ornithogalum* grows freely, even near the roadside. Plant *Scilla hyacinthoides*, and don't let the name *Scilla peruviana* mislead you. It is a Mediterranean native, coming up readily from seed and growing into ever-thicker clumps. *Tulipa clusiana*, *T. praecox*, and *T. saxatilis* flower early with delicate charm, although, sadly, in my garden tulips tend to disappear quietly. (A friend recommends: "Add *Tulipa sylvestris* to your garden and I promise you won't lose it.") The sea daffodil (*Pancratium maritimum*) appears in sandy coastal soil. The late-summer-flowering sea squill (*Urginea maritima*) sends up tall white spires, followed by large shiny leaves. Its bulbs were once used as rat poison and in Greece are hung on the door at the New Year to bring good luck. Also autumn-flowering are *Colchicum*, the rare silvery-pink *Merendera*, and the golden *Sternbergia lutea*. In shade use *Arum italicum*, friar's cowl (*Arisarum vulgare*), *Dracunculus* in the Araceae family, and all cyclamens for their attractively marbled leaves and easy ways; *Cyclamen hederifolium* flowers from summer to autumn. *Iris foetidissima* with its spectacular fruit heads in autumn/winter covers the ground in shade, while *I. unguicularis* grows wild under oak trees in Morocco.

Conceived in this manner, a self-sustaining, natural space is created for relaxation and enjoyment, a garden where insects, butterflies, and birds are as much at home as the family.

Mediterranean Flora

Strictly speaking, the Canary Islands are not considered part of the Mediterranean-climate region, but many of their plants, such as *Aeonium*, *Dracaena draco*, *Hedera canariensis*, *Phoenix canariensis*, and *Pinus canariensis* have been included for their easy use in the garden. On the other hand, runaway Mediterranean Basin weeds, such as the grasses *Ampelodesmos*, *Calycotome*, or *Spartium*, have been omitted. In order not to expose them to excessive harvesting, no mention is made of the rare and threatened ground orchids. With certain genera, for instance tulips, you may expect a longer list, yet most tulips come from the East and few are native to the Mediterranean Basin. The same goes for roses.

Trees and Palms
Abies cephalonica
    Southern Greek mountains
Abies pinsapo
    Mountains near Ronda,
    Southern Spain
Acer monspessulanum
    S Europe
Arbutus andrachne
    SE Europe
Arbutus unedo
    Western Mediterranean
Castanea sativa
    S Europe, N Africa, Asia Minor
Cedrus atlantica
    Atlas Mountains (Algeria, Morocco)
Cedrus libani
    Asia Minor, Syria
Celtis australis
    S Europe, N Africa, Asia minor
Ceratonia siliqua
    SW Asia, naturalized in the Mediterranean

Cercis siliquastrum
  Eastern Mediterranean
Chamaerops humilis
  SW Europe, N Africa
Crataegus azarolus
  N Africa, W Asia
Crataegus monogyna
  Europe, N Africa, W Asia
Cupressus sempervirens
  Mediterranean, W Asia
Dracaena draco
  Canary Is.
Ficus carica
  Introduced to the Mediterranean
  from W Asia
Fraxinus ornus
  S Europe, SW Asia
Juglans regia
  SE Europe, Himalaya, and China
Juniperus communis
  Europe, N America, Asia
Juniperus oxycedrus
  Mediterranean, W Asia
Juniperus phoenicea
  Mediterranean
Juniperus sabina
  S and C Europe to Caucasus
Laurus nobilis
  Mediterranean
Olea europaea var. europaea
Olea europaea var. oleaster
  (O. e. var. sylvestris)
Phoenix canariensis
  Canary Is.
Phoenix dactylifera
  N Africa, SW Asia
Phoenix theophrasti
  E Crete, SW Turkey
Pinus brutia
  E Mediterranean, N Africa
Pinus canariensis
  Canary Is.
Pinus halepensis
  Mediterranean, W Asia
Pinus nigra
  Europe (Austria to C Italy, Greece,
  and former Yugoslavia)
Pinus pinaster
  W Mediterranean
Pinus pinea
  Mediterranean
Platanus orientalis, deciduous
  SE Europe

Populus alba
  C and SE Europe
Populus nigra Italica
  S Europe, W Asia
  (introduced in the early 18th c.)
Prunus armeniaca
  S Europe
Prunus dulcis
  N Africa to W Asia
Prunus lusitanica
  Portugal, Spain
Prunus spinosa
  Europe, N Africa
Pyrus elaeagrifolia
  SE Europe, Greece, Crete
Quercus cerris, deciduous
  C Europe
Quercus coccifera
  Mediterranean
Quercus frainetto, deciduous
  SE Europe
Quercus ilex
  SW Europe
Quercus ilex var. rotundifolia, evergreen
  SW Europe
Quercus ithaburensis spp. macrolepis
  Balkans, SE Italy
Quercus lusitanica, deciduous
  Portugal, SW Spain, N Africa
Quercus pubescens, deciduous
  W, C, and S Europe
Quercus pyrenaica, deciduous
  SW Europe, N Italy
Quercus suber
  S Europe, N Africa
Rhamnus alaternus
  Mediterranean, Portugal
Taxus baccata
  Europe, Algeria, W Asia
Tetraclinis articulata
  Algeria, Morocco, Mogador,
  Malta, SE Spain
Ulmus minor (syn. U. carpinifolia)
  Europe, N Africa

Shrubs

Adenocarpus anagyrifolius
  Morocco
Adenocarpus decorticans
  Spain
Anthyllis barba-jovis
  Mediterranean
Artemisia abrotanum

Artemisia arborescens
Artemisia absinthium
Artemisia fragrans
Bupleurum fruticosum
  S Europe
Buxus balearica
  Balearic Is., SW Spain
Buxus sempervirens
  S Europe, N Africa, W Asia
Cistus albidus
  SW Europe, N Africa
Cistus clusii
  W Mediterranean, N Africa
Cistus creticus
  C Mediterranean, N Africa
Cistus crispus
  W Mediterranean
Cistus ladanifer
  Spain, France, N Africa
Cistus laurifolius
  Mediterranean
Cistus monspeliensis
  Mediterranean
Cistus munbyi
  Morocco
Cistus parviflorus
  Crete, Cyprus
Cistus populifolius
  Spain, France
Cistus x purpureus, wild hybrid bet-
  ween C. creticus and C. ladanifer
Cistus salviifolius
  Mediterranean
Cistus sintenisii
  N Greece, Albania
Cneorum tricoccon
  Endemic W Mediterranean
Colutea arborescens
  Mediterranean
Coronilla emerus
  C and E Mediterranean
Coronilla juncea
  Portugal, NW Africa
Coronilla valentina spp. glauca
  S Europe
Corylus avellana
  Europe, N Africa, N Africa
Cotinus coggygria
  C and S Europe to Himalayas
Cytisus battandieri
  Morocco

Mediterranean Dream Gardens

Cytisus monspessulanus
S Europe, N Africa
Cytisus multiflorus
Spain, Portugal, N. Africa
Cytisus x praecox, garden
Origin C. multiflorus x
C. purgans
Cytisus purpureus
C and SE Europe
Cytisus scoparius
Europe
Daphne gnidium
S Europe, N Africa
Daphne oleoides
S Europe to Himalaya
Daphne sericea
SE Europe
Elaeagnus angustifolia,
naturalized
S Europe, origin W Asia
Erica arborea
S Europe, N and E Africa
Erica multiflora
W and C Mediterranean
Euphorbia dendroides
Mediterranean
Genista cinerea and
many more
SW Europe, N Africa
Hypericum balearicum
Balearic Is.
Hypericum cambessedesii
Possibly spp. or var. of
H. hircinum
S Europe
Ilex aquifolium
W and S Europe, N Africa,
W Asia
Jasminum fruticans
Mediterranean
Lavandula angustifolia
Mediterranean
Lavandula dentata
SE Spain
Lavandula stoechas
Mediterranean
Limoniastrum monopetalum
W and C Mediterranean
Myrtus communis
Mediterranean, SW Europe

Nerium oleander
Mediterranean to SW Asia
Paliurus spina-christi
S Europe to Himalayas
Phillyrea angustifolia
S Europe, N Africa
Phillyrea latifolia
S Europe, Asia Minor
Phlomis cretica
S Greece, Crete
Phlomis crinita
S and E Spain, NW Africa
Phlomis cypria
Cyprus
Phlomis fruticosa
Mediterranean
Phlomis herba-venti
Mediterranean
Phlomis italica
Endemic Balearic Is.
Phlomis lanata
Crete
Phlomis lunarifolia
Cyprus, S Turkey
Phlomis lychnitis
Spain, S France
Phlomis purpurea
S Portugal, C and S Spain
Pistacia lentiscus
Mediterranean
Pistacia terebinthus
Mediterranean, Asia Minor
Pistacia vera
introduced from W Asia
Punica granatum
introduced from SW Asia
Pyracantha coccinea
S Europe, SW Asia
Rhamnus ludovici-salvatoris
E Spain, Balearic Is.
Rosmarinus officinalis
S Europe, Asia Minor
Ruta chalepensis
Mediterranean
Santolina chamaecyparissus
S France, Pyrenees
Senecio cineraria
(syn. bicolor spp. cineraria)
W and C Mediterranean
to Greece

Tamarix africana
Portugal, N Africa
Tamarix gallica
SW Europe
Teucrium chamaedrys
Mediterranean
Teucrium fruticans
W and C Mediterranean
Teucrium polium
Mediterranean
Thymelaea hirsuta
Endemic Mediterranean
Thymelaea tartonraira
Mediterranean
Thymus, many
Mediterranean
Viburnum tinus
Mediterranean, SE Europe
Vitex agnus-castus
Mediterranean to C Asia
Ziziphus lotus
Mediterranean
Ziziphus spina-christi
Cyprus, E Mediterranean

Perennials, Annuals, Cushions, Accents

Acanthus
Mediterranean
Achillea grandifolia
Europe
Achillea millefolium
Europe
Achillea ptarmica
Europe
Aeonium
Canary Is.
Ajuga reptans
Mediterranean
Alyssum montanum
Mountains of Spain
and France
Alyssum saxatile
C and E Mediterranean
Anchusa
Europe, Africa, W Asia
Antirrhinum
Old and New World
Aquilegia vulgaris
W, C, and S Europe

Asteriscus
Aubrieta deltoidea
Ballota pseudodictamnus
Bellis annuis
Bellis sylvestris
Buglossoides purpurocaerulea
Calendula
Campanula
Capparis spinosa
Centranthus
Cerastium tomentosum
Chrysanthemum coronarium
Convolvulus cneorum
Cynara scolymus
Dianthus
Digitalis dubia,
Endemic Balearic Is.
Digitalis obscura
Spain
Echium
Euphorbia characias
Euphorbia myrsinites
Ferula communis
Globularia
Gypsophila pilosa
E Mediterranean
Halimium lasianthum
Helianthemum
Helichrysum stoechas
Lavatera arborea
Limonium sinuatum
Lithodora diffusa
Lithodora rosmarinifolia
Lobularia maritima
Malva
Nepeta cataria
Spain to Turkey
Nigella damascena
Pastinaca lucida
Endemic Balearic Is.
Reseda
Ruscus aculeatus
Ruta angustifolia
W and C Mediterranean
Ruta graveolens
S Europe
Ruta montana
NW Africa to Turkey
and Balearic Is.

Salvia officinalis
Salvia ringens
   Greece
Salvia sclarea
   Mediterranean
Scabiosa
Sedum
Teucrium chamaedrys
   Mediterranean to W Asia
Teucrium flavum
   Mediterranean
Teucrium fruticans
   Iberia
Teucrium marum
   W Mediterranean
Teucrium orientale
   E Mediterranean
Teucrium polium
   Mediterranean to W Asia
Verbascum creticum
Verbascum dumulosum
   SW Turkey
Verbascum phoeniceum
Vinca difformis
Vinca minor
Viola

Bulbous Plants

Allium ampeloprasum
Allium flavum
Allium moly
Allium neapolitanum
Allium roseum
Allium schoenoprasum
Allium sphaerocephalon
Allium triquetrum
Androcymbium europaeum
Anemone blanda
Anemone coronaria
Anthericum liliago
Arisarum vulgare
Arum italicum
Arum maculatum
Arum pictum
Bellevalia ciliata
Biarum sp.
Colchicum autumnale
Crocus cambessedesii
Crocus flavus
Crocus goulimyi

Crocus minimus, endemic
Crocus pallasii
Crocus sativus
Crocus serotinus
Crocus sieberi
Cyclamen balearicum, endemic
Cyclamen coum
   (syn. C. orbiculatum)
   E Mediterranean
Cyclamen graecum
Cyclamen hederifolium
Cyclamen persicum
Cyclamen repandum
Dipcadi serotinum
Dracunculus muscivorus
   Balearic Is., Corsica, Sardinia
Dracunculus vulgaris
Fritillaria acmopetala
   E Mediterranean
Fritillaria graeca
   S and E Greece
Fritillaria hispanica
   Spain, Portugal
Fritillaria messanensis
Fritillaria persica
   S Turkey, Jordan, Israel
Gladiolus communis
   S Europe
Gladiolus illyricus
   Mediterranean
Gladiolus italicus
   S Europe
Gynandriris
Helleborus argutifolius
Helleborus foetidus
Helleborus lividus
Hermodactylus tuberosus
Hyacinthoides sp.
Iris attica
Iris foetidissima
Iris germanica
Iris lutescens
   NE Spain, S France, Italy
Iris planifolia
   W and C Mediterranean
Iris pseudacorus
   Europe and N Africa
   to Middle East
Iris pumila
   SE and EC Europe

Iris unguicularis
Iris xiphium
Leucojum aestivum
Leucojum autumnale
   W and C Mediterranean
Leucojum trichophyllum
   SW Spain, Morocco
Leucojum valentinum
   E Spain and Greece
Lilium candidum
   Mediterranean
Merendera filifolia
Muscari comosum
Muscari neglectum
Narcissus bulbocodium
Narcissus elegans
   W Mediterranean to
   Italy and Sicily
Narcissus jonquilla
Narcissus papyraceus
Narcissus serotinus
   Mediterranean
Narcissus tazetta
Narcissus viridiflorus
   S Spain, N Africa
Ornithogalum arabicum
Ornithogalum nutans
Ornithogalum umbellatum
Paeonia broteroi
Paeonia cambessedesii
Paeonia clusii
Paeonia mascula
Paeonia rhodia
Pancratium illyricum
Pancratium maritimum
Ranunculus
Romulea bulbocodium
Romulea linaresii
Scilla hispanica
Scilla hyacinthoides
Scilla peruviana
Sternbergia colchiciflora
Sternbergia lutea
Tulipa clusiana
Tulipa praecox
Tulipa saxatilis
Tulipa sylvestris
Urginea maritima
Urginea undulata

Climbers

Aristolochia sempervirens
   E Mediterranean
Asparagus acutifolius
Asparagus albus
Asparagus stipularis
Clematis cirrhosa
Clematis flammula
Clematis orientalis
Hedera canariensis
   Canary Is.
Hedera helix
Humulus lupulus
   S Europe, W Asia
Lonicera etrusca
Lonicera implexa
Rosa gallica
Rosa pimpinellifolia
   Europe
Rosa sempervirens
   Mediterranean
Rosa serafinii
   Mediterranean and
   SE Europe
Smilax aspera
Vitis vinifera
   Possibly introduced from
   Asia Minor, Caucasus

To these lists can be added
grains and cereals and such
fruits and vegetables as
cucumber, leek, melon, and
onion, and a wide range of
spices, including coriander,
cumin, and garlic.

Mediterranean Style
How to Create a Likeness

This section will demonstrate how a mediterranean "feel" can be achieved even if you live hundreds of miles away from the Mediterranean Sea. Behind all the features that we think of as typical of a mediterranean garden lie reasons stemming from the circumstances of life in this part of the world. Here I will summarize some of the most important of these features and suggest ways in which they may be re-created in more northerly climates. In this way, "mediterranean" as a garden style need not be limited to the Mediterranean-climate regions.

Containers find their place in all Mediterranean gardens.

For more ideas, see :

- Native Mediterranean Plants, page 21
- A House That Lies Well in Its Land, page 44
- The Mediterranean Garden, page 60
- A Garden in the Hills, page 138
- Living with Animals, page 162
- A Country Garden, page 168

In recent years, all things Mediterranean have become fashionable. "Mediterranean" as a garden style is often attempted but not always correctly interpreted. A potted palm, a few olive-oil jars, and a lonely yucca are hardly reason enough to call a dusty patio a mediterranean garden. If we mean to create the real thing, we must bear in mind that the mediterranean garden has been dictated by necessity since time immemorial, so that behind each of its features lies a reason. You will find below some of the ingredients for a true mediterranean garden. These may at first appear to resemble landscaping guidelines, but a closer look will show that they stem from the circumstances of mediterranean life.

Present-day mediterranean gardeners have been influenced by many factors, yet as a perusal of *The Mediterranean Garden*, the journal of the Mediterranean Garden Society (see Addresses), shows, we are all looking for mediterranean roots. We may wonder what grew here in past centuries, what still grows on the hillsides and in the fields around us, and what we should do with our poor, dry, wind-swept soil. However, not everyone who attempts to design a mediterranean garden actually lives in the Mediterranean Basin. Many people who live in northern regions are attracted by the Mediterranean lifestyle and would like to create at least a simulacrum of it.

Gravel and cushion shapes provide the Mediterranean look, even if the plants (*Euryops*) are not Mediterranean natives.

One letter I received reads: "I garden near the Belgian coast on sandy soil and my garden is small. Temperatures go down to -10° C. My aim is to re-create the Mediterranean in the garden using rocks and gravel and different levels. I love the scents as much as the flowers. During the summer, I put yuccas and agaves everywhere amidst the plants. Does anyone have any ideas as to what else I can do to create the mediterranean feel?" Am I wrong in assuming that many gardeners are wondering along the same lines?

Although a northern climate may not allow for a true Mediterranean garden, many gardeners may be tempted by undemanding mediterranean plants. Certainly gardeners who live in a relatively mild area or in a sheltered site can always create a likeness. A patio or the corner of a courtyard in a northern

The paving, cushion shapes, and light-colored walls are characteristic of the Mediterranean Basin.

A collection of pots in a courtyard is a good way to create a Mediterranean "feel." Note the restrained, earthy colors.

garden will often go well with the mediterranean style. A raised bed with a retaining wall may imitate mediterranean terracing and will also provide the good drainage that is paramount in mediterranean gardens. Thriving plants in containers can be plunged into the soil here; if they are then topped off with gravel, the artifice will not show. At the onset of winter, when the weather turns unfavorable, these potted plants can easily be moved indoors, although most mediterranean plants prefer a cool location to a heated room. (Generally speaking, it is not so much

the cold but the frost and faulty drainage that kill them.)

In the previous section, The Mediterranean Garden, you will find a more detailed discussion of the list below, but here for the sake of convenience, let me summarize:

• A courtyard or patio with attractive containers, or any level ground on which people may gather and sit outside

• Terraced land. A few steps, a leveled path, and a raised bed will do.

• A pergola with climbers for shade and scent (jasmine, for instance)

• Shade to give protection against the intense summer sun and in which to place a table for leisurely meals and a glass of local wine. For gardeners in northern climes an umbrella may do, since intense summer sun will rarely be their problem.

• Decorative paving. Try a mosaic with pebbles or pavers (to replace the sodden lawn), or simply use gravel.

• A small water feature (even a token one) or a tiny drip with, for instance, recirculated water. Remember that in all mediterranean regions water has always been scarce and was certainly never wasted.

• Containers of all sizes are a must.

• Decorative vases or a statue. A simple, well-chosen copy might do.

• Columns. To create a mediterranean likeness, a single column would be enough.

• Evergreen or gray-foliaged, drought-tolerant plants that require little watering, since a water-drenched look would spoil the image of a hot mediterranean summer garden.

• Topiary, which means evergreens clipped into shape. Box, cypress, and myrtle are the traditional elements, but you may find many alternatives.

• Cushion shapes to imitate the rounded volumes of many native plants.

• Cypresses are indispensable for a mediterranean feel, so have at least one.

• Plants repeated over and over (remember that the choice of plants available in the past was small).

• Fragrance and aromatic scent. To recall the *maquis*, plant thyme, for example, where it will be walked on.

• Palms and spiky, sword-leaved plants introduce structure and a southern feel.

• A reduced color palette. Color is beautifully replaced by the appealing interplay of glittering light and soothing shade. Splashing color around is a recent introduction.

• Grow your own food. Even a small patch would be sufficient. If we want to create the mediterranean look, we can do nothing better than planting structural artichokes, tall corn or maize, and ground-covering melons, or near a south-facing wall, almond, grape, fig, and lemon (see The Edible Garden, page 146). For almonds, you may have to settle for an ornamental one.

• Work with the seasons. Enjoy jubilant spring bloom and let the garden and the gardener rest over a hot summer.

Although all mediterranean gardens have an overall sameness, there is still plenty of room for each garden to display its own individuality. A list of the native mediterranean plants can be found in the preceding section, The Mediterranean Garden.

Decorative paving is another Mediterranean feature.

The Olive Grove
Spring Flowers, Autumn Harvest

An olive grove in spring is a wonderful sight, spreading at your feet a carpet of spring bulbs and wildflowers. Suggestions for waterwise planting near or under olive trees are provided in this section. Bulbs, for instance, thrive in these conditions and are easily grown. For open ground beside an olive grove, I suggest a wildflower meadow, which may evoke memories of childhood. I will even include a description of pressing olives so that you may be encouraged to press your own olive oil.

The bronze summer color of spurges enhances the view to the right of this majestic olive tree.

For more ideas, see:

- Native Mediterranean Plants, page 21
- A House That Lies Well in Its Land, page 44
- The Mediterranean Garden, page 60
- A Garden in the Hills, page 138
- Living with Animals, page 162
- A Country Garden, page 168

Majestic olive trees first drew my attention to a potential garden site on our sheep farm, adjacent to the fenced-in garden around the house. Surely it would be possible, I thought, to make use of these trees for a natural yet gardenlike landscape, but how? Since not much occurred to me right away, I started tidying up, as I always do when starting a new garden project. For once, thorny weeds did not abound. Good luck had it that, after this initial clearing, I was able to find an experienced person with an eye for bringing out the beauty of a good framework. As soon as the ancient trees had been shaped to their best advantage, we set out to remove a collapsed stone wall that blocked the view and cleared stones off the level ground for use as a fill nearby. When we discovered some beautifully aged stone slabs, we used them to build steps from one area to another. Gradually, the design emerged simply by tidying up. I believe that today's landscape architects call this "editing the landscape"—a process similar to that of the editor who "weeds" a manuscript, puts order into it, and brings out its inherent strengths. By the time summer arrived, the scene was left to itself, but not before a stone bench had been built beneath the oldest olive tree.

Note: Revolution may still be in fashion for some, but evolution proceeds step by step until gradually a balanced picture emerges in which no bulldozer has a role.

Open ground near the olive tree we have richly planted with native Mediterranean plants, such as the pink rock rose (*Cistus albidus*), lavender, and white *Iris germanica*.

When, on my return after a season away from the garden, I sat in the shade beneath the trees, my mind's eye envisioned a wonderful scene. The terrace with its ancient olive trees would be underplanted with mediterranean spring bulbs, and a few steps would lead to an inviting passage at the far end, imparting mystery to what lay beyond. A wall, already repaired, would embrace the lower terraces. Further back, bulky myrtle or oleander would block out the view of a country road, while a mass of prickly pears would clothe a patch of rubble. The setting could be even more attractive if one of those aged water tanks were part of it. Carefully restored, an old cistern is always an asset. Wooden garden furniture could accompany the stone bench. (In this context, fancy wrought-iron pieces would not have the right weight, and plastic—to my mind—is out of the question. For information about the repair of stonework, see A Country Garden, page 168.) And for those who can manage them, sheep grazing under olive trees add greatly to the atmosphere of a grove (see Living with Animals, page 162).

Trees and shrubs planted in an olive grove should be chosen with care and a sense of proportion, because nothing should interfere with the strong presence of ancient olive trees. The simpler the arrangement, the better. A carob tree (*Ceratonia* siliqua) might look right, or mock privet (*Phillyrea angustifolia*) and buckthorn (*Rhamnus alaternus*), with drifts of snowflake (*Leucojum*) in their shade. For an evergreen mass, choose mastic (*Pistacia lentiscus*) or myrtle, with *Nerium oleander* for summer blossom and laurustinus (*Viburnum tinus*) for winter color. For more flowers, add swaths of lavender, rock roses, rosemary, and salvias and generous patches of *Euphorbia*, *Helichrysum*, and *Santolina*. You can find the rare spurge olive (*Cneorum tricoccon*) and *Rhamnus ludovici-salvatoris* growing wild among olive trees. Honeysuckle (*Lonicera implexa*) may ascend a half-broken tree to disguise its mutilated branches, while the delicate *Clematis cirrhosa* or the vigorous *C. flammula* enjoy the cool root run of a wall. Cypresses or the mediterranean fan palm (*Chamaerops*) add exclamation points where needed. This choice of native Mediterranean plants can indeed be supplemented or replaced by those from other mediterranean-climate regions.

Bulbous plants, also called geophytes, suit an olive grove, and in a mediterranean-type climate provide color for much of the year. Plan cheerful groups planted near the trees, where they won't get

A restored stone wall accommodates the succulent *Sedum rubrotinctum*.

lost. Aim for a natural scene. A selection from the rich choice of mediterranean bulbs is suggested below. However, you can also try those from other mediterranean-climate regions, such as the South African Cape for instance—from *Aristea* all the way through the alphabet to *Watsonia*. The Cape is a treasure trove, where new species continue to be discovered.

In a coastal area, good spring bulbs are *Anemone*, *Kniphofia*, *Pancratium*, and *Ranunculus*, as well as most bulbs in the *Iridaceae* family (see below). In higher regions, anemone, crocus, hyacinth, iris, ixia, narcissus, ranunculus, and tulips, together with the taller *Helleborus*, *Hemerocallis*, and *Paeonia*, respond well to winter chilling. All survive the summer drought underground.

You can also enjoy the summer- and autumn-flowering small *Bulbocodium vernum*, or try *Colchicum*, *Crocus goulimyi*, *C. sativus*, and *C. speciosus*, together with *Cyclamen*, *Merendera*, *Sternbergia*, and *Urginea*. These all add splashes of color in a relatively flower-poor season. Most bulbous plants are easy to grow and often tend to naturalize. The bulbs of the mediterranean autumn crocus (*Sternbergia*), for instance, like to sit on a wall (or at its foot) and make

Terraces with olive and many other trees

The native Mediterranean autumn crocus (*Sternbergia lutea*) is a cheerful sight that may last for weeks. It is best planted in rich clumps and requires no care whatsoever.

Add Splashes of Color

Generally speaking, small plants are often the most suitable in the setting of an olive grove. You can plant dozens of narcissus species, for instance. Explore them all or opt for large drifts of the type you feel does particularly well for you. The choice below, from the Mediterranean Basin, can also be enriched by winter-, spring- and autumn-flowering bulbs from other mediterranean-climate regions, such as *Amaryllis belladonna* from the South African Cape or daylilies (*Hemerocallis*) from China. Consult also the list in the section on the Mediterranean Garden.

Cyclamen hederifolium in shade

The red-hot poker (*Kniphofia praecox x*), in South Africa

Anemone coronaria

Winter- and spring-flowering bulbs from the Mediterranean Basin
Allium
Anemone
Crocus
Cyclamen
Helleborus
Hyacinthus
Iris germanica
Iris unguicularis
Leucojum aestivum
Muscari
Narcissus
Ornithogalum
Paeonia
Ranunculus
Scilla
Tulipa

Anemone pavonina

Summer- and autumn-flowering bulbs from the Mediterranean Basin
Bulbocodium vernum
Colchicum
Crocus goulimyi
Crocus sativus
Cyclamen
Merendera filifolia
Sternbergia lutea
Urginea maritima

Watsonia, in South Africa

Iris germanica has few requirements.

Sternbergia lutea

Muscari armeniacum

Amaryllis belladonna

do with the merest trace of soil. *Cyclamen balearicum*, and lily turf (*Liriope*) in small patches, the ground-covering, winter-flowering Algerian iris (*Iris unguicu-laris*), and the South African *Agapanthus* in large patches will fit in very nicely with the olive trees. However, avoid the stately asphodel, which is invasive.

The bulbs from the *Iridaceae* family are particularly accommodating and easy to grow from seed. Let a few seeds (from your own garden?) drop into a crack or between the stones of a wall (not more than twice as deep as the size of the seed), and let the winter rain do the rest. Nothing more is needed. This works well with freesias, gladioli, or *Lapeirousia* and achieves the natural look you have in mind. The choice of bulbs from California and southern Australia is more limited. Nursery catalogues will provide inspiration, but your order may be delivered rather late, considering that in mediterranean regions bulbs should be in the ground before the first autumn rains.

Note: In spite of what the books may say, mediterranean gardeners know of only one way to store bulbs—in the ground, where they should be left year round.

The bulbous plants I have mentioned so far are drought-tolerant and require no irrigation, since their water needs are taken care of by winter rain. However, if

Olea europaea in this olive grove

the winter rain, which makes them grow and lets them store reserves for the season ahead, is insufficient, spring bulbs may show stunted growth as they emerge. In this case, replace that missing winter rain with a single copious watering. In summer, however, bulbous plants need to "bake" in ,the dry ground, and watering at that time would interrupt their natural growth cycle and should be avoided. The best flowering performance usually follows the hottest, driest summers. If you wish, you may fertilize the bulbs lightly after flowering.

I am writing this as the Mediterranean summer comes to an end, which is the moment for the stately sea squill (*Urginea maritima*) to flower. I once thought that this awakening was triggered by the first autumn rains, but last year the sea squill shot out of barren ground long before then. This year, the characteristic mediterranean summer drought was replaced by frequent rains, and I wondered if the deluged sea squill would appear earlier as a result. It was not so, however. Its flowering, I was told, is not triggered by rain but by the shortening days. I wonder how bulbs that lie a foot below ground sense the length of the days.

Maintaining an olive grove involves nothing more than corrective pruning. Once all dead wood and inward-growing branches have been cut out, a small chopper is used to remove new shoots at the base of the olive trees; a saw is unsuitable for this job since it leaves short stumps from which more shoots will grow. Withered, unsightly bulb leaves can be tucked under a nearby shrub, pulled up, or covered with mulch. As an alternative, my garden help plaits the leaves before tucking them under. The long, narrow leaves of narcissus are particularly suited to this task. Yet before such plaiting, you should wait until the vital juices that build up the bulbous growth for the following year have been drawn back from the leaves.

A Wildflower Garden

You have placed the trees and the shrubs and interred the bulbs, but more open ground may still require planting. The idea of a manicured lawn has not crossed your mind, of course, but how about a wildflower meadow? The following statement from the World Wildlife Fund is very persuasive:

"It is strange how we exclaim over the richness and diversity of natural parks and forests and yet settle for dreary monoculture when it comes to our own gardens. The use of synthetic fertilizers, weed killers, pesticides and other elaborate treatments may result in a lawn worthy of Wimbledon, but quite apart from the ecological damage incurred by using poisonous chemicals, the land becomes sterile. It can no longer feed insects such as butterflies and bees, which in turn attract birds and lizards. Why not experiment by allowing an unused patch of garden to revert gradually to a meadow? Choose a flat, sunny site and just let the grass grow. Resist the temptation to mow for 6 months to give plants a chance to flower and seed. Thereafter, mowing 3–5 times a year should be sufficient. If you stick to this cutting programme, you will encourage a natural lawn with a wide variety of short-stemmed, slow-growing flower and grass species which need no watering. You can cheat by scattering wild flower seeds. Poppies and violets, gypsophila, camomile and pimpernel will make their appearance after 1–2 seasons. Within 2–4 years, clovers, scabious, sage, dandelions and cornflowers should have colonized. Why spend hours weeding, watering, cutting, spraying and raking a lawn when a meadow, once established, takes care of itself?"

Plant bulbs and annuals beneath the trees for a rich tapestry of spring color.

Pressing Your Own Olive Oil

A Franciscan from Poljica near the Adriatic coast describes the olive harvest and the pressing in his simple, picturesque idiom: You harvest the olives on All Saints Day or thereabouts, in early November. You don't want to wait till the olives are overripe and start to rot, but then you don't want to take them when they are green either. You need ladders and sticks because there is lots of climbing and batting to do. Once you have harvested the olives, you gather up the sacks, take them home and pour them into basins or vats or, if you haven't got any, you spread them out on the floor. Then you let them rest a day or two and ripen up, come into their own. If the piles are big, you will want to stir them and air them out because otherwise they'll burn and their oil will burn your mouth. Next you crush them in a press. The women throw them in and the men work the press. But you don't pour out the liquid then and there. No, you let it stand for a bit so the best oil – what we call lanbik – rises to the surface. You pour that into wooden barrels and put what is left into sacks you have rinsed out a few times with boiling water. Then the men roll up their trouser legs and trample on it to squeeze the rest of the oil out. You scoop that oil up with a soup plate and pour it into a barrel and throw out the dregs—what we call murga (From Pedrag Matvejevic, *Mediterranean*, 1999).

Making oil is a tradition. Maintaining the purity of the oil by removing the marc, which is like removing the dregs from wine, is a great art. Straining is not enough. The desire for a pure, unadulterated product is so strong that procedures bordering on alchemy come into play. Oil can also be obtained from flax, almonds, myrtle, and palm, but the oil from the olive has always been preferred.

Preserving olives takes a good deal of effort. In the past they were soaked in the sea before being preserved with bay leaves, red peppers, and a few stalks of fennel. In western Crete, they preserve (black) olives in oil with a sprig of sage and some bitter-orange peel. Delicious.

Wild bellis (*Bellis annuuis*) carpet the ground under these olive trees each year.

If the soil is very degraded or compacted, you must be prepared to do a bit of weeding during the first year (thistles), until the cover closes in on the soil. In spring, wildflowers line mediterranean roadsides, producing a brilliant display for weeks on end. These same poppies, cornflowers, and resedas could give your meadow the true mediterranean feel, and wildflower seeds are easy to come by. What better way to cover the ground in your olive grove? Don't we all cherish memories of wildflower meadows? How about giving it a try?

A Coastal Garden
Your Haven by the Sea

This section on seaside mediterranean gardens deals with the vital issue of protection from the onslaught of sand- and salt-laden winds, for which I propose a creative use of windbreaks. I also provide a useful list of salt-resistant plants suitable for a coastal garden, as well as a thought-provoking recipe for that simplest of Mediterranean foods, stone soup. And, for a finale, an inspiring description of Jane Burke's seaside garden in Australia.

Coastal gardens have many different faces. From coastal cliffs, beaten all winter long by incoming waves, to golden sandy beaches, flat and shell-studded for miles, you can find many variations. What they all share, unlike inland gardens, is the salt content of the air and the prevailing coastal humidity. Wind and winter storms carry sand and salt-blast to all but the most protected sites, burning leaves, sometimes killing plants, and often resulting in lopsided growth. Where fogs are frequent, count on low light intensities. Another thing common to coastal gardens is a more temperate climate found in all places that are near water, be it a lake, a river, or the sea. This relative mildness spares such gardens both the coldest and the hottest days experienced by inland regions. Coastal gardens also share a view— the never-changing sea. Blue and green, or dark and threatening, rolling in or lashing around, it is always there, with perhaps a small boat bobbing about on the horizon.

A protected coast has many unspoiled coves.

For more ideas, see :
- A House That Lies Well in Its Land, page 44
- Scale and Proportion, page 52
- The Instant Garden, page 118
- Living under Pines, page 124
- Hedges, Screens, and Boundaries, page 180
- The Lazy Person's Dream Garden, page 186

Planning Your Seaside Site

Coastal soils are mostly sandy. They provide a light and well-drained growing medium but lack substance and dry out more quickly than you would like. Compost, added freely, improves moisture retention, as does a thick mulch. Under poor, sandy soil conditions, growth is slow, and a cautious initial plant selection is called for. Where coastal humidity prevails, it favors pathogens that may be fatal for feltlike leaves, and this too requires a careful choice of plants. Attention should also be paid to ventilation within or between plants wherever they are grown

The palazzo at the Hanbury Gardens in northern Italy overlooks the sea. Cypresses are a prominent element.

closely spaced. Planting sites require careful attention to topography, such as dunes or rocky coastlines, and existing water and flood courses. Also bear in mind the possibility of an occasional high tide. All these factors will influence the way you create your garden.

Note: A combination that needs no care whatsoever and will do well in poor, sandy soil consists of a few wispy *Tamarix* underplanted with white *Pancratium illyricum* and the later-flowering sea daffodil *P. maritimum*.

Dune stabilization may effectively be achieved, in this era of natural gardens, by planting coastal grasses and herbaceous plants where coastal dunes are threatened by the constant movement of the tides. These plants include the Mediterranean *Ammophila arenaria* and *Andropogon gerardii* (a magnificent, tall perennial grass with rich autumn colors), *Leymus* and *Pennisetum setaceum* (invasive), and the lower-growing *Sporobolus cryptandrus*. Succulents, together with native grasses, often survive best (*Aloe, Drosanthemum, Lampranthus*). The widely used Hottentot fig (*Carpobrotus*) has a coarse look, but its fruits are edible. Also suitable are compact,

Compact-growing plants protect others from the sea wind.

Tamarisk (*Tamarix gallica*)

felty, and silvery hairy plants such as the saltbush (*Atriplex*) and the cottonweed (*Otanthus maritimus*) with its large yellow flowers or *Lotus creticus* (silvery-leaved patches with fragrant yellow blooms). Hard-leaved agave and yucca provide a striking outline, while New Zealand flax (*Phormium tenax*) as an accent will tolerate an occasional flooding. The deciduous native sea buckthorn (*Hippophaë rhamnoides*) provides winter-long interest with its red berries. All these plants add beauty and fulfill an important stabilization function. If planted at the end of winter in compost-enriched, mulched soil, most of these species will be established by autumn and will stabilize the sand before the onset of winter storms.

Wind-exposed gardens depend on "first-row shelter," a technique favoring plants that grow naturally in seaside locations where sturdy plants can protect the relatively tender vegetation of the inner belt. Pine trees, for example, grow naturally to the water's edge and are often covered by foam. Other plants accustomed to sea breezes include the Australian pyramid tree (*Lagunaria*) and tea tree (*Leptospermum*), as well as kapuka (*Griselinia littoralis*) and the tall Christmas tree (*Metrosideros excelsa*) native to the beaches of New Zealand. Jerusalem thorn (*Parkinsonia*) from tropical America and *Schotia* from South Africa join in. Suitable plants are also Californian manzanita (*Arctostaphylos*) and buckwheat (*Eriogonum*) and the Mediterranean salt-bush (*Atriplex halimus*), buck-thorn (*Rhamnus alaternus*), and a well-shaped *Tamarix gallica*, the latter thriving on salty water. Its feathery outline softens the harsher, architectural design of sword-leaved plants. The dense growth and attractive foliage of these trees and shrubs will moderate the wind and define a boundary.

For a quick screen, use beefwood (*Casuarina verticillata*), the bulky *Myoporum insulare*, the pepper tree (*Schinus molle*), or Brisbane box (*Tristania conferta*). They may feature as a backdrop or as specimen trees and suit close stands. The lower-growing bottlebrush (*Callistemon viminalis*), rock roses (*Cistus*), broom (*Cytisus canariensis*), *Euryops pectinatus*, and *Westringia* all add colorful blooms. *Acacia redolens*, together with manzanita (*Arctostaphylos uva-ursi* 'Point Reyes') and coyote brush (*Baccharis pilularis*), will cover the soil. Large patches

of honey-suckle (*Lonicera japonica*) require nothing more than a yearly confining to the allotted space.

An inner protective belt may comprise the strawberry tree (*Arbutus unedo*), *Juniperus phoenicea*, Corsican or Aleppo pine (*Pinus nigra var. maritima* or *P. halepensis*), and pepper tree (*Schinus terebinthifolius*) to protect the garden from prevailing winds. Shrubs for this setting include the sun-loving Natal plum (*Carissa*), mirror plant (*Coprosma repens*), native hops (*Dodonaea viscosa*), silverberry (*Elaeagnus pungens*), *Escallonia*, mastic (*Pistacia lentiscus*), *Pittosporum tobira*, and many daisy bushes (*Olearia*). Under the shade of a tree, plant an Indian hawthorn (*Rhaphiolepis umbellulata*). *Acacia longifolia*, *Laurus nobilis*, and *Nerium oleander*, which grow well in sandy soil, may be sheared or kept low as a hedge. In their wind shadow, colorful *Coreopsis*, *Euryops pectinatus*, *Lantana*, African

Tiny clouds hover over the sea and promise rain, which never seems to arrive.

Stone Soup

Stone soup is known on virtually all the islands of the Ionian Sea. It was made by the Illyrians and the Greeks, by the Liburnians and the Etruscans, and is as ancient as Mediterranean poverty. Take two or three stones from a spot covered by the low tide. They should be neither too large nor too small and should be dark from having lain on the seabed. Cook them in rainwater until everything in the pores has had a chance to seep out. Add a few bay leaves and some thyme, a teaspoon of olive oil, and a teaspoon of wine vinegar. You will not need salt if you have chosen the proper stones (Pedrag Matvejevic, *Mediterranean*, 1999).

glaucoptera, or *A. podalyriifolia* contrast well with the particularly sturdy willow myrtle (*Agonis flexuosa*). Near the house, palms such as *Chamaerops humilis* and *Phoenix canariensis* add a southern touch. *Washingtonia filifera* tolerates salt at root level.

The climbing, autumn-flowering Cape honeysuckle (*Tecomaria capensis*) strikingly complements the gray mass of the salt-tolerant germander (*Teucrium fruticans*). With time, their entangling branches will become impenetrable. The trumpet creeper (*Campsis radicans*) and Boston ivy (*Parthenocissus tricuspidata*) quickly cover walls, while a chalice vine (*Solandra maxima*) with its giant egg-yolk-color flowers will brighten your winter days.

daisy (*Osteospermum ecklonis* and *O. fruticosum*) provide low-maintenance cover. The aromatic leaves of rosemary, lavender, and lavender cotton (*Santolina*) also have a contribution to make, while California lilac (*Ceanothus maritimus*), blue marguerite (*Felicia amelloides*), sea lavender (*Limonium*), and Russian sage (*Perovskia*) in large patches mirror the color of the sea. So much for the sturdy plants.

In a sunny corner sheltered from the wind, **tender deciduous trees and shrubs** will provide summer shade and striking blossom. Try silk tree (*Albizia julibrissin*), orchid tree (*Bauhinia variegata*), Barbados pride (*Caesalpinia pulcherrima*), the thorny floss silk tree (*Chorisia speciosa*), the flamboyant *Delonix regia*, coral tree (*Erythrina corallodendrum*), or before crape myrtle (*Lagerstroemia indica*). Evergreens include *Acacia baileyana* and *A. dealbata*, bottlebrush (*Callistemon viminalis*), and *Eucalyptus ficifolia*. All will provide a background for tender flowering shrubs such as *Bauhinia galpinii*, *Buddleja* (*B. asiatica*, *B. davidii*, *B. madagascariensis*), jessamine (*Cestrum*), Mexican orange (*Choisya ternata*), poinsettia (*Euphorbia pulcherrima*), *Hibiscus*, *Iochroma*, *Polygala*, yellow bells (*Stenolobium stans*), and yellow oleander (*Thevetia peruviana*). Gray *Acacia cultriformis*, *A.*

This bench, strategically placed to overlook the sea, is accompanied by dense evergreen foliage. The palms in the background add height.

Bulbous plants have a definite place in a coastal setting. Anemone, freesia, ranunculus, and sparaxis greet you with cheerful spring blooms. Tall red-hot poker (*Kniphofia*) or *Watsonia* stand out where plantings need height. The daylily (*Hemerocallis*) spreads steadily. In spring, *Romulea bulbocodium* paints the sand with shiny violet dots, while in late summer the brilliant white sea daffodil (*Pancratium maritimum*) perfumes the beach. On northern slopes among shrubby *Erica multiflora* and St. John's wort

(*Hypericum balearicum*), the bulbous sea squill (*Urginea maritima*) grows almost to the water's edge. *Hippeastrum* in terra-cotta pots may adorn a terrace.

Annuals, such as bellis, calendula, Chinese aster, pansy, and snapdragon provide splashes of summer color. Cosmos, petunia, portulaca, tagetes, nasturtium, and zinnia are short-lived yet incomparable for shallow soils.

Where water is available and you intend to use it, a labor-intensive—and therefore costly—lawn is possible. **Coastal grasses** (graded by salt tolerance from high to low) are *Paspalum vaginatum*, St. Augustine grass (*Stenotaphrum secundatum*), and kikuyu grass (*Pennisetum clandestinum*). However, carpets of drought-tolerant *Gazania rigens* or the succulent *Mesembryanthemum* tolerate salt-laden winds and provide a fairly successful alternative to a lawn. The roots of manzanita (*Arctostaphylos*) easily catch hold in the light soil, rapidly covering large patches. In sun, a well-tended "lawn" of Cape weed (*Arctotheca*), of African daisy (*Arctotis*), sea pink (*Armeria maritime*), saltbush (*Atriplex semibaccata*), *Lotus creticus*, or *Vittadinia australis*, once established, takes care of itself.

Only the simplest planting seems suitable to the grandiose spectacle of sea and sky. When the day draws to its close, sharply outlined dunes turn pale lavender and dark amethyst. Lucky is the gardener who can watch the evening sun sink into the sea or the full moon rise on a cloudless night out of mysterious, inky waters.

This scene in South Africa shows native vegetation growing all the way to the water's edge. Such perfect coloring would not be easy for a gardener to achieve, but we can always respect nature's creation.

Plants for Coastal Gardens

Mesembs (*Mesembryanthemum*) cover sandy patches near the sea.

South African *Arctotis acaulis* creates a carpet near the sea.

Argyranthemum, a South African daisy, grows in typical cushion shapes.

Trees, Shrubs, Palms
Acacia baileyana
Acacia cultriformis
Acacia dealbata
Acacia glaucoptera
Acacia longifolia, likes salt spray
Acacia podalyriifolia
Acacia redolens
Acacia saligna
Acca sellowiana
Agonis flexuosa
Albizia julibrissin
Arbutus unedo
Arctostaphylos 'Point Reyes'
Atriplex canescens
Atriplex halimus
Atriplex semibaccata
Aucuba japonica
Aurinia saxatilis
Baccharis pilularis
Bauhinia galpinii
Bauhinia variegata
Buddleja asiatica
Buddleja davidii
Buddleja madagascariensis
Caesalpinia pulcherrima
Callistemon viminalis
Carissa
Casuarina stricta
Ceanothus maritimus
Cestrum
Chamaerops humilis
Choisya ternata
Chorisia speciosa
Chrysanthemum frutescens
Cistus
Coprosma repens, likes salt spray
Cordyline australis
Corokia
Correa alba
Correa reflexa
Cotoneaster
Cupressus macrocarpa
Cupressus sempervirens
Cytisus canariensis, likes salt spray
Delonix regia
Dodonaea viscosa
Dovyalis caffra
Dracaena
Echium
Elaeagnus angustifolia
Elaeagnus x ebbingei
Elaeagnus pungens
Erica multiflora
Eriogonum

Erythrina corallodendrum
Escallonia macrantha
Eucalyptus ficifolia
Euonymus japonicus
Euphorbia pulcherrima
Euryops pectinatus
Genista
Grevillea robusta
Griselinia littoralis, likes salt spray
Halimium
Hebe
Hibiscus
Hippophaë rhamnoides
Hypericum balearicum
Iochroma
Juniperus chinensis
Juniperus conferta
Juniperus oxycedrus
Juniperus phoenicea
Lagerstroemia indica
Lagunaria patersonii
Lantana
Laurus nobilis
Lavandula angustifolia
Lavatera
Leptospermum
Leucadendron, likes salt spray
Leucophyta brownii
Leucospermum, likes salt spray
Melaleuca nesophila
Melaleuca quinquenervia
Melia azedarach
Metrosideros excelsa
Myoporum insulare
Nerium oleander
Olearia, many
Ozothamnus turbinatus
Parkinsonia aculeata
Perovskia
Phoenix canariensis
Phoenix dactylifera
Phormium tenax
Pinus brutia
Pinus canariensis
Pinus halepensis
Pinus nigra maritima
Pistacia lentiscus
Pittosporum crassifolium
Pittosporum tobira
Polygala
Populus alba
Pyracantha
Quercus ilex
Rhamnus alaternus
Rhaphiolepis umbellulata

Rhus integrifolia
Rhus lancea, brackish water
Robinia pseudoacacia
Rosmarinus officinalis
Santolina chamaecyparissus
Schotia
Schinus molle
Schinus terebinthifolius
Stenolobium stans
Tamarix gallica
Teucrium fruticans
Thevetia peruviana
Tipuana tipu, likes salt spray
Tristania conferta
Viburnum tinus
Viburnum tinus 'Lucidum'
Vittadinia australis
Washingtonia filifera
Westringia rosmariniformis

Climbers
Campsis radicans
Lonicera japonica
Parthenocissus tricuspidata
Solandra maxima, likes salt spray
Tecomaria capensis

Ground Cover, Succulents, Bulbous Plants
Agave
Aloe arborescens
Aloe thraski
Anemone
Antirrhinum majus
Aptenia
Arctotheca
Arctotis
Armeria maritima
Bellis
Calendula
Carpobrotus
Centaurea
Cerastium tomentosum
Coreopsis
Cosmos
Dianella revoluta
Drosanthemum
Erigeron
Eschscholzia californica
Felicia amelloides
Fragaria chiloensis
Freesia
Gazania rigens, likes salty winds
Hemerocallis
Hippeastrum

Ixia, sandy loam, do not disturb
Kniphofia
Lampranthus
Libertia ixioides
Limonium x perezii
Lotus creticus
Mentzelia lindleyi
Mesembryanthemum
Osteospermum ecklonis
Osteospermum fruticosum
Othantus maritimus
Pancratium illyricum
Pancratium maritimum
Penstemon heterophyllus
Petunia
Portulaca
Ranunculus asiaticus
Romulea bulbocodium, sandy dunes
Sparaxis tricolor
Tagetes
Tropaeolum
Urginea maritima
Viola
Watsonia
Yucca
Zinnia

Grasses
Ammophila arenaria
Andropogon gerardii
Leymus
Paspalum vaginatum
Pennisetum clandestinum
Pennisetum setaceum, invasive
Sporobolus cryptandrus
Stenotaphrum secundatum

Wild-growing Coastal Vegetation
Asparagus stipularis
Cistus salviifolius
Crithmum maritimum
Erica arborea
Erica multiflora
Hypericum balearicum
Juniperus phoenicea
Juniperus sabina
Phillyrea angustifolia
Pinus halepensis
Pinus pinea
Pistacia lentiscus

93

An Australian Beach Garden

This little beach cottage was built mostly with recycled material.

When I visited the mediterranean-climate regions in Australia, I hoped to see site-appropriate gardens using native flora, and had the great luck to be shown landscape designer Jane Burke's garden at Sorrento, Victoria. The garden impressed me with its sensitive approach. Fiona Brockhoff had a hand in the design in the early stages. The following is Jane's description of her own garden.

"A garden beside the sea is an idyllic notion. In reality, the harsh conditions often associated with coastal gardens can be a challenge in terms of plant selection and landscape design. This garden is close to the ocean beach at Sorrento/Victoria. With a southwesterly aspect, the site is exposed to relentless salt-laden winds and hot afternoon sunshine. The design strategy to accommodate these constraints incorporates plants that occur on the nearby dunes. Quaint, springy, rounded cushion bushes (*Leucophyta brownii*) are mixed with leafy shrubs like coast daisy (*Olearia axillaris*), coast everlasting (*Ozothamnus turbinatus*), white correa (*Correa alba*), and seaberry saltbush (*Rhagodia candolleana*). Various sedges and grasses grow among the shrubs, providing shape, texture, and color variation. Limestone rocks and recycled pier beams reinforce the coastal theme and give the garden definition and textural detail. Beach-combed treasures decorate the gravel surface. Shell grit is used here, with sea-blasted colored glass fragments and a lifetime collection of marine flotsam. Seaweed is used as a fertilizer mulch. These design elements, spaced on gravel terraces, create a visual link with the natural landscape of the coastal woodland southward to the ocean beach.

"Coastal dune plant communities present an interesting mosaic of generally glabrous foliage (coated with a waxy secretion—pale gray to pale green leaves) with some glaucous foliage (without surface ornamentation—or at least the upper surface of leaves shiny and usually darker green). Other characteristics include reduced leaves, succulence and salt glands. Many coastal plants produce edible fruits and berries. These salt-tolerant plants (halophytes) are adapted to severe conditions of wind and salt spray, low-nutrient soils, and constant attrition of wind-blown sediments.

"The dune sands that support these plants are low in organic matter and most trace elements. Water-holding capacity is extremely low. Once the dune plants are established, they are drought-

Jane Burke's coastal garden offers a fine example for other seaside gardeners.

resistant and require only an occasional application of slow-release fertilizers.

"Dune communities are subject to continual deposition of salts. The salts are blown by the wind in tiny water droplets called aerosols, which result from the forces of wave action and winds on the seashore. Along with sodium chloride, aerosols bring nutrients such as potassium and magnesium. This

may explain why many coastal plants fail when planted in exposed sites that are some distance from the sea.

"Calcium-carbonate based sand dunes, derived mainly from marine shells, have extremely low levels of organic matter and pH from neutral to alkaline. Deep organic mulching can increase acidity, increase water-holding capacity and decrease oxygen concentrations in soil pores. If you must mulch dune plants, use larger wood chips that degrade slowly and allow air to pass through to the soil below.

"Dune communities rarely form a continuous canopy. Gaps are caused by tree fall, sand erosion, and deposition. This association includes few understorey plants, except for herbs such as sea celery (*Apium prostratum*), with ground-covering bower spinach (*Tetragonia implexicoma*) and coast twin-leaf (*Zygophyllum ballardieri*). Most dune shrubs, sedges, and grasses require maximum sunshine and good ventilation. (Some may not flourish under canopy trees or in a site shaded from the afternoon sun.) Some coastal shrubs do tolerate a broader range of environments. *Correa reflexa* (green flower coastal form) and sea-berry saltbush (*Rhagodia candolleana*), with tussocks of knobby club-rush (*Isolepis nodosa*), coast tussock grass (*Poa poiformis*), and black anther flax-lily (*Dianella revoluta var. breviculmis*) are suitable for semi-shaded sites.

"The natural attributes of coastal plants may guarantee success in a difficult site. However, it is important to keep in mind that, like many other indigenous species now used in horticulture, these plants have specific requirements that are related to their ecology. Knowledge of the natural environment of any native species is useful as a guide for successful plant selection. The ecological requirements of cushion bush (*Leucophyta brownii*), for instance, are markedly different from those of most cottage plants. This species may be difficult to use in the competitive conditions of a cottage garden, with a regime of fertilizers and regular watering.

"Plants can be pruned to constrain the shape for hedging or to encourage a multi-stemmed habit for a squatter form. City gardens, exposed to the winds along the bay foreshore, can use these species in a formal or architectural style. One simple way to use this idea in small gardens is to create a relatively flat area dressed with a 15cm deep mulch of gravel fines (crusher dust). Gravel media will give textural contrast to the interesting forms of many dune plants and provides conditions similar to their natural habitat. The surface of the gravel layer is reflective, limiting heat transference to plant roots. Drainage is good and the water-holding capacity is improved. While gravel beds are low maintenance and inexpensive to construct, gravel is a perfect environment for seed germination and regular weeding is essential, as overdue removal of mature weeds disturbs the gravel and brings the subsoil to the surface.

"Autumn is the best time to plant. Do this after the gravel fines have been laid down, with the crown of the plant at, or slightly below, the gravel surface. Water tubes in well. Average rainfall should be sufficient for good growth, but weekly water will alleviate young plant stress. Tip-pruning of young shrubs in winter will improve plant shape."

The Swimming Pool Garden
An Escape from the Heat

This section describes how to integrate a pool into the garden. Even water-conserving gardeners can enjoy a swimming pool by filling it in winter when rainfall is usually plentiful and by using a pump to recirculate the water. A certain amount of care is needed in designing the planting. This garden makes use of heat-loving, litter-free plants, but there are a number of others that should be avoided. I have included here a helpful list of things to beware of from the point of view of both comfort and safety.

In hot, dry countries, the sight and sound of water conveys a comfortable feeling of coolness. The traditional landscaping of Near Eastern gardens was often focused on a rectangular body of water, a model that was eventually adopted by many cultures around the Mediterranean. Today, water is at such a premium that its use in the garden may be restricted to a shallow birdbath, although a naturalistic setting might include a time-worn water cistern. Even if waterwise gardening is your choice, you may still envisage a swimming pool. Once it has been filled with tap water or winter rain, modern equipment will keep its water clean for a long time.

A swimming pool, by its size and volume, makes an impact that requires careful incorporation into the general garden scheme (see also Chapter 2). In nature, water collects at the lowest spot, and you may site your pool accordingly if your landscaping plans and the topography of your land permit it. A swimming pool that takes up most of the garden space becomes a central feature, so its materials and

Water catches between the natural rocks and serves as a reservoir for times of need.

the plantings around it should fit the overall spirit of the garden. These features are best integrated into their surroundings and not seen as isolated elements. If you have chosen turquoise as the color of your pool tiles, the pool will attract attention. In this case, both the pool and its immediate surroundings should be worth looking at, with (in this particular case) turquoise treated as an integral part of the garden's color scheme. As an alternative, consider the color of gray slate. Give it a try. Slate looks more natural and at night turns the water into a mysterious darkness that reflects surrounding

For more ideas, see:
- Refreshing Shade, Delightful Scent, page 110
- The Instant Garden, page 119
- A Country Garden, page 168
- The Lazy Person's Dream Garden, page 186

trees and countless stars. Consider not only the pool's color, but also its depth. A shallow pool heats up quickly, which is an asset in cool off-seasons. In summer, however, it is a deep pool that offers refreshing coolness.

Paving material is available in bewildering variety, and your choice needs careful thought. Brick or tile paving heats up nicely during off-seasons, but is this what you will want under the hot summer sun? The surface should not be slippery but it should ideally feel soothing under bare feet. A wall made from the same or similar material may protect the pool from wind and possible noise, as well as provide a feeling of privacy. If you bear in mind that the sun is low in winter and high in summer, protective roofing over such a wall will catch the welcome morning and afternoon sun in winter and provide cherished shade in summer.

This well-planned pool garden is expertly incorporated into its setting, a mature oak wood. Note the natural color of the pool tiles (gray slate). Design by Caroline Menzel.

To keep the paving clean, a pebble mulch could cover the soil around nearby plantings. Alternatively, a raised bed and containers will confine the soil to the spots where you want it. Chlorine damage also needs to be considered. This chemical is tolerated by datura (*Brugmansia*), night jessamine (*Cestrum nocturnum*), palmito (*Chamaerops humilis*), Russian olive or silverberry (*Elaeagnus*), oleander, and tamarisk. The risk of damage can be minimized if chlorine levels are kept to a minimum and if a dividing strip of generous width is put between the pool and the plantings. Salt-water-treated pools should never be used for irrigation except for coastal plants, such as tamarisk.

Heat-loving and drought-tolerant plants are the order of the day because swimming pools are usually located in the warmest possible site on one's property. These plants thrive in full sun and demand little care. Tender species in containers, backed by a wall,

enjoy the heat and can be moved indoors over winter.

Near the pool, plant any palm you fancy; they are low-maintenance. So are sword-leaved plants, most of them in the Agavaceae family. They will not impose on water resources, and because they are practically litter-free, they can be planted right at the pool's edge. To add dramatic contrast, choose from among the cabbage tree (*Cordyline*), the dragon tree (*Dracaena*), New Zealand flax (*Phormium tenax*), and the spineless *Yucca gloriosa*. The equally spineless Australian spear lily (*Doryanthes palmeri*) and the giant *Beschorneria* and *Furcraea* from Mexico grow to an impressive size. Once they come into bloom—which does not happen often—their tall flower spikes are an unforgettable sight. Although sometimes hard to come by, all three are worth any amount of trouble it takes to get and keep them.

Flowering trees and shrubs planted away from the pool can be arranged to frame the principal feature of the garden. Evergreens are preferable because they create less litter than deciduous ones. Consider, for instance, some of my favorites, the

In this California pool garden, careful attention has been paid to the natural color of the water and the choice of the plants. Design by Chris Rosmini.

shiny-leaved kapuka (*Griselinia*), fruit-bearing guava (*Psidium*), and the long-flowering, thornless India hawthorn (*Rhaphiolepis*). The tall Brazilian pepper tree (*Schinus terebinthifolius*), Brisbane box (*Tristania conferta*), and pincushion hakea (*Hakea laurina*) add height. Give the bottlebrush (*Callistemon*) a spacious site, so that its startling flower brushes and graceful bearing can be appreciated. The same goes for pride of Madeira (*Echium*) and bird-of-paradise (*Strelitzia*), backed by crape myrtle (*Lagerstroemia*) and the dramatic cabbage tree (*Cussonia*). Low maintenance and long-lasting bloom are provided by *Coleonema*, *Euryops pectinatus*, blue marguerite (*Felicia amelloides*), and *Phylica ericoides*. Rosemary, grevillea (*Grevillea rosmarinifolia*), and *Westringia* add evergreen rounded masses. Accompany them with many pelargoniums.

Succulents thrive on heat-reflecting paving. Try, for instance, soft-textured *Agave attenuata*, winter-flowering *Aloe arborescens*, and *Kalanchoe*. Spreading *Sedum*, *Crassula*, and creeping succulents such as *Aptenia cordifolia* hug the ground. Again, the ever-present *Gazania* is a great standby. Not a succulent,

Agapanthus creates a weed-suppressing cover. Also consider ground-covering pebbles (though not for bare feet).

Many **climbers**, such as the wall-covering herald's trumpet (*Beaumontia grandiflora*), queen's wreath (*Petrea volubilis*), and the cup-of-gold vine (*Solandra maxima*), thrive in a hot, protected environment.

As **windbreaks**, choose the cypress pine (*Callitris*) or mediterranean arar (*Tetraclinis*) and accompany them with the bulky silver-tree (*Elaeagnus x ebbingei*), with a tea tree (*Leptospermum laevigatum*), paperbark (*Melaleuca*), or oleander (*Nerium oleander*).

A shady area should be an important part of your plan if you do not relish day-long exposure to African heat and you want to avoid the midday sun (today considered a threat to everyone's health). Once again, litter is a consideration. So choose palms or the evergreen mirror plant (*Coprosma repens*). Cut off the seeds of the Japanese aralia (*Fatsia japonica*) before they turn black. Or use a Chinese privet (*Ligustrum lucidum*) or *Myrtus communis* to back tall, large-leaved *Alocasia*, *Schefflera*, *Sparrmannia*, or *Strelitzia nicolai*. Except for the myrtle, these plants require weekly water. At their feet, *Clivia* with its long-lasting flowers can be used in shade to cover the ground, together with lily turf (*Liriope*) or *Ophiopogon*.

Around a pool, beware of:

• **Litter.** Fallen leaves, flowers, fruits, or pollen can create a maintenance problem that is aggravated by wind. For instance, the dainty spring blossom of olive trees throws a veil over the pool in no time. The African sumac (*Rhus lancea*) drops messy berries and is best confined to the background. It is also advisable to steer clear of eucalyptus in places where litter is a concern.

- **Thorns** of shrubs and succulents. Although it is litter-free, the formidable thorns of *Agave americana* make it unsuitable for a poolside.

- **Slippery paving** can lead to accidents.

- **Invasive roots** of fig and plane trees, of poplars and willows, are forever searching for water and will always find it, especially in a nearby pool.

- **Upheaving.** The Californian Washingtonia palm, for example, lifts the paving. Before choosing trees, first check with the builder and your nursery.

- **Shade.** The drought-tolerant *Magnolia grandiflora* gradually reaches majestic proportions and, with time, may overshadow a pool. Its location, like that of any large tree, should be given careful consideration.

- **Health.** Allergies are often caused by spring bloom (e.g., olive trees), while the scented blossom of mock orange (*Philadelphus*) attracts bees, which may sting.

Cotyledon orbiculata, easily grown from cuttings, will cover unsightly corners.

(More or Less) Litter-free Plants

Trees, Shrubs
Anisodontea
Brugmansia
Bupleurum
Callistemon citrinus
Callitris
Chamaerops humilis
Cinnamomum
Citrus
Coleonema
Coprosma repens
Cupressus
Cussonia paniculata
Cussonia spicata
Elaeagnus x ebbingei
Eriobotrya deflexa
Euryops
Fatsia japonica, partial shade
Feijoa
Grevillea rosmarinifolia
Griselinia lucida
Hakea laurina
Heteromeles arbutifolia
Hibiscus
Lagerstroemia indica
Lagunaria patersonii
Laurus nobilis
Leptospermum laevigatum
Leptospermum petersonii
Ligustrum lucidum
Magnolia grandiflora
Melaleuca
Myrsine africana
Myrtus communis
Nerium oleander
Phoenix canariensis
Phylica ericoides
Pittosporum, many
Polygala
Psidium
Rhaphiolepis

Rhus lancea, suckers
Schefflera actinophylla
Schinus terebinthifolius
Sparrmannia africana
Tetraclinis
Thryptomene
Tristania conferta
Tristania laurina
Umbellularia californica
Westringia
Widdringtonia

Perennials, Bulbous Plants
Agapanthus
Alocasia
Aptenia cordifolia
Arctotis
Canna
Capparis
Cerastium
Clivia
Crassula
Crinum
Dianella tasmanica
Dietes grandiflora, clumps
Dimorphotheca
Echium
Felicia amelloides
Gazania
Gerbera
Hedychium coronarium
Hedychium gardnerianum
Hemerocallis
Kniphofia uvaria
Leucophyta brownii
Liriope
Moraea iridioides, clumps

Ophiopogon
Osteospermum
Pelargonium
Sedum
Tanacetum
Zoysia tenuifolia

Accent Plants
Agave attenuata
Aloe arborescens
Beschorneria yuccoides
Cordyline australis
Cussonia paniculata
Cussonia spicata
Dasylirion
Doryanthes palmeri
Dracaena draco
Furcraea bedinghausii
Kalanchoe beharensis
Phormium tenax
Sansevieria trifasciata
Strelitzia nicolai
Strelitzia reginae
Yucca gloriosa

Vines
Beaumontia grandiflora
Jasminum azoricum
Jasminum revolutum
Jasminum sambac
Petrea volubilis
Solandra maxima
Solanum jasminoides
Thunbergia
Trachelospermum

Saving an Oak Woodland
A Personal Experience

Oak trees used to grow throughout the Mediterranean Basin, but no more. This means that oak conservation is a timely topic and, I believe, a subject worth for a garden project. This section refers to my own experience conserving oaks and growing suitable plants in proximity to them. I include here a discussion of the problem of honey fungus (*Armillaria mellea*), also called oak-root fungus, and a tribute to the Portola Valley Ranch in California as a successful example of oak conservation.

The Mediterranean countryside was once covered with trees, mostly oaks, which provided shelter for early man and protection from enemies invading from the sea. Many species of animals counted on the oaks for their food. It has often been claimed that shipbuilding did away with the Mediterranean woods; but in fact wood was cut wherever humans were present, for beams and doors, chairs and tables, pigsties and ladders, olive presses and flour mills, fencing and gates, and the burning of charcoal. Fields were set on fire so that newly sprouting grass that followed would provide fodder, but in the process all trees that stood in the way were burned. Fire also destroyed the underbrush, which had protected the tree seedlings and had provided mulch for the forest floor. The exposed soil was gradually washed away until only bare rock was left. You have seen this countless times. Humans took away the forest without a thought for replacing what they destroyed. Isn't it time we began to reverse that trend by replacing what has been harvested?

Nowadays, urban sprawl cuts into the few woodlands that remain. Bulldozers uproot trees, and Caterpillar tractors remove their debris. Too often uprooted vegetation is left to dry at the side of the road, where it causes a potential fire hazard. The plantings that take their place—lawns and backyards—seldom justify such violent action. Before all the woodlands around the Mediterranean are gone, there should be an effort made to preserve them, especially the oaks. Reforestation, or at least the planting of a small oak wood, is a commendable project, and the conservation of existing trees is a worthwhile theme for a garden.

Reviving Our Oak Woodland

For the better part of the last twenty years, I have been gardening on ten acres (four hectares) of land on our sheep farm, which is part of the last untouched wilderness areas in the western Mediterranean. Tucked away between the mountains and the sea, the fields lie at an altitude of around 1,000 feet (350m) with a mainly northwest exposure. Frost is rare, and yearly rainfall varies between 18 and 28 inches (48 and 73cm).

What I discovered when we first arrived was not

A fine oak with native drought-tolerant *Pistacia*, *Cistus*, and *Viburnum tinus*

handy refuge in sudden downpours! These oaks are dependable and have weathered many storms. They give me a sense of being rooted to the ground, yet their age—the oldest is five hundred years old, we were told—became a matter of concern. And so we got hooked on oak conservation.

Our first task was to repair the derelict fencing. Goats feed on whatever is within their reach, and before we arrived, they regularly broke through the fence, climbed into trees, or even used rocks as jumping platforms to get into greener pastures. At first our fence repairs brought no relief, since the goats then took to crawling beneath them. It took time and patience to locate these places and close them off. In the *maquis* landscape, oak grows in unfavorable conditions and will remain dwarfed and shrublike if grazed on by sheep or goats; with fencing, however, native shrubs in the same location may grow into small trees.

We looked in vain for oak seedlings, until one day we realized that the foot-high mounds with oaklike leaves were actually oaks of uncertain age. As with the wild olive, these "cushions" had smaller, spinier leaves than the full-grown trees, and decades of animal abuse had kept them about a foot high. I removed the small, twisted side shoots, leaving only what promised to become the future trunk. Once they were no longer grazed on, the plants seized their opportunity and in time became what they had wanted to be all their lives: trees. Their roots, already well established in their surroundings, are certainly sturdier than those of new, container-grown plants.

In the past, grazing allowed few seedlings to come up, while today oak, buckthorn (*Rhamnus*) and olive (*Olea*) appear abundantly in all fenced areas. Dozens of young trees are a living proof that it is not difficult to bring woods back to the Mediterranean. Where these plants grow too close together, the sturdiest ones can be selected as future trees and the interfering ones can be sheared, goat-wise, into cushions. As I write this, we have reached the moment when "editing" the trees in our garden has

the plant life that had existed here a few hundred years ago. We found overgrazed fields, a neglected pine forest (*Pinus halepensis*), and the remains of a centuries-old oak forest (*Quercus ilex*). These ancient oaks became the backbone of our garden and its principal theme. Some tree trunks are about 15 feet (5m) around when measured 3 feet (1m) above the ground, while others are hollow, which offers a

Now protected by a fence, colorful undergrowth has come up near the oak on the right. This scene in the author's garden is never watered.

become a necessity. For twenty years, we let the pines grow wherever they seeded themselves, since they protected the garden from northerly winds. In the meantime, oak trees reestablished themselves in the same area, and we must now remove some pines in favor of the oaks. We are doing so before the young pine trees become too large, which would make their removal more complicated.

Once our woodland was cleared of dead material and of the all-embracing brambles, the beauty of the centuries-old oaks emerged. This Mediterranean forest had retained what must have been part of its

leathery leaves. These evergreen ornamentals with neatly rounded shapes that grow to 36 inches (1m) are excellent candidates for garden use. Honeysuckle (*Lonicera implexa*) and white-flowered *Clematis cirrhosa* and *C. flammula* were exuberant climbers. The spiny *Smilax aspera* pulled everything within reach to the ground and remained hard to eradicate. A rich undergrowth comprised friar's cowl (*Arisarum vulgare*), *Cyclamen balearicum*, and many ground orchids. Around Christmastime, seasonal red berries adorned the butcher´s broom (*Ruscus aculeatus*). We did not find any strawberry trees (*Arbutus unedo*), rock roses (*Cistus*), or laurustinus (*Viburnum tinus*), but once introduced, they flourished. Pine trees or wild olive that interfered with the oaks were cut back or removed, and in open spaces the oaks developed rapidly.

Trouble in Paradise

Under the oak trees, a rich soil seemed to promise an Asian woodland. Irrigation was installed, and large patches of white-flowered azaleas and hydrangeas, tropical ginger, glorious tree peonies, and delicate tree ferns were planted. Silvery-white camellias contrasted with the dark oak trunks, while datura (*Brugmansia*), jasmine, and lilies perfumed the air. Plants throve on the virgin soil. The first year was like a dream come true.

The second year was another story. I should have known that **oak roots require dry summers!** Honey or oak-root fungus (*Armillaria mellea*) occurs naturally in oak woods, and when kept at bay by dry summers will do no harm. When watered, however, oak-root fungus comes to life and thrives, gradually choking the roots so that the trees die. I consulted with an eminent botanist with a faint hope at the back of my mind that there would be a way of keeping my Eden. "You knew it all the time," was all he said to me. It was the irrigation system. Reviewing plant after plant, I realized that many of them—the drought-tolerant ones such as the Mexican orange (*Choisya*), toyon (*Heteromeles*), *Plumbago*, and the thornless India hawthorn (*Rhaphiolepis*)—had been

original grandeur: shrubby mastic (*Pistacia lentiscus*) and shiny myrtle (*Myrtus communis*), together with a few mediterranean fan palms (*Chamaerops humilis*). Among our exciting finds were two western Mediterranean endemics, *Rhamnus ludovici-salvatoris* and the spurge olive (*Cneorum tricoccon*) with its olivelike

watered unnecessarily. I shed my unrealistic dreams: the water-demanding plants such as the clematis hybrids, azaleas, white ginger, tree ferns, and camellias had to go, and their replacement with drought-tolerant ones got under way.

There are, as I learned, many drought-tolerant plants from the Mediterranean Basin that make **good companions for oaks**. An important German botanical text offers this helpful advice:

In an open, sunny oak woodland grow *Arbutus unedo*, *Erica arborea*, *Juniperus oxycedrus*, *Myrtus communis*, **many** *Phillyrea*, *Pistacia lentiscus* and *Rhamnus alaternus*. Beneath them grow *Daphne gnidium* and *Euphorbia characias*. Fallen leaves are often the sole ground cover under oaks, but where there is sufficient light, box thrives (*Buxus balearica* **and** *B. sempervirens*). *Cneorum tricoccon* and *Rhamnus ludovici-salvatoris* are accompanied by a varied undergrowth of irises such as the sweetly perfumed *Iris unguicularis* and the discreet *I. foetidissima* with attractive seed capsules. They are joined by small patches of *Cyclamen balearicum*, by the flatly spreading *Teucrium chamaedrys*, by wide expanses of periwinkle *Vinca* and in deep shade by butcher´s broom *Ruscus aculeatus*. *Clematis flammula*, *Lonicera etrusca*, *L. implexa* and *Rosa semper-virens* soar into shrubs and trees, while an interesting range of Asparagus species hides among the shrubs into which they climb. (M. Rikli, *Das Pflanzenkleid der Mittelmeerlaender*, 1943; see Bibliography).

For even more possibilities and to avoid potential losses, it is best to choose plants that are considered armillaria-tolerant. Such trees include *Acer*, *Castanea sativa*, *Calocedrus decurrens*, *Celtis*, *Ceratonia*, *Cercis*, *Diospyros kaki*, *Ficus carica*, *Fraxinus*, *Pyrus communis*, pines, and other conifers. Taller shrubs include *Arbutus unedo*, *Cotinus coggygria*, *Elaeagnus angustifolia*, *Nerium oleander*, and *Vitex agnus-castus*. Smaller plants are *Arctostaphylos*, *Buxus*, *Ceanothus*, and *Phlomis*. Be inspired by this wide range of plants.

Oaks and Water

Oaks are watered by winter rain, which carries them through the summer. As we have seen, in summer one should never irrigate beneath an oak, especially near the trunk. Beyond the drip line, where a few oak roots still reach, a plant in need could receive a monthly summer watering, but only if the drainage is perfect. It thus is best to choose drought-tolerant plants and divide the area to be planted into zones:

Near the trunk: Choose drought-tolerant *Vinca difformis* and *Crassula multicava* for a totally undemanding, quick-spreading ground cover in deep shade. For the same location, yet slower to spread, consider *Cyclamen persicum*, *Helleborus*, *Iris foetidissima*, *I. unguicularis* (native to Moroccan and Algerian oak woods), *Liriope*, *Lonicera etrusca*, *Ophiopogon*, *Plectranthus arabicus*, and above all *Ruscus aculeatus* and *R. hypoglossum*. That's quite a generous choice for a difficult site. If you wish to grow water-demanding plants near the trunk of an oak, keep them in containers where they can be watered as needed.

Well away from the trunk and all the way to the drip line: Moderately shade-tolerant, although all reach for the light, are the drought-tolerant *Bupleurum fruticosum*, *Buxus*, *Choisya ternata*, *Dodonaea*, *Escallonia*, several *Hebe*, *Laurus nobilis*, *Mespilus germanica*, *Myoporum*, *Myrsine africana*, *Myrtus communis*, *Phillyrea*, *Rhamnus alaternus*, *Rhaphiolepis*. Most can be clipped low where required. Add also the climbing *Clematis cirrhosa* and *C. flammula* and the bulbous *I. japonica* (syn. *I. fimbriata*). Where sun reaches, plant *Acanthus*, *Agapanthus*, the mediterranean fan palm (*Chamaerops humilis*), *Eriocephalus africanus*, *Garrya elliptica*, *Griselinia lucida*, *Heteromeles arbutifolia*, *Phylica ericoides*, *Pistacia lentiscus*. Beyond the root zone, plant *Abelia x grandiflora*, *Coprosma*, *Correa*, *Euonymus japonicus*, *Fatsia japonica*, *Schefflera actinophylla*, *Spiraea* and many more.

Note: You can grow *Zantedeschia aethiopica* with winter rain and let it die down in summer.

Other Oak Lessons We Learned

Each oak species has a preferred location. Oak and the plants mentioned all have a suitable root system

In southern Spain, cork oak (*Quercus suber*) is planted for the cork it yields.

to endure bedrock with little overlying soil. Together with other trees and shrubs, they protect watersheds and thus maintain the quality of water. They also protect wildlife and ameliorate the climate since vegetative growth filters out air pollutants.

Oak trees are threatened not only by man but are also weakened by old age, declining winter rains, and possibly by the climate change, thus predisposing them to pests and disease. In Europe, an additional threat is *Cerambyx cerdo*, a brown-black beetle about three inches (8 cm) long with antennae of an equal length that bores holes into the trees. Sawdust on the ground bears witness to its work. Various poisons have been recommended but I have not used them. Since well-groomed trees are less vulnerable, we cut out all dead wood and re-balance the branch structure by shortening the longest and weakest branches to lessen their load. Up to now, trees have responded favorably.

A friend of mine "harvests" the beetles in the late evening hours of early summer when they leave the tree. Twilight hours are considered best, although the beetle can be found throughout the day and at other times of year. Alternatively, a piece of wire is used to extract the grubs. During the terribly dry summer of 2003, the occurrence of *Cerambyx cerdo* was minimal. As a result of declining oak forests in northern Europe, *Cerambyx cerdo*, which can be found in Europe and the Near East, is on the threatened species list.

Oak Conservation Efforts

The loss of native plants is not limited to the Mediterranean Basin. The winter rainfall belts in California, the Cape of South Africa, and south-western Australia face similar problems, and all tackle their challenges with ingenious means. In California, for instance, the preservation of native woodlands has become a prime commitment, and garden clubs and individuals contribute significantly toward this aim. The Santa Barbara Botanic Garden offers a certificate in California horticulture that includes the study of gardening under oaks that deals with appropriate oak species and healthy plant associations for them.

Portola Valley Ranch, designed by California landscape architect Nancy Hardesty, is an example of oak conservation that has worked successfully. Hardesty's guidelines include erosion control, the preservation of view corridors and animal habitat, and fire management. "Foremost, however," she says, "is the use of native plants from oak woodlands and chaparral, with evergreen trees and shrubs as a backbone to the design."

• Undergrowth in Californian oak woodlands includes California coffeeberry (*Rhamnus californica*, *R. crocea*), California lilac (*Ceanothus*), and toyon (*Heteromeles arbutifolia*).

• For the understory beyond the drip line of oak, choose *Garrya elliptica*, *Mahonia pinnata*, *Myrica californica*, *Prunus ilicifolia*, *Ribes quercetorum* and *R. viburnifolium*. Coyote (*Baccharis pilularis*), *Ceanothus griseus*, *Iris douglasiana*, the fern *Polystichum*, and *Satureja douglasii* make good ground covers.

• In mixed evergreen forests, many oaks, such as the very drought-tolerant *Quercus agrifolia*, *Q. chrysolepis*, *Q. douglasii*, *Q. kelloggii*, and *Q. lobata*, are ideally suited for slope stabilization. Accompany with *Acer macrophylla*, *Arbutus unedo*, *Sequoia sempervirens*, and *Umbellularia californica*.

• In chaparral-type landscapes thrive *Arctostaphylos*, *Baccharis*, *Ceanothus*, scrub oak, *Heteromeles arbutifolia*, *Prunus ilicifolia* and *Rhamnus californica* (closely related to the Mediterranean *R. alaternus*).

• For foothill woodlands *Arctostaphylos*, *Aesculus californica*, *Ceanothus*, and *Heteromeles arbutifolia* are right.

• On grasslands, flowering annuals and grasses help to maintain wildlife.

A final note: Seán O'Hara, the guru of "Mediterranean Climate Gardening, an Internet resource for gardeners in the various mediterranean climates throughout the world" (http://MediterraneanGardenSociety.org/discuss), writes: "Oaks in our gardens are certainly worth any amount of trouble we have to go to to keep them healthy. Those I know who do garden appropriately around oaks have found that this method of gardening suits them just fine since it is so much less labour and water intensive than what they did before."

Cymbidium orchids grow well on oak but need summer water and thus should not be planted there.

Plants for an Oak Woodland

These plants, once established, are drought-tolerant and do not require irrigation. They thus suit oak woods, where no summer water should be applied

Trees, Shrubs, Palms

Acer macrophylla
Aesculus californica
Arbutus unedo
Arctostaphylos
Artemisia
Buxus balearica
Buxus sempervirens
Calocedrus decurrens
Castanea sativa
Ceanothus griseus
Celtis
Ceratonia
Cercis
Chamaerops humilis, sun
Choisya
Cistus
Cneorum tricoccon
Cotinus coggygria
Diospyros kaki
Elaeagnus angustifolia
Erica arborea
Eriocephalus africanus
Euphorbia characias
Ficus carica
Fraxinus

Garrya elliptica
Griselinia lucida, sun
Heteromeles arbutifolia
Juniperus oxycedrus
Mahonia pinnata
Myrica californica
Myrtus communis
Nerium oleander
Phillyrea
Phlomis
Phylica ericoides, sun
Pistacia lentiscus, sun
Plumbago
Prunus ilicifolia
Pyrus communis
Rhamnus alaternus
Rhamnus californica
Rhamnus crocea
Rhamnus ludovici-salvatoris
Rhaphiolepis
Ribes quercetorum
Ribes viburnifolium
Sequoia sempervirens
Umbellularia californica
Viburnum tinus
Vitex agnus-castus

Ground Covers, Bulbous Plants

Acanthus
Agapanthus, sun
Arisarum vulgare
Asparagus sp.
Baccharis pilularis
Cyclamen balearicum
Daphne gnidium
Iris douglasiana
Iris foetidissima
Iris unguicularis
Ruscus aculeatus
Ruscus hypoglossum
Satureja douglasii
Teucrium chamaedrys
Vinca
Zantedeschia aethiopica

Climbers

Clematis cirrhosa
Clematis flammula
Lonicera etrusca
Lonicera implexa
Rosa sempervirens

Near the Trunk

Arthropodium
Crassula multicava
Cyclamen persicum
Fragaria chiloensis
Helleborus
Iris foetidissima
Iris unguicularis
Liriope
Lonicera etrusca

Myrsine africana
Ophiopogon
Ruscus aculeatus
Ruscus hypoglossum
Vinca difformis

Away from the Trunk (toward the drip line)

Arbutus unedo
Bupleurum fruticosum
Buxus
Choisya ternata
Dodonaea
Escallonia
Hebe, several
Hemerocallis
Iris japonica (syn. I. fimbriata)
Laurus nobilis
Mespilus germanica
Myoporum
Myrtus communis
Phillyrea
Rhamnus alaternus
Rhaphiolepis

Beyond the Root Zone (preferably in shade with occasional summer water)

Abelia x grandiflora
Coprosma
Correa
Euonymus japonicus
Fatsia japonica
Schefflera
Spiraea

Refreshing Shade, Delightful Scent
A Cool Summer Hideaway

While the merciless summer sun beats down on the countryside, cool shade will keep you refreshed, especially if your garden is enriched with a water feature and with scented white flowers and cypresses clipped into shape or soaring to the sky. Indeed, in the hot mediterranean summers, shade is of paramount importance—for both plants and humans. This section explores the means of creating shade, considers the aesthetic effects created by the delightful play of shade and light, reminds us of the risks of solar radiation, and discusses plants suitable for a shady garden. A range of tropical plants, often bewitchingly scented, suits this garden, too. Two lists are given here—one of drought-tolerant plants that grow in shade (a few with weekly summer water) and another one of scented plants for shade. A shade garden is best for the gardener who likes to cater to the demands of the plants and who is familiar with their exposure requirements. Beginners may start with a small area to get the feel of mediterranean gardening in shade.

Over the hottest summer months, mediterranean gardeners put their gardening efforts into low gear. A cool terrace or the shade of a pergola or tree tempts most of us—certainly more than garden work. We seek out the cool areas in our garden and wonder why we didn't plan for more shade in the past.

The Mogul gardens in Kashmir met the challenges of heat with inspired solutions. Water in hot, dry summers conveys coolness, and many ancient garden designs are based on water. In these Kashmiri gardens—summer residences for the few—water features were fed by melting snow from the mountains, which remained white all summer long. Open, colonnaded pavilions invited a cooling draft and the trees provided shade. We may not be able to copy their artistry, but we can always be inspired by it. Simple methods include setting up a tarpaulin in summer where the sun hits most or leaving a door in a wall open to invite a draft, but there are many more attractive solutions to summer heat.

The mediterranean gardener may set up a terrace covered by rambling climbers, or perhaps trace the path of a pergola, or even take advantage of a cool north-facing wall. Dark, shade-giving cypresses and scented white flowers, accompanied by the sound of dripping water, are well suited to confined areas surrounded by tall buildings or hidden in a backyard on a bustling street. Cool summer shade can also be found beneath the wide-spreading crown of a tree, where the family might gather for a meal or for recreation. Shade can mean a cool patio or a busy courtyard. Yours will be a garden where you can listen to bees humming and the leaves rustling or where you have set aside a peaceful corner in which to hear the silence.

There are many different types of shade. Many Australian trees cast light shade, whereas darkness creeps in under mediterranean oaks. Yet the filtered, dappled, intermittent, or moving shade under the canopy of a tall tree or beneath a pergola will benefit most shade-loving plants. During the hottest summers, filtered shade with a few hours of sun during the day may please even sun-loving mediter-ranean plants. On the other hand, most exotic climbers will race up into the tree tops to reach as much light as possible. However, remember that confined conditions, such as dense shade, are disliked by a range of native plants such as *Arbutus*, *Laurus nobilis*, *Myrtus communis*, and *Viburnum tinus*. To thrive, they require circulating air and sun.

If you intend to use the garden throughout the year, you will need deciduous trees, such as the Chinese flame tree (*Koelreuteria*), to let the winter sun through (when what you want is warmth) and to shade your garden in summer when you will appreciate a cooling breeze. Accompany these with the delicate bridal wreath (*Spiraea cantoniensis*). The right balance between sun and shade is sometimes tricky to achieve, but it is worth careful thought. If you are not pressed for time, you can work it out throughout the year.

Note: A garden with dense shade may be of no use in winter. It also limits the choice of plants and flowers.

Today, shade in the sun-drenched mediterranean environment has an additional function. Time and again we are advised to keep out of the sun during the hottest midday and afternoon hours, when the solar radiation is strongest and when it is an act of bravery to venture out into the scorching sun. Instead of staying indoors, why not create a shade

The rose 'New Dawn' casts delightful shade and light onto the paving.

garden? Establishing gentle summer shade may require patience; after all, plants take time to grow. All the more reason, then, to apply careful planning. Consult the Instant Garden project on page 118 for the way to achieve quick results and for a list of pioneer plants, both of which will provide valuable tips on how to speed up the process.

My tip: Summer shade is best planned during blazing midsummer heat, for this is the moment when one is likely to find the best solutions. As I envision the shade garden, winter winds are howling round the house, straining my imagination.

Whether cool shade is achieved by a pergola or an arbor, by a covered terrace or by trees, aim for a ray of sun to play on leaves, to lighten a corner, or to be reflected in water (perhaps a birdbath). The play of shade and light has always been an essential component of mediterranean gardens.

A shade garden is not necessarily water-consuming. Parts of the garden can be paved, for instance, as a tree-shaded patio for summer meals (if you avoid heat-absorbing materials). Stonework will remain cool on the hottest midsummer day. An old cistern lovingly restored, a small fountain with ferns, the sound of water dripping on rock— even the smallest trickle gives a soothing effect, achieved with minimal (recirculated) water. It does not require more than a pail of water to refresh the floor, to cool the leaves, and to provide ease to the gardener who sits out at night.

Shade abounds in Charles Shoup's formal Greek garden, where a trickle of water cools the air.

A shade garden thrives best on a light, humus-enriched, and well-mulched soil. Where soil conditions are problematic, extensive paving and a number of containers can always be arranged for without much difficulty. A raised bed for choice plants spares us the difficult task of digging in the hard, stony soil that is a frequent feature in mediterranean lands. Where competing tree roots leave little hope for planting, plants can first be potted and the pots then sunk in the ground (if you wish to do so) or moved around to achieve a pleasing effect.

The Power of Scent...

In order to be fully enjoyed, a shade garden needs scent. Scents have an emotional impact that visual impressions often lack. Whether it is the aromatic scent of herbs on a summer day or the heady perfume of tropical flowers on a warm night, fragrance always adds an extra dimension. People will go to great lengths to track down the source of an appealing fragrance. Note, however, that many plants require full sun to release their delicate scent and would not be suitable for a shade garden.

Fragrance, bewitching scent, a heady perfume, a tasty aroma, or an appealing smell— all can be part of the shade garden. Plants have scented flowers, such as honeysuckle (*Lonicera*) and Chilean jasmine (*Mandevilla*), or leaves that give off scent when crushed (*pelargoniums*, mint) or when a passer-by brushes against them (many herbs). Aroma is triggered by different stimuli. Plants of the Mediterranean landscape (*maquis* or *garrigue*), for instance, give off scent in the hot mid-day sun to protect themselves from dehydration; they have not been included in the list of plants for a shade garden. Many tropical plants pervade the evening air with bewitching scent in order to attract the moth on which they rely for fertilization (see the informative book *Sex in Your Garden*, 1997). Often iridescent white or pale cream-colored flowers such as jessamine (*Cestrum*) attract our attention in the twilight. Although most jasmines have a far-reaching scent, none beats star jasmine (*Trachelospermum*). Early in the year, almost in winter, the exquisite perfume of *Viburnum carlesii* is a delightful surprise.

You may wonder why *Elaeagnus x ebbingei* and *Osmanthus* figure on the scent list. Their flowers are insignificant, yet they send out their powerful fragrance far and wide. Passersby are often puzzled until they have found the source of their delight. The delicate perfume of violets, on the other hand, is only perceived if one goes down on one's knees.

…and Color

Color plays its part in a scented shade garden. Light colors give a feel of coolness, in the form of paint on the wall or of flowers you mean to grow. Light-colored pink and cream flowers with an occasional heliotrope introduce light into a shade garden. Shiny green leaves such as those of the tall *Alocasia* or *Aucuba japonica* provide a perfect foil for flowers in cool colors. A white garden has always had—and still has—its adepts, and this shade-garden project would suit such a white-flowered garden best. In the evening, silvery white flowers shine in the darkness and their scent replaces color. Remember: Hot colors such as red, orange, and also yellow mean "sun" and give a feeling of warmth. Recently, however, clivia (*Clivia miniata* var. *citrina*) comes also in pale, creamy yellow and is worth a try for its polished leaves and drought tolerance.

Maintaining a Shade Garden

A shade garden often does best with weekly water, but if it is carefully designed with the right drought-tolerant plants, it may be able to survive with little watering. In any case, you will be able to manage with minimal water if you group plants according to

The shade in this woodland is intermittent, which favors *Hemerocallis* at left.

their water requirements. For instance, grow water-demanding plants together, ideally near the house. Potted and watered according to their needs, they can be located where they highlight the setting and thus justify the water expenditure.

Maintenance of a scented shade garden is low if plants are chosen carefully to suit the site. In winter an annual cutting back lets light through and avoids confined locations where pests and diseases like to lurk.

Plant Selection

Choosing plants in a garden that is planned for shade requires careful thought. It also requires a good knowledge of the demands that the plants will make on us and is probably not for the beginner. The range of plants that thrive in total shade and with little water is limited, but it can be enriched by those plants that like to have their roots in cool shade and their heads in the sun. Palms are a good example, as are many of the climbers. Planted in shade, most climbers tend to race up to reach sun and light, as does the Bengal sky vine (*Thunbergia grandiflora*), so that their flowers are out of sight. Other plants need full sun to grow well yet provide soothing shade beneath them for summer meals.

Note: for a range of plants that grow in shade without additional summer water, see the list of plants suitable for sites near oak trunks in Saving an Oak Woodland, page 109.

A **mass of shiny, evergreen foliage as a background** is a must in a shade garden. Carob (*Ceratonia siliqua*), New Zealand laurel (*Corynocarpus laevigatus*), *Magnolia grandiflora*, or buckthorn (*Rhamnus alaternus*) qualify as good shade trees. The polished leaves of kapuka (*Griselinia lucida*), myrtle (*Myrtus communis*), English laurel (*Prunus laurocerasus*), *Viburnum suspensum*, and of many *Pittosporum* provide volume. The mirror plant (*Coprosma repens*) and holly (*Ilex*) tolerate heavy shade. Totally maintenance-free, the long-flowering Indian hawthorn (*Rhaphiolepis indica*) will be one of your best shrubs. You simply cannot go wrong; its clean, polished foliage is unequaled, and it goes on

producing its white or pink flowers for a long period. To cover an unsightly wall, a row of slender tall cypresses comes to mind. Have at least one palm, say *Phoenix canariensis*, in order to listen to the rustling sound of its fronds when a light breeze arises during a summer afternoon.

Note: Velvety-gray leaves seldom thrive in shade.

Well worth the weekly water it needs, the shiny-leaved, summer-flowering ginger (*Hedychium coronarium*) makes a bold statement and has one of the most bewitching scents I know. In dappled shade, it creates a perfumed corner together with flowering maple (*Abutilon* 'Boule de Neige'), with begonia, datura (*Brugmansia*), fuchsia, impatiens, jasmine, and lilies. Early-blooming *Iris japonica* thrives in shade. If you have foliage in mind, then add the spectacular, large-leaved elephant's ear (*Alocasia*). *Fatsia* bears football-size flower heads—a midwinter sight. It is the large-leaved plants that require weekly watering, or at any rate do better with it. With large leaves you can create a tropical atmosphere.

Fairly tolerant of drought are *Abelia* x *grandiflora*, bush anemone (*Carpenteria californica*), Mexican orange (*Choisya ternata*), and *Escallonia*. However, the ground beneath trees and tall shrubs is often

Even a small flower composition can lighten a shady evergreen site.

This walkway, with time, will become more shaded as the climbers grow (*Podranea ricasoliana*).

robbed of water. To enjoy their flowers, "waste" a bit of water on them. Planted nearby and watered together, the late-summer-flowering Japanese anemone (*Anemone japonica*) covers their bare bases.

As an evergreen ground cover in shade, carpet bugle (*Ajuga reptans*) and periwinkle (*Vinca minor*), accompanied by the delicate violet (*Viola odorata*), form the flattest of carpets. *Coprosma* x *kirkii* 'Variegata' lights up a dark corner, while a dense carpet of lily turf (*Liriope*) or of the similar *Ophiopogon* will with time smother all weeds. Evergreen *Agapanthus*, butcher's broom (*Ruscus hypoglossum*), and false Solomon's seal (*Smilacina racemosa*), planted en masse, will cover the ground densely. The Gladwin iris (*Iris foetidissima*) takes care of a forgotten dry corner in total shade, while *Iris douglasiana* and *I. unguicularis* 'Alba' carpet the ground under oak.

Exquisite bulbous plants flourish in this setting. *Anemone blanda* 'White Splendor', *Arum italicum*, many *Cyclamen*, snowdrop (*Galanthus*), snowflake (*Leucojum*), and bluebell (*Scilla campanulata*) herald

spring and are all easy to come by. The Californian *Dichelostemma ida-maia* flourishes in light soil and dry shade. In summer, the stately *Lilium speciosum* and other lilies, planted deeply in humus-rich soil, will repay your trouble with their delicious scent. The blood lilies (*Haemanthus albiflos*, *Scadoxus puniceus*, and *Veltheimia*) delight all who search for rare treasures.

In a sunny corner, beyond the mottled shade and framed by glossy evergreens, add white-flowered *Allium grandiflorum* and *Gladiolus colvillei* 'The Bride' for the cool feel they impart. Or group small, white spring bulbs such as *Chionodoxa*, *Crocus*, *Hyacinthus*, *Muscari*, *Ornithogalum*, and *Puschkinia*. The Madonna lily (*Lilium candidum*) differs from all other lilies in that it follows the mediterranean winter-rain cycle. Shallowly autumn-planted in a sunny spot, it flowers in spring.

Large-leaved climbers, such as the lizard plant (*Tetrastigma*), will rapidly provide shade by covering a pergola, for instance. Large-flowered clematis hybrids bring color to a hidden corner. Wisteria

Centranthus ruber 'Albus' needs no watering.

shoots will grow up and up toward the sky and carry their scent into the house. Many jasmines are appealing, but their overbearing exuberance, which is often time-consuming to control, should be remembered. Accent plants, such as the cast-iron plant (*Aspidistra*) and the New Zealand flax (*Phormium tenax*), are tolerant of most conditions. So are *Cordyline* and *Yucca*.

Many shade-loving or shade-tolerant plants grow well in containers. Box and laurel are easily sheared into shape. Alternatively, you might choose *Sarcococca* with its insignificant-looking yet delightfully scented flowers. The inquisitive roots of the bear's breeches (*Acanthus*) are held at bay in a container, so that one can enjoy their large, exuberant leaves without being overwhelmed. Cycads convey a sense of permanence, and *Cymbidium* orchids confer a touch of luxury. Add some ferns and remember, too, that the calla lily (*Zantedeschia*) thrives under most conditions. Depending on their hardiness, container plants can be brought indoors to overwinter. There are many possibilities for flowers in shade, not necessarily at the expense of water.

Drought-Tolerant Shade Lovers

Established plants that need weekly watering in summer are noted. For scent, see the list of scented plants below.

Sun-loving Trees that Provide Shade

Ceratonia siliqua
Corynocarpus laevigatus
Cupressus
Jacaranda
Magnolia grandiflora, large
Phoenix canariensis
Pittosporum tobira
Rhamnus alaternus, reliable
Taxus baccata, large tree

Shrubs for Shade
Abelia x *grandiflora*
Abutilon 'Boule de Neige'
Arctostaphylos densiflora
Aucuba japonica, dense shade
Brugmansia
Bupleurum fruticosum,
   half-shade
Buxus microphylla
Buxus sempervirens
Chamaerops humilis
Choisya ternata
Cneorum tricoccon,
   light shade
Coprosma repens
Cordyline, accent plant
Dais cotinifolia
Escallonia
x *Fatshedera lizei*,
   weekly water
Fatsia japonica, weekly water
Fuchsia, weekly water
Garrya elliptica,
   monthly water

Griselinia lucida,
   bi-weekly water
Hebe, large-leaved ones
Heteromeles
Laurus nobilis
Ligustrum
Mahonia x *media* 'Charity'
Mahonia pinnata
Myrtus communis
Osmanthus fragrans
Pittosporum crassifolium
Pittosporum tobira
Pittosporum undulatum
Prunus laurocerasus
Prunus lusitanicus
Rhaphiolepis indica
Schefflera, weekly water
Spiraea cantoniensis
Viburnum suspensum,
   weekly water

Climbers to the Sun
Clematis armandii
Clematis cirrhosa
Jasminum officinale
Pandorea pandorana,
   occasional water
Parthenocissus, quick
Solanum jasminoides,
   bi-weekly water

Camellia japonica suits cool shade.

Sollya heterophylla,
   occasional water
Tetrastigma voinierianum
   large leaves
Thunbergia grandiflora
   'Alba'
Trachelospermum
   jasminoides, some water
Wisteria, weekly to
   monthly water

Perennials that Cover the Ground in Shade

Acanthus
Ajuga reptans,
   weekly water
Anemone japonica,
   weekly water
Aquilegia
Aspidistra elatior,
   tolerates dark shade
Coprosma x kirkii,
   flat ground cover
Cymbidium,
   occasional water
Digitalis, white-flowered
   ones, weekly water
Erigeron karvinskianus,
   ground cover
Fragaria californica
Hedychium coronarium,
   weekly water, heat
Helleborus
Hosta, weekly water
Impatiens walleriana,
   water as needed
Paeonia, occasional water
Phormium tenax,
   accent plant
Ruscus hypoglossum
Smilacina racemosa,
   weekly water
Streptocarpus,
   weekly water
Trachelium caeruleum,
   monthly water
Vinca rosea 'Alba',
   ground cover
Vinca tricolor, ramping

Bulbous Plants

Acanthus mollis
Agapanthus,
   occasional water
Allium grandiflorum
Anemone blanda
   'White Splendour'
Anemone coronaria,
   weekly water
Arisarum vulgare,
   dainty, summer-dry
Arum italicum, summer-dry
Chionodoxa, summer-dry
Clivia miniata var. *citrina,*
   creamy-yellow
Crinum,
   white, weekly water
Crocus, dry summers
Cyclamen, dry summers
Cymbidium,
   occasional water
Dichelostemma ida-maia,
   dry shade
Galanthus, dry summers
Gladiolus colvillei
   'The Bride'
Haemanthus albiflos,
   winter-flowering
Hemerocallis, weekly water
Iris douglasiana, under oak
Iris foetidissima, evergreen
Iris innominata,
   woodland, evergreen

Scented Plants for Shade

For a cool effect, choose white flowers.
A weekly watering will not overwater nor
will it let the plants listed below go thirsty.

Trees and Shrubs with Scented Flowers

Alocasia odora
Bouvardia longiflora, exquisite
Brugmansia candida, best scent
Carissa grandiflora,
   only light shade
Carpenteria californica
Cestrum nocturnum
Choisya ternata
Citrus limon, requires sun
Elaeagnus x ebbingei,
   only light shade
Elaeagnus pungens,
   only light shade
Gardenia
Heliotropum arborescens
Murraya paniculata, heat
Osmanthus heterophyllus
Pittosporum
Sarcococca ruscifolia,
   tolerates dense shade
Viburnum bodnantense
Viburnum x burkwoodii
Viburnum carlesii
Viburnum deben

Climbers, Trailers

Beaumontia grandiflora
Clematis armandii
Gelsemium sempervirens,
   flowers yellow
Ipomoea alba
Jasminum odoratissimum
Jasminum polyanthum
Jasminum sambac

Lonicera fragrantissima
Mandevilla laxa
Solandra maxima, flowers yellow
Stephanotis floribunda
Trachelospermum jasminoides
Wisteria sinensis 'Alba'

Crinum x powellii 'Album'
has a powerful scent.

Ground Cover and Bulbous Plants

Convallaria majalis
Crinum
Crocus chrysanthus,
   no summer water
Freesia, no summer water
Hedychium coronarium, heat
Hyacinthus, no summer water
Iris unguicularis 'Alba'
Lilium, many
Narcissus tazetta 'Paper White'
Polianthes tuberosa
Viola odorata

The Instant Garden
Quick Results for the Impatient Gardener

I have not forgotten gardeners who are pressed for time, and in this section, I cater to their needs by explaining how to achieve rapid growth to cover a garden area. Not all plants are slow to establish themselves, and I have described here plants that may be used to achieve a finished look very quickly, including annuals that will provide instant color. Most of the plants I suggest are drought-tolerant, or at least waterwise. Furthermore, I have included a special tip—pioneer plants for a quick green mass. At first sight, this project seems to cover the same ground as the Lazy Person´s Dream Garden, but this time I write about speed rather than labor-saving techniques.

Although all of us hope to live with our garden as it matures and eventually harvest the fruits of our toil, under certain circumstances a garden may be ours for a short period only. What about when you rent a house for a single summer, or at most a year, but would like to see flowering plants right from the start? And there are many other situations where a rapid result is required: when you want to protect your new garden against the salt air produced by a stormy sea or to hide a recently built skyscraper—as fast as possible. Or you may simply be impatient, as many of us are.

Annuals may come to your assistance for a single summer, but once their season is over, you will notice the gap they leave. Why not use fast-growing perennials and woody plants, invest a bit of time in choosing the right ones, and place a bowl of annuals by your front door to gladden your visitors' hearts—and your own?

To speed up the growth of your garden, reflect on what you want to achieve. You may not want to invest in permanent paving, but a lawnmower can

Soft paint quickly spruced up a French garden.

For more ideas, see :

define garden areas immediately by cutting a grass path into a meadow. Gravel spruces up the appearance of the garden from the moment it is spread. Plan your choice of plants carefully. Cypress and all sword-leaved plants such as New Zealand flax (*Phormium*) and yuccas provide a full-grown look almost from the start.

Not all plants give quick results. A plant that assumes its mature landscape role in about four years is considered very fast. A fast-growing pine may gain about 2 feet (60cm) annually, to which a green-fingered gardener can add a few more inches. Neighbors will share their wealth of experience with you and nurseries will advise, but remember that each garden has its own rapid-growing plants and that small treasures, lovely as they are, are likely to make little headway in a short time.

A plant's performance will only be as good as the conditions you offer it. In order to shoot up with the speed of a racehorse, most plants need attention to their growing needs. Heat-requiring plants really do need heat to progress, while shade lovers require shade and without it will collapse in the hottest locations. Take the time to search for suitable planting sites with suitable soil and the right exposure. These are all of paramount importance.

Shade is what facilitates a quick start, and mulch is what gets soil life going, whereas stress factors such as wind, drought, and lack of soil tend to limit rapid growth. Time spent on the careful preparation of a well-drained planting hole, with adequate plant food placed at the bottom, will later be rewarded by speedier growth. Weekly water seems adequate for most plants, but refrain from overwatering and overfertilizing since *more* is not necessarily *better*. Plants that have been forced are easily weakened and may become prone to pests and diseases.

Note: For quick results, consider close planting, which under normal conditions is not always the best thing to do.

Eucalyptus trees grow quickly, and the myoporums will soon become significant in size.

Well-rooted plants get you off to a quick start. At the garden center, look for container-grown but not pot-bound specimens. If you are in doubt, remove the plant from the pot to investigate the roots and examine the new leaves for healthy, sturdy growth. Buy only the best quality—a higher initial investment will pay dividends later on.

Note: Plants in gallon containers are usually healthier. And avoid those grown in pure peat; they dry out quickly and will be reluctant to grow into the surrounding soil when transplanted.

A garden full of quick-growing plants may become labor-intensive over the years as such plants often need massive cutting back. Since it will take a lot of plants to replace a lawn, easily propagated plants are a cost-effective choice.

Make ample use of pioneer plants, a special category. These are reliable, stalwart plants that produce quick results for a temporary cover and will create an effect within a year. Fast-growing and undemanding, they provide valuable initial shade to get a garden going, and they cover the soil and put a protective coat over it, as nature does when left to do so. They gradually build up the soil and improve soil life by creating a favorable growing medium. Many plants get going right away, whereas others require a period to establish themselves before shooting up. But some of the quickest plants are, in the long run, often difficult to keep within bounds if growing conditions are too much to their liking. They may even become invasive and at a later stage may have to go.

Drought-tolerant (and, of course, quick) are Sydney golden wattle (*Acacia longifolia*), California lilac (*Ceanothus* 'Frosty Blue'), and ngaio (*Myoporum laetum*), chosen with a view to evergreen foliage and flowering. They grow fast under almost any conditions. Also choose from among blackwood (*Acacia melanoxylon*), *Cupressus arizonica* var. *glabra*, shamel ash (*Fraxinus uhdei*), black locust (*Robinia pseudoacacia*), and the pepper tree (*Schinus molle*), a fast-growing pioneer tree in shade. Plant a western redbud (*Cercis occidentalis*) for winter sun and summer shade, and enjoy its long-lasting spring blossom. The shrubby blue hibiscus (*Alyogyne huegeli*) adds blooms, backed by the glossy green Chinese privet (*Ligustrum lucidum*). The yellow flowers of the flannel bush (*Fremontodendron*) stand out for weeks.

If you have towering heights in mind, plant *Eucalyptus viminalis*, one of the quickest trees, but choose a site where its litter will not create problems. In a protected corner, a large-leaved, white-flowered *Catalpa bignonioides* is a spectacular sight. To quickly improve a view that lacks interest,

use cypress. Tall specimens will have to be firmly staked until their roots have taken hold. Although most plants don't look like much when newly planted, sword-leaved cabbage tree (*Cordyline*), dragon tree (*Dracaena*), New Zealand flax (*Phormium*), and *Yucca*, though not fast-growing, have style from the start. The same goes for palms.

For a quick, colorful foreground, use *Coreopsis*, sea lavender (*Limonium*), all *Pelargonium*, and many *Salvia*. *Cotoneaster* 'Lowfast' races along to simulate a lawn, helped by California lilac (*Ceanothus* 'Joyce Coulter'), *Hypericum calycinum*, or *Lantana montevidensis*. Marvel of Peru (*Mirabilis jalapa*), planted as seeds or fleshy roots, is unequaled for immediate, brilliant color. Cuttings of African daisies (*Dimorphotheca* or *Osteospermum*) or *Argyranthemum frutescens* from the Canary Islands flower the same year.

Annuals, such as marigold (*Calendula officinalis*) and California poppy (*Eschscholzia californica*), naturalize readily. Nasturtiums (*Tropaeolum majus*) are accommodating in the extreme and will climb into or onto whatever lies in their path. On the Canary Islands, they cover vast expanses of stony no-man's-land with yellow and orange flowers, giving the site an air of joyful radiance. Observe a nasturtium's light green leaves, held high on an elegantly fragile stem, each one positioned to shade the ground. Scatter seed where you wish it to grow. Later pull out surplus plants and pot them up to be held in reserve for quick emergency repairs. The painter Monet used nasturtiums extensively in his garden at Giverny. The sunflower (*Helianthus annuus*), honored by the painter Van Gogh, thrives on virgin soil, reaches towering heights in its first year, and makes a spectacular display in front of light gray rock. In its shade, the tall sunflower creates favorable growing conditions for slower plants.

Succulents are easy, but ask for the quick ones, such as *Crassula multicava* or *Sedum telephium*.

If you mean to structure a view, plant a *Cordyline*.

Aptenia cordifolia, a succulent and a quick ground cover, climbs in full sun over rocks or spreads over gravel and, together with closely planted *Lampranthus*, forms colorful carpets in no time. Succulents should not be underestimated. Together with trees, shrubs, climbers, and bulbous plants, they fill an important role in a drought-tolerant garden. However, they do need a discerning eye to assign them the right place, as an eye catcher, a winter bloomer, or an undemanding ground cover.

Add immediate interest to your garden with large, spectacular leaves. The castor bean (*Ricinus communis*) has leaves that are either red-tinged or shiny green and can be used to fill the space designated for a future large shrub or tree. Although its seeds are poisonous, we had our summer lunches in its shade for years without incident. *Ricinus* needs minimum care. For an emergency supply, place a few seeds in a pot and let them grow. (If children are around, cut off the seed heads.) On a large scale, a fig tree satisfies the same need, but its roots are difficult to eradicate if they have been allowed to grow between rocks. The spectacular honey flower (*Melianthus major*) grows with such eagerness in rich soil that you can almost watch it. The Japanese aralia (*Fatsia japonica*) makes a good display from the start. Given dappled shade and moderate water, it gains in beauty and stature as it grows.

A hedge planted with oleander (*Nerium oleander*), or an access path bordered by it, will flower in its first summer, its evergreen foliage a perfect foil for the flowers (variegated leaves would blur the design). Thorny silverberry (*Elaeagnus pungens*) and firethorn (*Pyracantha*) will grow into impenetrable hedges, protecting you from intruders. Their small scented white flowers and the edible red fruits of the former are added benefits.

Climbers are often speedy growers, for instance, *Bignonia*, chalice vine (*Solandra*), potato vine (*Solanum*), and roses. Many passifloras will find their way up into a tree. Others require positioning, tying-in, or corrective pruning, which will eliminate some summer growth. The vigorously spreading honeysuckle (*Lonicera japonica*) suits unfavorable, difficult sites. It creates a first cover, from which other plants come up, and over the years it will deposit valuable vegetable matter. Periwinkle (*Vinca difformis*) is a miracle plant, covering the ground in sun or shade and establishing itself in one winter as ground cover on a low bank. Pretty blue flowers come up en masse to light up a dark corner in early spring. Once it is established, long shoots strike root wherever they reach and also climb into shrubs. Pull up a few, pot up for a season, or plant right away in shade. If you cut it back annually to about one foot, it will form neat mounds. This particular periwinkle, given time, tends to invade; but experiment also with others.

Bulbous plants are invaluable for a quick effect. A few large bulbs of *Gladiolus* hybrids and of amaryllis (*Hippeastrum*) or the rhizomes of bearded irises and calla lilies (*Zantedeschia*) make themselves noticed the first year. Smaller bulbs are preferably planted in numbers for mass performance (*Sparaxis, Sternbergia*). All make the most of themselves if backed by evergreen foliage. *Agapanthus*, one of the best to shade the ground quickly, often flowers in its first year and can be divided as early as its second year. Planted in shade, *Iris japonica* soon covers the ground under tall shrubs with its graceful foliage and delights us in spring with its flowers.

Container plants will contribute to rapid growth where the glare of the sun needs mellowing or a neighboring view requires concealment, as on a terrace or balcony. Container-grown *Dombeya* and African linden (*Sparrmannia*) carry large leaves and spectacular flowers from late winter to spring. Flowering maple (*Abutilon*) flowers year round. Take advantage of the graceful foliage of the super-quick tree of heaven (*Ailanthus altissima*). If you are tempted by its easy ways and carried away by its rapid growth, remember that the restricted planting site of a container will help confine the roots. The same goes for African sumac (*Rhus lancea*).

The following plants are what I call garden stalwarts.

• *Abelia*, an exquisitely scented flowering shrub with an arching habit and striking autumn color, soon covers a sizeable patch in half-shade (occasional summer water).

• *Artemisia absinthum*, the common wormwood, brings a lovely gray cloud to your garden in no time at all. Its fine feathery leaves successfully contrast or harmonize with other plantings.

• *Buxus sempervirens* or *B. balearica* stand up to summer heat and drought when such stalwarts as *Coronilla*, *Phormium tenax*, or even young holm oak (*Quercus ilex*) wince.

• *Echium candicans*, *E. pininana* and other echiums are among the best drought survivors. They enliven the garden with their striking white to blue inflorescences (red with the biennial *E. wildpretii*) and occasionally seed themselves.

• *Elaeagnus* x *ebbingei* and the silverberry (*E. pungens*) are unbeatable for vigor. Each covers 36 square feet (2 x 2m) or more in a few years. Place them where nothing else will grow.

• *Eriocephalus africanus*, the kapok bush, is one of the best survivors in poor soil and drought. Its white winter flowers are small, yet their mass is spectacular. Easy and quick to grow from cuttings.

• *Euonymus japonicus*, with apple-green spring foliage, takes almost any growing conditions but prefers semi-shade to strongly reflected heat.

• *Lavandula*, in my experience, takes time to fill its allotted space. With you, lavender may react differently and should certainly be tried, once you have asked for suitable species. The same goes for rosemary.

• *Phlomis fruticosa*, *P. italica*, and *P. russeliana* cover the soil in hot, dry spots. Jerusalem sage is totally drought-tolerant and also animal-resistant.

• *Tanacetum parthenium* offers help without being asked. An attractive, undemanding ground cover, the feverfew flourishes on a mere suspicion of soil. Mulch and a modicum of water keep it happy. It self-seeds with ease, so pot up seedlings for later use.

• *Teucrium fruticans*, the bush germander, reaches far and wide with gray feltlike shoots. Its flowers are negligible, but its low demands are noteworthy.

The drought-tolerant *Mirabilis jalopa* flowers in a year.

A Selection for Quick Results

Trees

Acacia longifolia
Acacia melanoxylon, invasive
Ailanthus altissima, invasive
Callistemon citrinus
Cassia excelsa
Casuarina cunninghamiana, fine-textured
Casuarina equisetifolia
Catalpa bignonioides
Cercis occidentalis
Cupressus arizonica var. *glabra*
Cupresssus sempervirens
Eriobotrya deflexa, no alkaline soil
Eriobotrya japonica, tolerates alkaline soil
Eucalyptus viminalis, manna gum, very fast
Fraxinus ornus
Fraxinus uhdei, evergreen
Grevillea robusta
Hakea laurina
Lagerstroemia indica, infrequent deep water
Leptospermum lanigerum
Ligustrum lucidum
Melaleuca nesophila
Morus alba
Myoporum laetum, a coastal screen
Parkinsonia aculeata
Paulownia tomentosa
Pinus, many
Platanus x *acerifolia*, beware allergies
Populus nigra
Rhamnus
Rhus lancea, suckers when young
Robinia pseudoacacia
Schinus molle
Tecoma stans
Tipuana tipu
Tristania conferta, no alkalinity
Washingtonia, lifts paving

Shrubs

Abelia x *grandiflora*, no coastal wind
Abutilon
Alyogyne huegeli, for coastal conditions
Artemisia
Buddleja davidii
Buddleja madagascariensis
Callistemon citrinus, wide tolerances
Ceanothus 'Frosty Blue', tolerates wind, heat
Ceanothus 'Snow Flurry', as above
Cercis occidentalis
Cestrum
Choisya ternata
Cistus, wide tolerances
Convolvulus cneorum
Cordyline
Cotinus coggygria, drainage, wind-tolerant
Cotoneaster lacteus, sun and shade
Cytisus x *praecox*, beware seeding
Dombeya
Dracaena
Echium fastuosum, pride of Madeira
Elaeagnus x *ebbingei*
Elaeagnus pungens
Eriocephalus africanus
Eriogonum arborescens and others
Escallonia
Euonymus
Euryops pectinatus, no alkaline soil
Fatsia japonica
Fremontodendron hybrids
Genista lydia, one month in bloom
Grevillea 'Canberra', barrier plant
Hebe
Hibiscus
Hypericum calycinum
Lantana
Lavandula angustifolia
Lavandula dentata is slower
Ligustrum japonicum, tolerates shade, wind
Melianthus major
Nerium oleander, full sun
Phormium tenax, widest tolerances
Prunus laurocerasus
Pyracantha coccinea, quick hedge
Rhus, some species
Rosa
Sparrmannia africana
Tamarix
Teucrium fruticans
Viburnum tinus
Westringia rosmariniformis
Yucca

Vines

Campsis radicans
Lonicera hildebrandiana
Macfadyena unguis-cati
Parthenocissus tricuspidata
Passiflora
Podranea ricasoliana
Solandra
Solanum jasminoides
Tecoma capensis
Tetrastigma voinierianum
Vitis vinifer

Living under Pines
A Peaceful Summer Retreat

Pines are a characteristic feature of the Mediterranean, but not all plants will thrive beneath them. This section describes plants that grow well and look good in association with pines. It also discusses the danger of fire during the long summer when pine needles exude their resinous scent, and how one may minimize the risks. A list of fire-retardant and labor-saving plants is given. The pine processionary caterpillar (*Thaumetopoea pityocampa*), a pest in many parts of Europe, is discussed in colorful terms.

The Aleppo pine (*Pinus halepensis*) grows to the water's edge.

For more ideas, see :

Let's imagine that your garden is part of a pine wood, or that a stand of pine trees grows on your land. My mind conjures up the smell of resin, dry needles carpeting the ground, hot summer afternoons spent reading in the shade. "What can I do with this garden?" you may ask, and I am tempted to reply "Leave it as is."

Let's say that when your house was being built, you succeeded in preserving the pine trees. You should allow them to grow to their full size, each with sufficient space to encourage the development of a sound, healthy network of branches. Dense and light-absorbing stands of pine need to be opened up to provide air circulation. Eliminate any trees that interfere with ventilation or with the growth of other, stronger trees, along with those that are ailing. Young specimens up to 3 feet tall (1m) tolerate being cut back, like box, and will fill out year after year (growth resumes only where needles grow, not from bare wood). Sticky resin will exude from damaged bark, but pines recover readily.

As they decompose on the forest floor, the soft pine needles use up whatever nitrogen is available, so it is necessary to add nitrogen to support plants that grow under pines. Pines also acidify the soil. On the other hand, a floor of pine needles makes a clean and attractive ground cover. The yellow autumn crocus (*Sternbergia*) will come up in large patches where you have planted the brown bulbs, throwing a cloth of gold under the pine trees.

It is known that pines, being tolerant of a wide range of conditions, tend to be invasive, so they should not be introduced where slow-growing oaks or fine old olive trees dominate. Yet a well-managed pine woodland is always preferable to bare rock and provides us with many amenities, including solid shade, a weed-suppressing ground cover, and a perfect place for children to roam and play. Pine

Pinus halepensis towers over a seventeenth-century watchtower on the Spanish coast.

trees grow well near the coast. So let's take advantage of them.

Pine Companions

The pine-tree garden is quick and easy to care for, and the plants described below, once established, do not need summer water or special care. After initial clearing, set up your hammock between the trees or move a deck chair out to enjoy the scene at leisure. A few tall shrubs such as a strawberry tree (*Arbutus unedo*) and laurustinus (*Viburnum tinus*) in sun or myrtle (*Myrtus*

Three rare *Cneorum tricoccon* have come up below the rocks in a pine wood.

communis) in dappled shade may conceal any sights you prefer not to see. Firethorn (*Pyracantha*), with its striking flowers, long-lasting berries, and formidable thorns, is a good substitute for costly fencing.

But perhaps you are seeking a wider plant range or more flowers. To my mind, an evergreen carob (*Ceratonia siliqua*) would look right with pines. In a clearing, you could add deciduous flowering trees such as the Judas tree (*Cercis siliquastrum*), hawthorn (*Crataegus*), or almond (*Prunus dulcis*). Choose silverberry (*Elaeagnus*) for its sweet scent; plant juniper (*Juniperus oxycedrus*) or sweet bay (*Laurus nobilis*) for bulk; add *Nerium oleander*, tobira (*Pittosporum*) or a few *Pistacia*. All rock roses (*Cistus*), broom (*Cytisus*), and *Genista*, several *Hypericum* (*H. balearicum*), *Jasminum fruticans*, Jerusalem sage (*Phlomis fruticosa*), lavender, rosemary, and sage flower and will thrive in the sun.

On a northern slope near pine trees, the spurge olive (*Cneorum tricoccon*), *Erica multiflora*, *Rhamnus ludovici-salvatoris*, *Helleborus*, and *Paeonia* grow wild in deep, well-drained soil, where their roots find a cool run under the rocks. They are happy in those places where the snow from an occasional snowfall lingers longest. The summer-flowering *Clematis flammula* will climb high to cover a tree with its spectacular white foam, while the delicate winter-flowering *C. cirrhosa* scrambles through a shrub and

adds quiet charm. The sky-reaching *Rosa sempervirens* is content in the driest site. Honeysuckle (*Lonicera*) is a constant presence while crocus, cyclamen, and early irises carpet the ground.

From other continents comes an additional group of plants that would be appropriate in this setting for sites in full sun without summer water: manzanita (*Arctostaphylos*), blueblossom (*Ceanothus*), and flannel bush (*Fremontodendron*) from California; buchu (*Agathosma*) with erica-like foliage from the Cape; and *Pimelea* from Australia, to mention just a few. Wild olive (*Olea*) or oleaster (*Elaeagnus*) do not belong in woodland, nor do pelargoniums and succulents; they like full sun and should be eliminated where they look miserable.

Pine Processionary Caterpillars

This pest (*Thaumetopoea pityocampa*), which is covered with poisonous hairs, occasionally occurs in Europe in pine forests, where its conspicuous white cocoon can be seen from afar. The eggs, laid early in August and protected by a white fluffy cylinder, hatch out in September, when the minute caterpillars begin to feed nightly on the pine needles and to prepare provisional nests, moving ever higher in the chosen tree. Once the nights turn cold, they start on the big final "nest," or cocoon. About mid-March they abandon this shelter, descend in a single file and, still in a single file, search for a suitable spot to chrysalize, turning into tiny cocoons, from which they will emerge the next spring as tender moths. Control is difficult, yet some gardeners cut off by hand all those nests that can be reached. And they use a gun to blow up the cocoons beyond reach. Cautionary note: Use protective gear, do not touch or stand beneath the nests of these caterpillars, which can be fatal to cats and dogs.

Where the ground has not been planted, pine needles provide a clean cover under the pines.

Rock roses, golden coronillas, bupleurums, and ericas thrive without watering under pine trees.

Plants for a Pine Wood

The following are not necessarily fire-retardant.
Most require a sunny location.

Agathosma

Arbutus unedo

Arctostaphylos

Ceanothus

Ceratonia siliqua

Cercis

Cistus

Clematis cirrhosa

Clematis flammula

Cneorum tricoccon

Crataegus

Crocus

Cyclamen

Cytisus

Dodonaea

Elaeagnus

Erica multiflora

Fremontodendron

Genista

Helleborus

Hypericum balearicum

Iris foetidissima

Iris unguicularis

Jasminum fruticans

Juniperus oxycedrus

Laurus lusitanica

Laurus nobilis

Lonicera

Myrtus communis

Nerium oleander

Paeonia

Phlomis fruticosa

Pimelea

Pistacia

Pittosporum

Prunus dulcis

Pyracantha

Rhamnus ludovici-salvatoris

Rosa sempervirens

Fire Prevention

As the destruction of nature progresses with lamentable rapidity, conservation has become an important part of our approach to gardening, with an increasingly prominent role being given to Mediterranean native plants and fire prevention.

Where periodic fires are a threat, total clearing of the ground (which invites erosion) has often been used as a means of preventing fires. Today, however, prevention is better achieved by the sensible use of fire-retardant plants. Plants cannot stop fire, but hazards may be reduced by replacing highly combustible vegetation, such as cypress, eucalyptus, juniper, and pine, with plants that possess a low fuel content, such as saltbush (*Atriplex*), bottlebrush (*Callistemon*), carob (*Ceratonia siliqua*), *Myoporum*, African daisy (*Osteospermum*), geranium (*Pelargonium*), and islay (*Prunus ilicifolia*). Low-growing, water-retaining succulents have the greatest fire-retarding potential.

Waterwise guidelines in fire-prone regions are the same as in any other mediterranean garden, but a few additional steps are required:

• Remove all dry vegetation, debris, and dead wood (firewood included).

• Replace flammable woody mulches with gravel or pebbles.

• Pave the area around the barbecue and choose adjacent plants with care.

• Eliminate wooden garden features (furniture, deck, fences)

• Install water outlets at each corner of the house with two hoses long enough to reach all round it, including the roof, and keep them ready during the fire season.

• Provide easy access for fire-fighting equipment.

Under normal circumstances, an occasional watering is sufficient to keep most recommended species healthy and to maintain sufficient moisture. But when there is an impending danger of fire, aim for a high water content in plant tissues, especially in areas that are not irrigated. In the areas most threatened, install wide-reaching sprinklers, provided that water is available in fire periods. Remember that untimely watering may finish off drought-tolerant plants, although this is a minor evil compared to the destruction wrought by fire.

Study the topography and wind patterns in your area. Fire moves most quickly upward (the chimney action in cypress trees) and more slowly on level ground, so long as the wind doesn't increase its speed. Therefore, avoid planting larger shrubs or trees below the house. Instead, place them *above* buildings or at the top of the land. To keep ground fires from spreading into tree canopies or onto the roof, remove any branches that touch the ground or hang over a building and take out all dead or inward-growing branches.

Eliminate plants with a high oil content or woody litter (such as *Acacia*). Instead, select those with year-round high moisture levels. In a wildfire, dry brush burns with great intensity. Mow the dry grass and replace it with a ground-covering "green belt," grouping plants by size, color, leaf shape, and texture, just as you would do in any other garden. A maximum height of 10 inches (25cm) is recommended. Planting is vital to keep the grass from growing back.

Cutting back woody plants encourages juicy, green growth. If your garden borders on a native landscape, carry this task beyond its confines, extending fire protection as you achieve a gradual, eye-pleasing transition from the garden to the wild.

Note: The fire tolerance of plants is displayed mainly in their ability to resprout from protected tissues. Examples include the buds on the rootstock of various *Eucalyptus*, *Hakea*, *Leucospermum*, and *Protea* species. Oak, too, often resprouts when burned. Manzanita (*Arctostaphylos*), *Banksia*, *Juniperus*, *Protea*, and the invasive *Hakea* depend on fire to facilitate seed release and dispersal and to enhance germination.

Low-growing succulents are fire-retardant. *Agave attenuata* is in the foreground, *Aeonium* and *Aloe* farther back.

Maintenance in a fire-retardant garden is greater than in other gardens but is helped by good planning and a watchful eye. If maintenance is carried out in winter, you will enjoy a flowering garden once summer arrives.

The latest thinking on fire-retardation in California recommends the establishment of four zones on one's property and the planting of a belt at least 50 yards wide (50m) around the house. However, any of the recommendations given above and below will lead you a long way along the fire-retardant path. Whenever you replace a plant, choose one of the fire-retardant species, gradually replacing high-fuel vegetation while still achieving an aesthetically pleasing landscape.

• **Zone 1.** Close to the house, replace cypress or pine by the lower-growing citrus and guava (*Acca*). Low-growing succulents have the greatest fire-retardant capacity, as their tissues contain maximum water (succulents such as *Aeonium*, *Crassula*, *Drosanthemum floribundum*, *Lampranthus*, and *Sedum*), but consider also sea pink (*Armeria*), pomegranate (*Punica granatum* 'Nana'), and the wide-spreading star jasmine (*Trachelospermum*). The fleshy rosettes of aloe cover expanses of rock that are otherwise difficult to plant, enriching garden color in winter with orange or yellow flower spikes. For cheerful blooms, make ample use of South African bulbous plants, including *Agapanthus* and red-hot poker (*Kniphofia*); tuck in bulbs between a uniform carpet of treasure flower (*Gazania*) or use daylily (*Hemerocallis*) for large expanses. Clumps of tall fortnight lilies (*Dietes bicolor* and *D. iridioides*) add height. Carpets of yarrow (*Achillea*), *Artemisia caucasica*, lavender cotton (*Santolina chamaecyparissus*, *S. virens*), or *Verbena peruviana* may be highlighted by an occasional *Agave*, New Zealand flax (*Phormium tenax*), or the trunkless *Yucca whipplei*. A well-grown prickly pear (*Opuntia*) silhouetted against the sky or the sea is a glorious sight. If you long for a climber on the house, use the quick-growing trumpet creeper (*Campsis radicans*) or

Cape honeysuckle (*Tecomaria capensis*). Let the potato vine (*Solanum jasminoides*) cover a shade wall or a *Wisteria* adorn your balcony (control its size and cut out all dead wood)..

• **Zone 2.** At a distance of about 30 feet (10m) beyond the house, redbud (*Cercis occidentalis*), pepper tree (*Schinus molle*), and the tall and quick-growing palm (*Washingtonia robusta*) are considered safe if well watered. For green masses in restrained quantities, use the evergreen currant (*Ribes viburnifolium*), yellow oleander (*Thevetia peruviana*), or oleander (*Nerium oleander*, low-growing cultivars) as a quiet background for gray *Artemisia*, Australian saltbush (*Atriplex semibaccata*), dusty miller (*Senecio cineraria*), or vibrant California poppy (*Eschscholzia californica*). The bottlebrush (*Callistemon*) is a good choice from Australian gardens.

• **Zone 3.** About 90 feet (30m) farther out and spaced about 20 feet (6–7m) apart, you can use evergreen carob (*Ceratonia siliqua*), buckthorn (*Rhamnus alaternus*), coffeeberry (*R. californica*), African sumac (*Rhus lancea*), or lemonade berry (*R. integrifolia*). Underplant these with the lowest ground covers to avoid the potential for a "fire ladder." Periwinkle (*Vinca*), which should be cut back periodically, would do well in tree shade.

• **Zone 4.** An outer belt can be planted 150 feet (50m) from the house, with the less fire-retardant manzanita (*Arctostaphylos hookeri*) and bearberry (*A. uva-ursi*), Natal plum (*Carissa*), California lilac (*Ceanothus gloriosus*, *C. griseus horizontalis*), rock roses (*Cistus*), California holly (*Heteromeles arbutifolia*), coffeeberry (*Rhamnus californica*) and redberry (*R. crocea*), and rosemary (*Rosmarinus officinalis* 'Prostratus'). Use also matilija poppy (*Romneya coulteri*), the glory of the chaparral.

Fire-Retardant Plants

"All-purpose" indicates both fire retardation
and erosion control
Group 1, best fire retardation
Group 2, medium fire retardation
Group 3, least fire retardation

Paeonia cambessedesii

Acacia redolens, group 3
Acca sellowiana
Achillea tomentosa
Aeonium, group 1
Agapanthus
Agave americana, group 1
Agave attenuata, group 1
Agave victoriae-reginae, group 1
Agonis
Aloe aristata, group 1
Aloe brevifolia, group 1
Arctostaphylos hookeri, group 3
Arctostaphylos uva-ursi, group 3
Arctotheca calendula
Armeria maritima
Artemisia
  (low-growing species)
Atriplex cuneata
Atriplex gardneri
Atriplex semibaccata,
  all-purpose
Baccharis pilularis
  var. prostrata, group 1
Brachychiton

Callistemon citrinus
Callistemon viminalis
Campsis radicans
Carissa grandiflora, group 3
Carpobrotus edulis, group 1
Ceanothus gloriosus
Ceanothus griseus
  var. horizontalis
Ceanothus prostratus, group 3
Cerastium tomentosum
Ceratonia siliqua
Cercis occidentalis
Cistus species, group 3
Citrus species, evergreen,
  leathery-leaved
Convolvulus cneorum
Cotoneaster dammeri, group 3
Crassula, group 1
Delosperma, group 1
Dietes bicolor
Dietes iridioides
Drosanthemum, group 1
Erica arborea
Erigeron karvinskianus
Eschscholzia
Euonymus fortunei
  var. radicans
Galvezia
Gazania
Griselinia

Beschorneria yuccoides
sheds no litter.

Helianthemum
  nummularium, group 3
Hemerocallis
Heteromeles arbutifolia (zone 4)
Hypericum calycinum, group 3
Kniphofia
Lagunaria patersonii
Lampranthus, group 1
Lantana montevidensis
Lippia canescens var. repens
Lonicera japonica 'Halliana'
Myoporum parvifolium
  var. prostrata
Nerium oleander,
  low-growing 'Mrs. Roeding'
Nerium oleander,
  low-growing 'Petite Salmon'
Opuntia, group 1
Osteospermum fruticosum,
  all-purpose
Pelargonium peltatum,
  all-purpose
Phormium tenax
Pittosporum tobira
  'Wheeler's Dwarf'
Pittosporum undulatum
Portulacaria afra
Potentilla verna
Prunus ilicifolia
Prunus lyonii (zone 4)
Punica granatum 'Nana'
Pyracantha 'Santa Cruz',
  knee-high

Quercus spp.
Rhamnus alaternus
Rhamnus californica (zone 4)
Rhus integrifolia
Rhus lancea, evergreen species
Ribes viburnifolium
Romneya coulteri
Rosmarinus officinalis,
  prostratus group
Salvia sonomensis
Santolina chamaecyparissus
Santolina virens
Satureja montana
Schinus molle,
  properly watered
Sedum, group 1
Senecio cineraria
Senecio serpens, group 1
Solanum jasminoides
Succulents, all group 1
Tecoma capensis
Teucrium chamaedrys, group 3
Teucrium fruticans
Thevetia peruviana
Trachelospermum jasminoides
Tristania conferta
Tulbaghia violacea
Verbena peruviana
Vinca difformis
Vinca minor
Washingtonia spp.
Wisteria
Yucca whipplei, trunkless

Gardening among Rocks
A Garden for All Seasons

Many mediterranean gardens are distinctly rocky. This garden project draws attention to the great potential of natural rock, describes how the gardener may make the most of this challenging condition, and explains which tools to use. Not only do rocks provide the excellent drainage that many native Mediterranean plants need, but they also set them off aesthetically. The imaginative use of succulents in rock gardens is suggested, followed by a plant list for rocky ground.

Gardening among rocks makes great gardens that become even better after the plants spread.

For more ideas, see:
- Surviving Summer Drought, page 34
- A Garden Has Its Own Mind, page 40
- A Garden in the Hills, page 138
- A Country Garden, page 168

Selecting the Site. Rocky outcrops, usually a consequence of centuries of erosion, should be considered your raw material in working with your mediterranean garden. If you find these on your site, then many gardeners will envy you for the opportunities you have to indulge in gardening among rocks. Do not fret about the lack of soil, and do not worry about the bare look of the rocks. Instead, make the most of your ready-made rock garden, without having to cart around a single rock or stone. Remember, the best rock gardens are built by nature.

Rocks have a highly sculptural quality, and it is worth all your attention and perseverance to bring this out carefully. Try to adapt the design of the garden to its location and climatic conditions. More often than not, a natural rockscape harmonizes agreeably with the surrounding countryside and bedrock is what anchors the house to its ground. Look for good proportions and for a harmonious relation between space and mass.

Nature will provide the rocks, the trees, and the ground cover. If the land has not yet been interfered with by man, the gardener will have to remove brambles, lift broken tree limbs, and shape the existing trees to their best advantage. In time, the course of a path will suggest itself, as well as the siting of a level area for a bench under trees. While it is sometimes necessary to rearrange a few rocks for purposes of design or for purely practical reasons, such as creating a path, leave them in place wherever possible.

Apart from anything else, the rocks hold back the soil. Not everyone has a cart strong enough to carry heavy stones or rocks, but you can make good use of an aluminum ladder and two to four strong people.

Rocks provide good growing conditions for roots that can find a cool root run and secure anchorage in the soil beneath them. Innumerable plants benefit from the backdrop of sculptural rocks and their contrasting textures, as well as from their reflected warmth. During winter, rocks provide quick-drying beds for trailing plant shoots. Once you have decided on the stones and rocks, you will cover the earth between them with suitable plants. Stone walls, terracing, and stepping stones can also be considered ways of gardening among rocks.

Design Considerations

In a site rich in microclimates, choose the plants in relation and in proportion to the rocks they are intended to accompany. Plants should not blur the attractive outlines of the rocks, nor should they clutter them with litter. Think of clean rock as an easily maintained ground cover. Ideally, colors should be selected to complement the shades of the rocks. Rocks will bring out the natural beauty of plants, in much the same way as a frame does with a painting. One successful way of giving visual priority to the rock is to use large quantities of a limited variety of plants.

Small treasures easily get lost in the garden, yet among rocks they may find a secure site. Scree (fine gravel on well-draining soil) complements natural rock harmoniously and is ideal for rare plants and small bulbs whose progress can be supervised with ease. Fine scree can also be used as a seed bed.

The sculptural quality of these rocks is enhanced by a spare planting of Mediterranean plants clipped into rounded shapes.

Plant Requirements

Besides the normal mediterranean winter rain, plant requirements include excellent drainage, fertile open soil (add compost, sand, vermiculite), and good air circulation. Occasionally an earthy fill is needed. In places where soil could slip through, cracks should be blocked at the bottom. As the years go by, spent flowers and dust will decompose, gradually forming soil.

My tip: There is no tool better than a crowbar to deepen a crack in the rock for planting or to move a whole rock a bit to the side.

It is important to match suitable plants to convenient planting sites. Plants native to the region are usually the best choice, for their roots know well

Large rocks provide a dramatic background to this garden, which was established on underlying bedrock with very little soil.

how to find a way through rock. Varying in size from a tiny sprig to a full-sized tree, native plants grow naturally on rocky outcrops, accompanied by lavender, aromatic rock roses, rosemary, and the smaller herbs—marjoram, savory, and thyme. As a matter of fact, many cushion shapes and most herbs qualify as suitable candidates for the garden among rocks. Other plants for a flowering rockscape include yarrow (*Achillea*), rockcress (*Arabis*), small artemisias, *Alyssum*, *Aubrieta*, basket-of-gold (*Aurinia*), maiden pink (*Dianthus*), Geranium, broom (*Genista*), sun rose (*Helianthemum*), candytuft (*Iberis*), and *Phlox*. Hellebores and peonies suit a northern exposure. Cypress, selected junipers, and thuja, together with sword plants (*Yucca*), add height. Plants from other continents include *Carissas*, *Correas*, *Cotoneasters*, *Grevilleas*, and *Melaleucas*.

Consider habitat-related planting in your rock garden, it is of prime importance. Nowadays, plants are often assembled for their visual effect without any thought given to their often far-away native homes. For instance, Jerusalem sage (*Phlomis*), helichrysums, and lavender cotton (*Santolina*) from the dry *maquis* are used for their muted grays, together with cannas from the humid tropics for their strong colors and summer-dry thistles for their height. All have different growing requirements and health problems will eventually result. Lavender is recommended for a herbaceous border, although it grows best where its leaves rest upon dry rock and where its roots can search out humidity deep between rocks. Many thistles, such as carline thistles (*Carlina*) and true thistles (*Cirsium*), have no place in a mediterranean garden, where most are considered an invasive weed. Some gardeners make an exception for globe thistles (*Echinops*).

One need not rely only on rock-garden vegetation. A range of bulbous plants takes advantage of rock crevices, where they are well protected during their summer dormancy and where their seeds will later germinate. Crocuses, freesias, and montbretias

Even bedrock can be used to create a garden. Drought-tolerant shrubs and a cypress grow in the crevices, and *Coronilla* lends color.

do especially well in cracks. Many irises provide flowers throughout the year. Succulents are a further possibility. They come from faraway places such as Mexico or South Africa, *Aeonium* from the Canary Islands; almost none are native to the Mediterranean Basin.

Yet succulents are invaluable in places where there is little soil. Quite a few demand nothing more than a dry place on which to rest their leaves; sometimes a crack is all they need to let their roots find their way down into cool darkness. In fact, succulents abhor cold, sodden ground and are much better off on a stony bed. Many succulents love a rocky corner into which they can huddle and from which they gradually grow outward into formidable cushions. However, not all succulents qualify, not all are sufficiently hardy, and it may take a bit of experience to know what and how much can be demanded of them. Since little expense is involved, however, and if you are prepared to be patient, you may as well give it a try. Whenever I swap a few succulent bits and pieces with gardening friends, I look forward to returning a few months later to the spot where I planted them, to see how they have arranged their leaf rosettes and what their flowers look like, and, of course, whether life in our garden suits them. Their ingenuous modesty often surprises and delights me.

On many rocky sites, you can garden not only in full sun but also under the shade of trees. The choice of suitable plants varies widely but, in such a location, relies more on leaves than on flowers. For woodlands, avoid tulips and daffodils that are native to the open steppes, but make free use of bulbous arums and friar's cowl (*Arisarum*), *Cyclamen*, snowdrop (*Galanthus*), snowflake (*Leucojum*), or *Ranunculus*, framed by spurge olive (*Cneorum tricoccon*) or box. Bugle (*Ajuga*), strawberry (*Fragaria*), lily turf (*Liriope*), and the similar *Ophiopogon*, together with periwinkle (*Vinca*), reliably cover the ground in shade. Try every peony you can lay your hands on and plant tall foxgloves (*Digitalis*) under pines. All these combine to give delight in spring and early summer. With the autumn rains, fresh-leaved *Acanthus* and *Aquilegia* will come up. Winter pleasures include many hellebores, the colorful seed pods of *Iris foetidissima* and the delicate scent of *Iris unguicularis*. Beware, however, the invasive plants, which are often difficult to dislodge once they have thrust their roots into a rock crevice. This includes *Asphodelus*, *Centranthus*, many *Allium*, and *Oxalis*.

Many gardeners have recently taken to growing their own *Aloe vera*. Known as the first-aid plant, this aloe is said to have antibiotic properties that clean, soothe, and heal. It seems to contain compounds that promote the removal of dead skin and stimulate the normal growth of living cells. Aloe is also believed to be good for healing burns and wounds by stopping pain and reducing the risk of infection and scarring. Most aloes grow well in mediterranean gardens.

Plants for a Rocky Site

Trees, Shrubby Plants
Artemisia
Baeckea ramosissima
Buxus balearica
Buxus sempervirens
Ceratostigma plumbaginoides
Cistus
Cneorum tricoccon
Correa
Cotoneaster
Cupressus
Erica carnea
Erica multiflora
Euphorbia
Genista
Grevillea rosmarinifolia
Halimium ocymoides
Hypericum
Juniperus
Lavandula
Melaleuca thymifolia
Myoporum parvifolium
Origanum majorana
Punica granatum 'Nana'
Rosmarinus
Ruta
Salvia
Satureja
Senecio
Stachys
Tanacetum
Teucrium
Thuja
Thymus

Flowering Plants
Acanthus
Achillea
Ajuga
Aloe
Alyssum
Aquilegia
Aubrieta
Centranthus (invasive)
Dianthus
Digitalis
Fragaria
Geranium
Helianthemum
Helleborus argutifolius
Iberis
Paeonia, in shade
Pelargonium spp.
Phlox
Satureja
Sedum
Thymus
Vinca

Bulbous Plants
Arum
Arisarum, in shade
Crocus
Cyclamen
Freesia
Fritillaria meleagris
Galanthus
Iris foetidissima, in shade
Iris unguicularis
Leucojum
Lilium
Liriope
Montbretia
Ophiopogon
Ranunculus
Scilla peruviana

If you insert a succulent cutting between rocks, it will gradually assume its typical outline.

A Garden in the Hills
The Art of Terracing

As coastlines worldwide become more congested, urban sprawl is now spreading further inland on higher, sloped ground. More people are leaving the busy tourist areas along the coast and going inland in search of the unhurried life they used to lead. Many of these people will find themselves gardening on terraces or on sloped ground for the first time. Terraced hill gardens, inspired by traditional Mediterranean terraces, require careful attention to topography. Soil erosion, exposure, and frost are among the challenges presented by this kind of garden. This section discusses terracing, ground covers, and the role played by pathways in conserving soil and avoiding erosion. Terracing is ideal for native Mediterranean plants, which demand perfect drainage; a list of suitable plants is provided.

A friend who lives in western Crete writes: "No one understands why we did not go for a coastal plot of land. Yet to me our mountain provides an infinitely better view than the sea. Every day it looks different. In summer its appearance changes from light gray to sandy gold; in early winter it has a brooding quality, seeming light purple or dark gray. When we cannot see it at all, then we know that our monsoon-like rain is on its way. Around Christmas rain falls as snow on the heights, and the Omalos plain at 3,000 feet (1000m) may be under 6 feet (2m) of snow. My

For more ideas, see :

favorite view is when we sit in our garden in the sun and see the snow-covered peaks in the distance. On every evening that it is possible, we sit on our roof terrace, watch the sun disappear from the peaks, and never tire of it."

Exposure

Like rock outcrops, hill sites and hillsides require a gardener to pay close attention to the topography. Where such gardens border on surviving *maquis* or woodland, hill gardens are best integrated into the overall landscape. They offer a challenging set of conditions for plant growth and create specific climatic corners for special plants. Exposure and erosion are significant factors in these gardens.

Terraces have been used since Roman times. In fact, often planted with olive or almond trees, they are a prominent feature of the Mediterranean landscape. Their retaining walls hold back the soil, provide natural drainage, and help prevent erosion. Even in areas of low rainfall, terracing is necessary to palliate the effects of sudden, violent downpours. Maintaining and restoring terraces will be one of your chief preoccupations. For minor terracing, you may be able to make do with a level path or a raised bed.

First, consider your exposure. Inland gardens are exposed to continental influences and endure sharper contrasts in daily and seasonal temperature fluctuations than do lowland or coastal regions. Daytime tem-

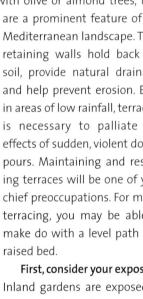

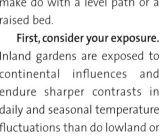

These ancient terraces, after invading pine trees were cleared and grain planted, turn a lovely golden color in summer.

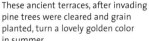
Ancient terracing is seldom restored with such care as in Louisa Jones's and Bernard Dupont's garden. A recent storm opened up the trees at the top.

peratures may soar, and nights are usually colder than in lower regions. Remember to use exposure wisely—just as you would in any other type of garden. Your garden may be exposed to the north or to the full south. When and where does the sun reach it and how about this in winter? With inland gardens, these questions require extra care.

Science reveals that trees exposed to heavy winds have a stronger wood structure, which enables them to endure the weight of occasional snow. A light cover of snow does little harm—indeed, it pulls a protective cover over the plants—but the weight of a heavy snowfall, especially if followed by rain and then freezing temperatures, puts too much strain on most branches, which may crack and break. If you garden in an area where snow occurs, you will want to keep this in mind when it comes to choosing your plants.

Frost is rare in coastal regions where the sea tempers climatic conditions, but it may occur inland in regions that are also often hotter in summer. Cold air is heavier than warm air and, like a fluid, will settle in the lowest-lying areas. Frost does likewise. Winter may also bring "radiation" frost, which occurs when low air humidity, low temperatures, and a lack of wind and cloud cover coincide. During relatively warm days and bright nights, soil and plants radiate their heat into space. A prolonged exposure to these conditions can bring about a fall in temperature to freezing point or below, when ice crystals in the plant tissues will interfere with their ability to function. Plant buds may resume spring growth, but where conductive tissues are impaired, the whole plant will collapse. Remember that mature woody tissues will limit the damage, so in early autumn reduce irrigation to induce dormancy in tender plants and to promote the growth of woody tissues at the onset of the cold season.

Tip: Cuttings taken from parts of the frost-damaged plant that are still green may survive.

Radiation frost, depending on its length, is more dangerous for the garden than periods of low above-freezing temperatures. As a protective measure, drain frosty air to lower land or operate an overhead sprinkler over the frost period, for water will warm the area by a few critical degrees. Also, use overhead screening (horticultural fleece, netting) or tie a few branches over those plants that are at risk. Alternatively, wrap them in thick layers of paper, cardboard, or straw and remove those once the frost is over. A thick layer of mulch is helpful since protected parts of the plant may resprout. And do remember to provide a well-drained soil.

Tip: Plant a tree in areas where frost may occur in your garden, as trees may help protect the tender plants beneath them.

Erosion

Once exposure has been dealt with, you must consider erosion. As a consequence of erosion, hilly sites may consist of wind-swept terrain with poor, shallow, or virtually nonexistent soil over dry rock, which makes the building up of soil another of your aims. It is not too difficult to rebuild soil where ample mulch is used. In order to halt erosion on a gentle slope that runs down to the fields of burned brown earth, make an effort to bring all original terraces back to life.

An important step in combating erosion is to establish vegetation. Plants are attractive soil stabilizers that hold the soil together. Hillside gardens need not be barren land but can be incorporated into a three-dimensional design. There is an ample range of plant material suitable for erosion control that copes efficiently with difficult conditions. However, plants for these sites must be chosen with care. Choose sturdy plants, like the California matilija poppy (*Romneya*), as their well-developed root system will keep the soil in place. Roots—both the shallow ones and the deep-reaching ones—can be fibrous, well-knit, or carrot-like, depending on the species.

Drought-tolerant plants are an excellent choice, since they avoid the need for irrigation on fragile slopes and their root systems are usually sturdy. They are easy to maintain and need no further care once established. Planting them in autumn guarantees that they will become established before the summer heat gets under way. Keep the planting holes horizontal and hold them up with well-placed stones. While the

A high wall holds up the access road to a traditional dwelling, and a large tree balances the different levels

Steps efficiently negotiate changes in level.

Apricot trees (*Prunus armeniaca*) flourish in the protected site of a clearing.

Extensive stonework has prevented erosion on the sloping ground in this Greek garden, justifying the initial expense. Design by Charles Shoup.

plant is in the process of becoming established, dig a depression, or berm, around it to hold water. This will make watering easier and prevents run-off. Later, avoid watering slopes that are planted with drought-tolerant plants—they can do without!

Tip: On steep slopes, use protective jute netting through which plants can grow while becoming established.

Plant deep-rooted trees such as *Acacia longifolia*, carob (*Ceratonia siliqua*), the colorful Judas tree (*Cercis siliquastrum*), and African sumac (*Rhus lancea*). Accompany them with cheerful shrubs, such as California lilac (*Ceanothus*), rock roses (*Cistus*), cotoneaster, buckwheat (*Eriogonum*), with the recommended creeping mahonia (*Mahonia repens*), or with oleander (*Nerium oleander*) and lemonade berry (*Rhus integrifolia*). Pioneer plants will grow quickly (see Plants for Quick Results, page 123).

In inland mediterranean gardens, many deciduous trees and shrubs are at the edge of their southern distribution. Being of northern origin, they prefer the well-drained, north-facing slopes that you find here; they ensure a cool root run, which benefits cherries, for example. On the other hand, in an inland garden many evergreens are at their northernmost limit, which explains their preference for a southern exposure. For a southern terrace, see The Edible Garden (page 146) for the plants that will flourish and bear fruit. Tender plants such as the heat-loving Australian *Acacia*, *Cassia*, and *Melaleuca*, as well as many species of *Euphorbia*, thrive here. In your garden, however, microclimates will affect both groups.

The wide range of deciduous flowering trees and shrubs is encouraged by chilly periods. Being leafless for months, deciduous trees are suitable for places where you want to receive the winter sun. Later they will delight you with their exuberant blossom, while in summer their foliage provides welcome shade. Choose from among Spanish chestnut (*Castanea sativa*), *Catalpa bignonioides*, the empress tree (*Paulownia tomentosa*), many *Prunus* and *Malus*, pink-flowered locust (*Robinia boyntonii*), the Japanese pagoda tree (*Sophora*), mountain ash (*Sorbus*), and snowbell (*Styrax officinale*). Where frost is rare, the coral tree (*Erythrina crista-galli*) and *Jacaranda mimosifolia* thrive. Flowering shrubs such as *Deutzia*, mock orange (*Philadelphus*), *Spiraea*, lilac (*Syringa*), and *Viburnum* will bloom in succession for weeks. The smoke tree (*Cotinus coggygria*) makes a great background for golden forsythia or laburnum.

In summer, confederate rose (*Hibiscus mutabilis*) and rose of Sharon (*H. syriacus*) carry on the show, together with false spiraea (*Sorbaria*) and the chaste tree (*Vitex agnus-castus*). Colorful fruiting shrubs, such as cotoneaster, hawthorn (*Crataegus*), evergreen California holly (*Heteromeles*), and firethorn (*Pyracantha*), attract birds in autumn and early

Terracing has here been carried out on a grand scale. Design by Charles Shoup.

winter. For still more flowers, you can underplant with colorful bulbs.

Note: In a hill garden, one either looks down upon a flowering crown of California buckeye (*Aesculus californica*) and golden rain tree (*Koelreuteria paniculata*), or up into the colorful canopy of a Judas tree (*Cercis siliquastrum*).

In hill gardens, **evergreen trees and shrubs enhance conifers**, such as arborvitae, cedars, cypress, juniper, and pine. Loquat (*Eriobotrya*) and *Magnolia grandiflora* are good choices. Countless evergreen shrubs delight you with a long flowering period or sweet scent (*Arbutus andrachne, A. menziesii, A. unedo, Arctostaphylos, Ceanothus, Cistus, Cytisus, Daphne, Escallonia, Euonymus, Ligustrum, Mahonia repens, Photinia*).

Many perennials are common to both inland and coastal areas and, together with ground covers and an extensive use of native plants, will fit well into the surrounding indigenous plant communities. These may consist of mediterranean broom (*Genista*), carob (*Ceratonia siliqua*), rock rose (*Cistus*), clematis, everlasting flower (*Helichrysum*), Jerusalem sage (*Phlomis*), a Judas tree (*Cercis siliquastrum*), and juniper, oak, olive, pine, pomegranate (*Punica granatum*), and tree heath (*Erica arborea*). Large patches of multi-colored African daisies (*Osteospermum fruticosum*) and of *Pelargonium peltatum*, are efficient ground covers, beautifully set off by the light gray foliage of a deep-rooted saltbush (*Atriplex semibaccata*). Quickly expanding, the starry-eyed Australian *Myoporum parvifolium* var. *prostrate* and the slower Californian coyote bush (*Baccharis pilularis*) cover bare soil while their inquisitive roots anchor them in the ground. Accompany them with the undemanding succulents; but it is best to avoid Hottentot fig (*Carpobrotus*), whose heavy mass may make it slip and, in the process, pull down the soil. For smaller plants, try foxglove (*Digitalis*) and mullein (*Verbascum*).

Bulbous plants add color throughout the year. Hellebores (*Helleborus argutifolius*) and peonies (*Paeonia broteroi* and *P. cambessedesii*) delight in humus-enriched, well-mulched soil in cool shade at the foot of a rock. Among these are some of my favorite plants for their easy, year-round presence.

Spring-blooming anemones, crocuses, daffodils, hyacinths, narcissi, ranunculi, and tulips respond to winter chilling and retreat underground during the summer drought. *Agapanthus*, *Amaryllis belladonna*, daylily (*Hemerocallis*), red-hot poker (*Kniphofia*) and sea squill (*Urginea*) provide a summer display (tall lilies require weekly water). Autumn-flowering *Colchicum*, *Crocus*, *Cyclamen*, *Merendera*, and the golden autumn crocus (*Sternbergia lutea*) add colorful splashes.

Plants for Terraced Land and Erosion Control

Most plants have been mentioned in the text. They are drought-tolerant unless otherwise noted. However, their water requirements depend largely on soil and on position.

Helleborus lividus, seen in the wild

Trees

Acacia longifolia, deep-rooted
Acacia melanoxylon
Aesculus californica
Arbutus andrachne
Arbutus menziesii
Arbutus unedo
Cassia
Castanea sativa, deep-rooted
Catalpa bignonioides,
    deep-rooted
Catalpa speciosa, weekly water
Cedrus
Celtis species
Ceratonia siliqua, deep-rooted
Cercis siliquastrum, deep-rooted
Cupressus
Eriobotrya, water for
    better fruits
Erythrina crista-galli,
    short-lived frost
Fraxinus dipetala
Fraxinus velutina
Ginkgo biloba
Jacaranda mimosifolia,
    short-lived frost
Juglans californica
Juglans hindsii
Juniperus, deep-rooted
Koelreuteria paniculata
Magnolia grandiflora
Melaleuca
Morus nigra
Olea europaea
Paulownia tomentosa
Pinus monophylla, deep-rooted
Pistacia chinensis
Platycladus orientalis
Populus fremontii
Prunus dulcis
Quercus, deep-rooted
Rhus lancea, deep-rooted
Robinia hispida 'Rosea'
Salix lasiolepis
Sophora
Sorbus
Styrax officinale

Shrubs

Arctostaphylos
Ceanothus spp., deep-rooted
Cistus spp., deep-rooted
Coronilla glauca
Cotinus coggygria
Cotoneaster, deep-rooted
Crataegus, deep-rooted
Cytisus
Deutzia
Echium fastuosum
Erica arborea
Erica multiflora
Eriocephalus africanus
Eriogonum fasciculatum,
    deep-rooted
Escallonia
Euonymus, deep-rooted
Euphorbia, many
Forsythia
Genista
Heteromeles
Hibiscus mutabilis,
    occasional summer water
Hibiscus syriacus,
    occasional summer water
Jasminum mesnyi
Jasminum nudiflorum
Laburnum
Lantana
Lavandula spp.
Leonotus leonuris
Ligustrum
Mahonia repens, deep-rooted
Myrsine africana
Nerium oleander, deep-rooted
Philadelphus
Photinia
Punica granatum
Pyracantha, deep-rooted
Rhamnus crocea
Rhamnus ilicifolia

Rhus aromatica
Rhus integrifolia, deep-rooted
Rhus laurina
Rhus trilobata
Ribes viburnifolium
Rosa multiflora
Rosa rugosa
Sambucus caerulea
Sorbaria
Spiraea douglasii
Symphoricarpos
Syringa, occasional
    summer water
Viburnum
Vitex agnus-castus

Ground Covers, Perennials, Succulents

Acacia redolens
Achillea tomentosa
Arctotis grandis
Ajuga reptans
Aptenia cordifolia
Arctostaphylos uva-ursi
Arctotheca calendula
Atriplex semibaccata
Baccharis pilularis
Carpobrotus
Coprosma x kirkii
Delosperma spp.
Digitalis
Drosanthemum spp.
Gazania spp.
Halimium
Hedera
Helianthemum nummularium
Helichrysum
Hypericum calycinum
Lampranthus spp.
Mesembryanthemum
Myoporum parvifolium
Osteospermum fruticosum
Pelargonium peltatum,
    weekly summer water
Phlomis fruticosa
Romneya coulteri, deep-rooted
Rosmarinus officinalis
Santolina chamaecyparissus
Verbascum
Vinca

Vines

Bougainvillea
Cissus antartica
Cissus glauca
Clematis lasiantha and others
Euonymus fortunei,
    prostrate form
Lonicera hispidula
Lonicera japonica
Parthenocissus quinquefolia
Rhoicissus capensis
Rosa banksiae
Tetrastigma voinierlanum
Trachelospermum jasminoides
Vitis vinifera
Wisteria

Bulbous Plants

Agapanthus,
    monthly summer water
Amaryllis belladonna
Anemone
Colchicum
Crocus
Cyclamen
Helleborus argutifolius
Hemerocallis
Hyacinthus
Iris douglasiana
Kniphofia
Lilium, weekly summer water
Merendera
Narcissus
Paeonia broteroi
Paeonia cambessedesii
Ranunculus
Sternbergia
Tulipa
Urginea maritima

The Edible Garden
Fruits and Vegetables for Your Table

This enthusiastically researched section on the edible plants that can be grown in a mediterranean garden starts with a look at those known to have been cultivated in antiquity. Lemon trees, either planted out or in containers, adorn the courtyard. Trees with tasty fruits and nuts, suitable for a modern waterwise orchard, are described, as well as appetizing vegetables and herbs, spices, and seeds for a waterwise *potager*. An inspirational plant list follows, including also exotic choices. The section ends with a timely word of warning about potentially harmful plants.

Storing the rich harvest, Mediterranean style

For more ideas, see :

Before the Mediterranean peoples cultivated grain or planted fruit trees from Asia, they lived on the seeds, bulbs, leaves, and fruit of the plants they found growing wild. Sloe (*Prunus spinosa*), for instance, has been found in Neolithic settlements in Italy. We learn that Theophrastus, who lived as early as 372–287 B.C., gives precise information on the cultivation of almond, fig, grape, olive, pear, and pomegranate. The small nuts of the wild almond (*Prunus webbii*) were considered a delicacy when mixed with honey. The preferred vegetables were those that tolerated dry summers, such as purslane (*Portulaca oleracea*). The wild carrot (*Daucus carota*) provided a tasty vegetable when cooked. The tender young leaves of chicory (*Cichorium intibus*), also cooked, were eaten with oil and vinegar as a salad, and their value as a diuretic was appreciated. The bulbs of the grape hyacinth (*Muscari comosum*) were well liked when cooked or pickled and are still eaten by the Greeks to mark the beginning of Lent. A paste made of quince (*Cydonia oblonga*) is prepared these days in Greece as *melomeli*. Today's owners of beach gardens may plant samphire (*Crithmum maritimum*) and eat the juicy leaves, cooked in wine or as a salad, if they do not choose to preserve them like capers.

Most of these plants were appreciated not only

In this young garden grow vegetables, flowers, and fruit trees. Several paths make access easy.

for their culinary but also for their medicinal properties. Valerian (*Valeriana dioscoridis*) was used by the ancient Greeks as a tranquilizer and today still figures as such. Mastic (*Pistacia lentiscus*) yields a white resin that freshens the breath and is today used as an ingredient in chewing gum. An eighteenth-century sultan is said to have requisitioned half of the harvest for his harem. I doubt, however, that lavender is still used as an antidote to poisoning. Many wild-growing plants have powerful dyeing characteristics: for example, the roots of alkanet (*Alkanna tinctoria*) produce a strong red dye for wool, and saffron (*Crocus sativus*) is used to flavor and color food.

The plants that fed mankind in earlier times, such as the olive, the fig, and the grapevine (and carob for animals), are also the plants that will provide a solid, undemanding framework for your Edible Garden. In order to survive the many vagaries of the climate, these plants had to be dependable. Readers seeking further inspiration will enjoy *Greek Wild Flowers and Plant Lore in Ancient Greece* by Hellmut Baumann (see Bibliography); the outstanding photographs provide a vivid picture of the rich Greek flora and striking countryside.

It is fashionable to grow food in home gardens today, and mediterranean climate conditions allow the sun to let fruits ripen to a delicious sweetness. The Edible Garden appeals to all age groups, and it won't be long before the search for new edible varieties turns into a family game. It may well be that in the more distant future (or even in the near

Louisa Jones's *potager* in Southern France is a delightful combination of all kinds of vegetables and flowers.

future), there will no longer be sufficient water available for flower gardens, so that we shall bless the day we turned to the water-conserving Edible Garden.

This garden of edible plants is dear to my heart; indeed, I am so enthusiastic that new possibilities constantly occur to me. I find it hard to restrain myself from rushing out and starting to plant them then and there, or mentally harvesting the fruit I recommend. Besides its utility, the Edible Garden can be of great beauty. Plants such as the architectural artichoke (*Cynara scolymus*) have attractive foliage and an interesting texture. Almond trees blossoming

in winter are an unforgettable sight.

Evergreen shrubs and trees grow in the Edible Garden, as do ground covers and climbers. They bear juicy fruit and vitamin-laden nuts, or they add tasty vegetables and new spices to your dishes. Choose from a wide array; there is ample material for a good-sized garden. Even if your garden is no larger than a reasonable-sized balcony or a small courtyard, you can still grow edible plants. For example, pineapple guava (*Acca sellowiana*) and the yellow guava (*Psidium guajava*) are both excellent container plants. And even a narrow windowsill can accommodate herbs.

Fruit trees can be grown by themselves in an **orchard**, bordering a path, or incorporated into other plantings. They do not need more care than other plants in your garden, although most will do well in a sunny site protected from the wind, such as near a wall of your house or on a southern terrace. A cypress hedge acts as a windbreak (but beware its foraging roots). Cherry and apple, pear and quince thrive in the sunnier spots of a north-exposed garden. Other requirements include good soil quality (incorporate compost), free drainage, generous mulching, and reasonable air circulation, achieved by a setting away from a wall and judicious pruning. You should attend to these factors, because strong, healthy plants produce better fruit.

Many plants mentioned here, indeed, more than half, have been chosen for their drought tolerance. Those that need an occasional watering are indicated. Fig trees, for instance, need a hot, dry summer and autumn to bear juicy, sweet fruit; asparagus grows wild and thrives on natural winter rain, while kumquat (*Fortunella japonica*) will require weekly summer water. The raspberry (*Rubus idaeus*), which demands water twice weekly in summer to produce the best berries, has been included as an isolated luxury. Drought tolerance depends on many factors, such as the depth of the soil, the position, and also the degree of establishment of the plants. Older trees will do with less water than those recently planted. The Edible Garden can therefore manage with little water, which means that it is also labor-saving and thus economical—if the plants have been chosen judiciously. The extensive and detailed list of edible plants may provide many design ideas. It goes without saying that native edible plants, although they have been transplanted from their natural site into the garden, still remain drought-tolerant.

Trees

If you are lucky, an evergreen tree such as a carob (*Ceratonia siliqua*) with shiny foliage already grows on your land. It prefers a sheltered location. Relished by children as an alternative to chocolate, its pods contain a sweet pulp (50 percent sugar) and are eaten either green or dry (as an anti-diarrheal remedy). Today they fetch good prices on the market. Carob beans contain large, hard seeds (carats), which in ancient times were used by jewelers and goldsmiths. Carat (35 grains) is still the unit of weight for diamonds and the measure for purity of gold in alloys, pure gold being 24 carat.

Grow loquat (*Eriobotrya japonica*), introduced in 1787 from Eastern Asia, for its evergreen, large, shiny

Olive and lemon trees make an attractive combination.

Persimmon foliage and fruits (*Diospyros kaki*) are an asset to every garden and easy to grow.

The evergreen oak (*Quercus ilex* var. *ballota*), grafted onto *Q. ilex*, bears sweet acorns that can be eaten raw or cooked in the same way as chestnuts. In cooler mountainous regions, try the deciduous Spanish or sweet chestnut (*Castanea sativa*).

If you can water weekly in summer, consider planting such attractive small trees as the pineapple guava (*Acca sellowiana*). Not only its fruits but also its flowers are edible, yet who would eat such pretty things? If available, plant strawberry guava (*Psidium littorale*), the taller *P. guajava*, or the Chilean guava (*Ugni molinae*), all belonging to the myrtle family.

The spectacular flowering of deciduous fruiting trees contrasts beautifully with the dark evergreen foliage of avocado, carob, or oak. Almond trees (*Prunus dulcis*) and apricot trees (*P. armeniaca*) light up a garden scene in late winter with their early bloom. But plant apricot only in those places where drainage is excellent. The easily grown plum or prune (*Prunus* x *domestica*) will give you long-lasting harvests if you select wisely from among the many varieties. Sloe (*Prunus spinosa*) grows wild and flowers exuberantly in spring. Once its pealike fruits have ripened well into winter and colder temperatures have turned them sweet, you can pick them, a few at a time, for their vitamin content whenever you pass by.

foliage, its sweetly scented flowers in mid-winter and its early, tasty fruit. Thin for larger fruit and mulch heavily or give it occasional, say bi-monthly, water in summer.

Note: Birds and bees also enjoy the fruit, so protect with netting or expect the birds and insects to have their share.

Evergreen olive trees (*Olea europaea*) may already grow on your land, and even quite old trees can be transplanted. In autumn, preserve the olives or press your own oil. Equipment for home use is on the market today and conveniently replaces the labor-intensive olive press. See also The Olive Grove (page 78).

The evergreen rounded avocado tree (*Persea americana*) has attractive, large, leathery leaves. It requires weekly summer water and heavy mulching. Old varieties grew to considerable heights, but modern early-fruiting varieties are offered in manageable sizes. If you have enough space, grow three for the best fruit bearing. Branching to the ground

The juicy persimmon is harvested before it falls to the ground.

protects the young, tender stems. Dead branches in older trees are later removed, and the inside of the tree turns hollow (for children to hide in).

Remember to plant a deciduous persimmon tree (*Diospyros kaki*), which does not demand water. Smallish cream-color flowers are followed by tomato-like sweet fruits, also called *kaki*. Autumn foliage turns the tree to flame.

Tip: Harvest the fruit before it is ripe and leave it to over-ripen in the kitchen or cellar where persimmons can be stored for a long time.

The deciduous fig tree (*Ficus carica*) is easy to grow, but remember that its roots are invasive. For the sweetest fruit, plant in full sun and withhold water after the plant is established. Choose a variety that bears early or late fruit—or have both.

Although the silkworm feeds on the leaves of the deciduous black mulberry (*Morus nigra*), and the gardener eats its blackberry-like fruits, best relegate the tree to a distant corner, because the juice of the berries stains.

The deciduous Chinese jujube (*Ziziphus jujuba*) bears sweet, datelike fruit that can be candied. Its deep roots and wide tolerances make it a desirable tree for gardens where growing conditions are difficult.

Oranges grow in the same location.

You can graft the deciduous medlar (*Mespilus germanica*) onto the wild hawthorn (*Crataegus monogyna*) wherever the latter comes up on its own. Or do likewise with the azarole (*Crataegus azarolus*). The small, undemanding, and drought-tolerant medlar is appreciated for its appealing rosettes of light green leaves, which surround a creamy-white flower that resembles a single, small camellia. The fruit is eaten over-ripe in late autumn. Its mushy taste is not to everyone's liking, but you will either acquire a taste for it or you can mellow its tartness by cooking.

Tip: If you live near a village, you may find a qualified person who will bring the grafting material from his orchard to do the grafting. When the work is over, have a glass of wine together. Later, give him a basket of fruit for his wife and slip a small banknote into his hand, which he refuses to accept—and yet keeps. What better way to spend a sunny winter afternoon!

In mountainous regions, deciduous cherries (*Prunus avium*) thrive on northern slopes in deep soil and on terraced land. They like underground water or weekly summer irrigation. The same conditions suit deciduous pear (*Pyrus communis*) and quince (*Cydonia oblonga*), which is outstanding for its flowers and is fairly resistant to disease. The Kaffir plum (*Harpephyllum caffrum*) suits frost-free regions. Its dark red fruits resemble olives.

Note: Peaches (*Prunus persica*) are prone to disease, so I prefer not to grow them.

If my garden were just a bit warmer and if I had the time to find a supplier, I would plant the wind-resistant and drought-tolerant star apple (*Chrysophyllum cainito*) from the West Indies. I remember a giant evergreen mango tree (*Mangifera indica*), casting dark shade over the tepid waters of a swimming pool on which floated exquisite orange-color fruits. Juicy mangos are best eaten in the bathtub, so the swimming pool seemed like the right location. The mango tree requires heat and some water.

In a protected spot, enjoy the confusingly wide range of citrus fruit such as clementines (the earliest to bear), grapefruit, lemons, or mandarins. Oranges are the tenderest of the lot, often a prey to pests. So,

A cherry tree (*Prunus avium*) grows well in colder regions. On a sunny day, have lunch under its flowering canopy and in autumn invite everybody for the harvest.

The barbary fig (*Opuntia ficus-indica*) is not only a formidable barrier but also produces delicious, colourful fruits.

Shrubs and Perennials

Now that we have covered the trees, let's think about the shrubs. The decorative fruits of the evergreen strawberry tree (*Arbutus unedo*) are at first yellow and insipid, but when fully ripe, after a long hot summer, they turn from burnt orange to dark red and become sweet. Use them to adorn salads.

In its native South Africa, the fruits of the drought-tolerant Natal plum (*Carissa macrocarpa*) are said to be used for a sauce. I always ask my South African visitors whether the bright red fruits of the carissas in our garden are edible, and most of these gardeners wax lyrical about their culinary qualities. Yet the white sap of the branches looks so poisonous to me that I have never dared try the fruit. However, the shiny evergreen foliage and the white starlike flowers are exquisite.

The evergreen, large-leaved tree tomato (*Cyphomandra betacea*), deciduous in cooler regions and not really a tree, grows fast but can fall prey to sucking insects. The fruit is slightly acid. Give it weekly water.

Evergreen and spiny, the Kei apple (*Dovyalis caffra*) grows to nearly 9 feet (3m) and, if frequently sheared, forms an impenetrable thicket, which I refer to as the Edible Garden's hedge. Yellow acid fruits (which are few if the hedge is sheared) are used to make preserves. For more spines, consider sea buckthorn (*Hippophaë*), whose vitamin-rich berries are used for preserves, and also see *Opuntia* (below).

The creamy flowers of the drought-tolerant *Elaeagnus* x *ebbingei* are followed by small, vitamin-rich fruits. They make up in taste what they lack in size and are excellent for jellies. You can also eat them raw.

The Oregon grape (*Mahonia aquifolium*) and the California holly grape (*M. pinnata*) are evergreen. Their edible blue-black berries become very juicy if they are given an occasional watering during the driest months.

if you intend to grow them, be prepared to water and to attend to health problems. Inquire locally for the best varieties. All citrus trees grow well in containers, and their flowers scent the air for weeks. Their leaves make an agreeable infusion. See The Andalusian Courtyard (page 176). The rose apple (*Syzygium jambos*) and the taller Australian brush cherry (*S. panicultum*) prefer a protected site with weekly water.

Many nuts grow well in mediterranean gardens. Pecan (*Carya illinoinensis*), Southern California black walnut (*Juglans californica*), and English walnut (*J. regia*) like a cool, deep root run, while the pinyon pine (*Pinus pinea*) and pistachio (*Pistacia vera*), a relative of *P. lentiscus*, enjoy open, dry locations. Almonds have already been pointed out, but did I mention the hazelnut?

The fruit of the statuesque fig cactus or prickly pear (*Opuntia ficus-indica*), once it has been peeled, is refreshing. Handle the fruit carefully to avoid touching its bristles (use thick rubber gloves). A sculptural addition to the garden, spiny opuntias also serve as a fence. Additionally, they have been used to great effect as a succulent fire-wall around houses where forest fires regularly occur. (See also A Country Garden, page 168.)

The perennial strawberry tomato (*Physalis pruinosa*) and the Cape gooseberry (*P. peruviana*) bear small yellow fruits. Give them weekly water. It appears that the Mexican husk tomato or tomatillo (*P. ixocarpa*) is completely drought-tolerant and if not staked will happily trail along the ground. All are easy to grow from seed.

The deciduous, drought-tolerant pomegranate (*Punica granatum*) was already used in the very earliest Mediterranean times. Its bronzy leaves are a lovely sight in spring, and its orange flowers are followed by exquisite juicy fruits. Use the fruit to prepare refreshing drinks or make a tart jelly to accompany turkey. This excellent container plant is best with occasional summer water.

Raspberries (*Rubus idaeus*) do well in our garden, although canes given to friends have a varying success rate. They do best with full sun and twice-weekly watering.

This old vine (*Vitis vinifera*) will soon cover itself with spring foliage.

Climbers

The kiwi fruit (*Actinidia deliciosa*) is easy, decorative, and well worth the weekly summer water it needs. It likes a fertile soil in sun, generous mulching, and a support on which to climb. Single, creamy, spring flowers are pretty. To obtain fruit, plant both male and female plants, or for a smaller garden choose a self-fertile variety such as 'Blake.'

The lovely Chilean bell-flower (*Lapageria*) is difficult to obtain and a challenge to grow, for the seed loses its viability after a very short time. The exquisite waxy white or pink flower is edible, but it's almost too beautiful to eat.

The ceriman, or Swiss-cheese plant (*Monstera deliciosa*), thrives on a hot, covered terrace and is suitable for cultivation in containers with occasional water. The fruit is edible, I am told (for tropical fruit salads?), and I regret not having tasted it when I lived in South America.

Most passionflowers like a cool root run and a nearby shrub or tree to climb into or ramble over, which makes an ideal choice if you are looking for an edible climber to cover an unsightly shed. They make do with weekly summer water, but they dislike wind and object to being trained. The fruits of *Passiflora edulis* fall to the ground when ripe and can be used to make refreshing drinks. *P. ligularis*, another edible passiflora, grows in the Andes at freezing temperatures. The fruit keeps for a long time and can be eaten with a spoon or used for juices. The exotic flowers of *P. mollissima*, surrounded by large leaves, are followed by banana-shape small fruits. The melon-size fruits of the heat-loving *P. quadrangularis*, however, taste insipid.

Passionflowers, such as *Passiflora manicata* x *antioquiensis*, grow in Mediterranean gardens, and most produce fruits.

We found this grape of uncertain origin in our old orchard, where it produces small grapes that are good for wine making.

Stauntonia hexaphylla races up into a tree in no time and its shiny red fruits make up for the small, unexciting flowers. I almost forgot to mention the traditional Mediterranean grapevine (*Vitis vinifera*), which covers many a pergola. But you probably grow it already, and not only for its drought-tolerant qualities.

Ground Covers

Once trees, shrubs, and climbers have been planted, you will be looking for ground covers. The peanut (*Arachis hypogaea*), a summer annual with pretty flowers and underground fruits, prefers an open, sunny patch. The undemanding succulent Hottentot fig (*Carpobrotus edulis*) rapidly covers large expanses in hot sun and bears edible fruit. The wild strawberry (*Fragaria vesca*) covers the ground willingly, even more so with occasional water. It also favors rock crevices.

The wide choice of scented-leaved pelargoniums is a gift from South Africa to your edible garden. Undemanding and drought-tolerant, these reliable ground covers vary in height from, say, 8 to 32 inches (20–80cm) and are easy to grow from cuttings. A friend uses *P. crispum* to impart a lemon flavor to rice, much as lemon grass (*Cymbopogon citrates*) does. The leaves of the following can be used to impart many flavors to your cooking: Apple—*Pelargonium odoratissimum*; peppermint—*Pelargonium tomen-*

Fragaria vesca, the well-known wild strawberry, grows into a carpet.

tosum; nutmeg—*Pelargonium fragrans*; rose—*Pelargonium capitatum* and *P. graveolens*.

New Zealand spinach (*Tetragonia expansa*), not a spinach but a succulent in the Aizoaceae family, is a reliable ground cover in sunny sites. It is tastiest in spring, when the leaves are tender, and it goes dormant in summer. For tender growth, cut back in winter. It is easy to grow from seed and likes an occasional watering.

Not everyone realizes that all parts of the nasturtium (*Tropaeolum majus*) are edible. An excellent ground cover in sun, the nasturtium produces colorful flowers to adorn a salad, while its peppery leaves will enrich a herb mixture and its buds (and seeds) can be pickled.

All parts of *Tropaeolum majus*, a quick-growing ground cover, are edible.

Vegetables

You probably already grow tomatoes, runner beans, cucumbers, and melons. How about a few more interesting plants? Green asparagus (*Asparagus stipularis*) with its feathery foliage occurs wild in woods and in the *maquis*, where it can climb into shrubs by means of small hooks or spill over a wall. Asparagus can also be grown in the garden. The tender shoots are collected as they emerge from the ground and, once cooked, are eaten as a vegetable or in a salad. The same goes for butcher's broom or box holly (*Ruscus aculeatus*).

In times of famine, people have eaten the heart of the Mediterranean palmito (*Chamaerops humilis*). Palms only grow from the central point; once that is removed, the plant dies. Who, today, would dream of sacrificing a palm for culinary purposes?

The often spectacular leaves of vegetables are star performers in a flower garden. The architectural leaves of the common globe artichoke (*Cynara scolymus*), planted individually or in groups, are an asset to any garden. Its flower buds are eaten. Cardoon (*Cynara cardunculus*) is grown for its edible leafstalks rather than for flower buds. Full sun and weekly watering suit both.

Many roots, bulbs, and tubers are used for cooking. The drought-tolerant sweet potato (*Ipomoea batatas*), for instance, has swollen, edible tubers that have to be dug up. The bulbous roots of *Moraea fugax* can be eaten as a vegetable, yet again I can't help thinking that the flowers are too lovely to sacrifice such a plant. I feel the same way about the grape hyacinth (*Muscari*).

The tender shoots of the nasty *Smilax aspera* can be cooked like asparagus, thus gradually putting an end to its vigorous growth and helping to clear it off

Artichokes (the buds) and daylilies (the flowers) are both edible.

the land—a satisfying prospect to anyone whose hands have been badly scratched by this plant.

Do you grow sweet corn (*Zea mays*) to give height to your plantings? With salt or sugar, toasted or roasted, corn makes a wealth of great dishes.

Herbs, Spices, and Seeds

Oregano, rosemary, sage, thyme, coriander (*Coriandrum sativum*), cumin (*Cuminum cyminum*), and caraway (*Carum carvi*) are native Mediterranean herbs and spices. Grow all of them! They can find a place in even the smallest garden—provided only that there is sun. The best locations are near the kitchen door or the barbecue. Many herbs, not only chamomile and mint, can be dried for infusions and will make up your own pharmacy.

Onions, leeks, garlic, and chives complete your kitchen garden (*Allium cepa, A. porrum, A. sativum,* and *A. schoenoprasum*). Lorenzo, a stonemason, tells me to discard the onions that flower (they are no good for the kitchen, he says) and to harvest the remainder. These are also the ones to be planted for next year's crop. Following his advice, we harvest two weeks after the flowers have come up and plant garlic cloves around Christmas. Once the first leaves appear, fertilize lightly with charcoal ashes.

Canna edulis, grown from seed, is flowering in my garden this year for the first time. Called *achira* in Peru, it needs weekly water. The large tubers, when mashed into a pulp, washed, and strained, provide a kind of arrowroot substitute.

Plant a caper bush (*Capparis spinosa*) into a hot, south-facing wall. You pickle the flower buds (not the fruit) in vinegar, but leave some for their lovely white powder-puff blooms. The small, hot pepper (*Capsicum frutescens*) is a pretty miniature bush. Place a potted

Small peppers (*Capsicum frutescens*) add zip to dishes.

one on your outdoor dining table for guests to help themselves. Be warned, though: you may find the peppers too hot.

Try *Catha edulis* tea sweetened with honey (Arab style), or follow Captain Cook's example by brewing your tea from the leaves of the tea tree (*Leptospermum scoparium*).

The stigmas of *Crocus sativus* yield saffron, but you will need at least a basketful of flowers to harvest even a small quantity. Lemon grass (*Cymbopogon citratus*) is strongly lemon scented and is widely used as an infusion and in Asian cooking. Use the seeds of juniper (*Juniperus communis*) for their strong aroma.

Remember the indigenous laurel or bay tree (*Laurus nobilis*)? It is slow to start but grows into a large evergreen mass and does well in containers. Myrtle (*Myrtus communis*) was in ancient Greece sacred to Aphrodite. Its dark-blue berries, cooked and concentrated, yielded a popular hair dye and also a remedy against intestinal ailments. It is still eaten

Cherry trees (*Prunus avium*) flower early in the year.

today; this morning I tried the small fruits and found them agreeably spicy.

Many buckthorn species are edible. *Rhamnus crocea* from western North America was eaten by the Apache Indians. It is said that the berries' red color was absorbed into their bloodstream and tinged their skin.

Vitex agnus-castus seed is often used as a replacement for pepper. It is supposed to encourage chastity, hence the name "monks' pepper."

Ginger (*Zingiber officinale*) has edible spicy roots, and its large leaves are a valuable asset. Choose a hot location in half shade, protected from the midday sun. In cooler regions and where drainage is poor, lift winter-dormant roots and replant in spring. Its water demands are moderate.

As the garden leaves me little time for the kitchen, I find that spicy sauces give instant taste to insipid dishes. I put herbs, onion, garlic, and a few pepper seeds into the blender, add a carrot, pepper or tomato to give body, and let the blender run, adding oil as for a mayonnaise. The same thing can be done with olives. This sauce keeps well in the refrigerator.

Edible Plants

I have given the common names here, as the botanical names may not be immediately recognizable to the hungry gardener.

Acca sellowiana, pineapple guava
Actinidia deliciosa, Chinese gooseberry
Alkanna tinctoria
Allium cepa, onion
Allium porrum, leek
Allium sativum, garlic
Allium schoenoprasum, chives
Anacardium occidentale, cashew
Annona cherimola, cherimoya
Arachis hypogaea, peanut
Arbutus unedo, strawberry tree
Arctostaphylos, bearberry, manzanita
Asparagus stipularis
Canna edulis, achira
Capparis spinosa, caper
Capsicum, miniature peppers, spicy
Carissa macrocarpa, Natal plum
Carpobrotus edulis, Hottentot fig
Carum carvi, caraway
Carya illinoinensis, pecan
Castanea sativa, Spanish chestnut
Catha edulis, khat, Arabian tea
Ceratonia siliqua, carob
Chamaemelum nobile, chamomile
Chrysophyllum cainito, star apple
Cichorium intibus, chicory
Citrus aurantium, bitter orange
Citrus limon, lemon
Citrus x paradisi, grapefruit
Citrus reticulata, clementine, mandarin
Citrus sinensis, sweet orange
Coriandrum sativum, coriander
Crataegus azarolus, azarole
Crataegus monogyna, hawthorn
Crithmum maritimum, samphire
Crocus sativus, saffron
Cydonia oblonga, quince
Cymbopogon citratus, lemon grass
Cynara scolymus, artichoke
Cyphomandra betacea, tree tomato
Daucus carota, wild carrot

Diospyros kaki, persimmon, kaki
Dovyalis caffra, Kei apple
Elaeagnus x ebbingei, oleaster
Eriobotrya japonica, loquat
Ficus carica, fig
Fragaria vesca, wild strawberry
Fortunella japonica, kumquat
Harpephyllum caffrum, Kaffir plum
Hippophaë rhamnoides, buckthorn
Ipomoea batatas, sweet potato
Juglans californica, walnut
Juniperus communis, juniper
Lapageria, Chilean bellflower
Laurus nobilis, bay laurel
Lavandula, lavender
Leptospermum scoparium, tea tree
Mahonia aquifolium, Oregon grape
Mahonia pinnata, California grape holly
Mangifera indica, mango
Mentha, mint
Mespilus germanica, medlar
Monstera deliciosa, ceriman
Moraea fugax (M. edulis)
Morus nigra, black mulberry
Muscari comosum, tassel hyacinth
Myrtus communis, myrtle
Olea europaea, olive
Opuntia ficus-indica, prickly pear
Origanum majorana, marjoram
Passiflora edulis, granadilla
Passiflora ligularis, sweet granadilla
Passiflora mollissima, banana
    passionfruit
Passiflora quadrangularis, giant granadilla
Pelargonium, scented-leaved ones
Persea americana, avocado pear
Physalis peruviana, ground cherry, poha,
    or Cape gooseberry
Physalis pruinosa, strawberry tomato
Pinus pinea, pinyon
Pistacia lentiscus, mastic

Pistacia vera, pistachio
Portulaca oleracea, purslane
Prunus armeniaca, apricot
Prunus avium, cherry
Prunus dulcis, almond
Prunus x domestica, plum
Prunus spinosa, sloe
Prunus webbii, wild almond
Psidium guajava, yellow guava
Psidium littorale, strawberry guava, purple
Punica granatum, pomegranate
Pyrus communis, pear
Quercus ilex var. ballota, sweet acorns
Rhamnus crocea, redberry
Rosmarinus officinalis, rosemary
Rubus idaeus, raspberry
Ruscus aculeatus, box holly
Ruta graveolens, rue
Salvia officinalis, sage
Smilax aspera, prickly climber
Stauntonia hexaphylla, purple fruits
Syzygium jambos, rose apple
Syzygium paniculatum, brush cherry
Thymus, thyme
Tropaeolum majus, nasturtium
Ugni molinae, Chilean guava
Valeriana, valerian
Vitex agnus-castus, false pepper
Vitis vinifera, grapevine
Zea mays, sweet corn
Zingiber officinale, ginger
Ziziphus jujuba, Chinese jujube

Poisonous *Vinca difformis* covers the ground under oak.

Potentially Harmful Plants

A word about potentially harmful plants seems necessary, since many of them exist in all gardens. But don't worry! We have all encountered them in the gardens of our childhood and yet we are still around. We may have relished the red berries of yew (*Taxus baccata*) and delighted in their pink pulp, but we took care not to bite into their seeds or to chew on the leaves. All the same, poisonous plants should be excluded from a garden that features mostly edible plants, and certainly from all places where children roam. When collecting wild fruits, make use of a reliable field guide, and when in doubt reject your find. The same goes for fungi. Be sure never to touch your eyes while working in the garden.

Wintersweet, or poison-arrow plant (*Acokanthera oblongifolia*), perfumes the air with its white flowers. Because its fruit resembles an olive, it could be taken to the kitchen by mistake. In Africa the entire plant is traditionally cooked until a resinlike paste remains; this is hidden in a tall tree and used as arrow poison.

Can something as beautiful as datura (*Brugmansia*) be so toxic? When the late-afternoon sun illuminates its large leaves and turns the white trumpets iridescent, one wants to kneel in admiration, dizzied by the bewitching scent. For years I have removed yellowing leaves and spent flowers, and I still wonder where the poison lies. Yet I have made it a practice to wear garden gloves, and I always wash my hands before touching my eyes or any food.

All foxglove (*Digitalis*) contain cardio-active glycosides, which vary from one species to another. It is the leaves that contain the valued but highly poisonous medicinal digitalis.

Plants with milky sap, spurge (*Euphorbia dendroides*), for example, may cause damage to skin or eyes when they are being pruned. Wear protective glasses, and in an emergency seek medical advice. The same goes for *Agave americana*.

Oleander (*Nerium oleander*) grows in every southern garden. It is so poisonous that no animal will nibble at it. Be sure not to use it for barbecue skewers or firewood!

Several plants in the Apocynaceae family (*Nerium*, *Trachelospermum*, *Vinca*) are poisonous. So are many bulbs (*Amaryllis belladonna*, *Colchicum*, *Urginea maritima*). *Merendera* inhibits cell division.

Potentially Harmful Plants

Most of the plants grown in gardens do not pose any risks to humans. However, potential damage that may be caused by the plants listed below runs the gamut from skin or eye irritants to intestinal poisoning. Toxic plants, depending on the quantities consumed, may cause no more than a mild illness, but a few may cause severe poisoning. (Consult *Poisonous Plants of South Africa* by B. van Wyk et al., 2002). When you seek medical advice, do so immediately and remember to take along a sample of the plant concerned. Do not try to make the person vomit.

Acokanthera, very poisonous
Agave americana, vicious thorns
Amaryllis belladonna, poisonous
Brugmansia, poisonous
Cestrum purpureum
Colchicum autumnale, very poisonous
Corynocarpus laevigatus
Cytisus, all
Daphne, poisonous, skin irritant
Digitalis purpurea, very poisonous
Euonymus, poisonous
Euphorbia, poisonous, severe eye irritant
Gelsemium sempervirens, very poisonous
Gloriosa superba, very poisonous
Hedera, poisonous
Helleborus, poisonous
Ilex
Illicium anisatum, berries are poisonous
Indigofera, poisonous to livestock
Juniperus sabina, poisonous
Laburnum, poisonous
Lantana, poisonous
Ligustrum, most species poisonous

All parts of *Acocanthera* are poisonous.

The seeds of *Ricinus* are highly toxic.

Melia azedarach,
   fruits highly poisonous
Merendera, inhibits cell division
Moraea collina, poisonous to cattle
Narcissus, poisonous
Nerium oleander, very poisonous
Nicotiana glauca, very poisonous
Ornithogalum, several very poisonous
Passiflora quadrangularis,
   the decomposing roots are
   poisonous, not the fruit
Plumbago
Plumeria

Prunus laurocerasus, poisonous
Rhamnus catharticus
Ricinus communis, very poisonous
Ruta, severe skin irritant in
   bright sunlight
Taxus baccata, very poisonous
Thevetia neriifolia
Trachelospermum
Urginea maritima, rat poison
Vinca
Wisteria, poisonous
Zantedeschia aethiopica, poisonous

Living with Animals
My Sheep Park

In the spirit of the late Thomas Church, a distinguished California landscape architect who believed that "animals belong to the landscape," I have found that for every garden there are animals to suit its size and conditions, whether they are wild or domesticated. In this section, I will discuss how to grow plants to attract birds, butterflies, and bees and how to train dogs to stop garden-destructive behavior. I will also describe my own experience with sheep and explore the range of plants that are not eaten by them. I will also suggest plants that deer are unlikely to eat.

As an animal lover, I have always encouraged animals to share my garden, but not all types of animals. A huge bulldog, for example, would not be easy to garden around, and some animals can cause damage. But tortoises and hedgehogs are attractive (and no-maintenance) garden dwellers, and horses and sheep can add beauty to the landscape if you live in the country. In spring the faint sound of the humming bees fills the days, just as the nightingale's jubilant song fills the nights. A slender, quick-footed weasel darts out from beneath a nearby rock, while birds move off to safer branches. A colony of geckos, the color of the surrounding rock, peek out from a crack, all neatly aligned, facing the sun like tourists on a beach. Frogs, salamanders, grasshoppers—welcome them all. I have not mentioned snakes, which, depending on the region you live in, rate between harmless and even beneficial to extremely dangerous. Ask your neighbors for advice on these garden creatures.

For grazing animals, turn a meadow into a pasture. To avoid its being over-trampled, all you need

Ducks and their brood are fascinating to watch.

do is fence it into three sections to be grazed in rotation. Animals will mow the grass free of charge; in fact, sheep will keep grass as closely trimmed as a golf course. Horses and cows qualify as good grazers, but goats, which can climb into trees, will make a nuisance of themselves and are believed to have done more for plant extinction in the Mediterranean than humans. Although I tend to feel uneasy about keeping animals behind bars, I remember a minute courtyard planted with a low tree and scented shrubs, roofed with wire mesh to keep the animals inside. Birds flew from branch to branch, tortoises crawled in the sand, and ducks watched over their broods.

Songbirds are not only a joy to watch but their presence is also a sound horticultural practice in our changing environment. Do you have the opportunity, as I did this morning, of watching a small gray

For more ideas, see:
- The Olive Grove, page 78
- Living under Pines, page 124
- A Country Garden, page 168

bird with a shiny white breast picking a branch clean of all insects? Relentlessly, untiringly, he cleaned each bud, picking up any insects that had fallen and leaving his "plate" clean. As long as we have such helpers, we don't need poisonous sprays!

The following plants can provide birds with fruits or seeds, as well as nesting material. Birds are attracted by the strawberry tree (*Arbutus*), Natal plum (*Carissa*), dogwood (*Cornus*), cotoneaster, silverberry (*Elaeagnus*), loquat (*Eriobotrya*), toyon (*Heteromeles*), lantana, and privet (*Ligustrum*). They delight in the fruits of California wax myrtle (*Myrica*), *Photinia*, cherry (*Prunus*), currant (*Ribes*), mountain ash (*Sorbus*), and snowberry (*Symphoricarpos*). Add the climbing honeysuckle (*Lonicera*), ground-covering Indian mock strawberry (*Duchesnea indica*), or wild strawberry (*Fragaria chiloensis*). Nectar-feeding birds prefer long tubular flowers, such as datura (*Brugmansia*), fuchsia, red-hot poker (*Kniphofia*), penstemon, and sage (*Salvia azurea*), and they bring their exotic world into the garden. Watch birds feast on the seeds of the spectacular sunflower (*Helianthus annuus*). The thorny firethorn (*Pyracantha*) provides nesting sites as an additional benefit.

Note: For bird advice, in the U.S. contact the Audubon Society at www.audubon.org; in the U.K., contact the Royal Society for the Protection of Birds (RSPB) at www.rspb.org.uk

Butterflies, a charming but increasingly rare inhabitant of the garden scene, are lured by nectar-rich heliotrope (*Heliotropum arborescens*), rue (*Ruta graveolens*), and fennel (*Foeniculum vulgare*), by long tubular composites such as artichoke (*Cynara scolymus*), and globe thistle (*Echinops*), and by members of the milkweed family Asclepiaceae, *Buddleja*, and *Sedum* 'Autumn Joy'.

Bees are attracted to *Abelia*, *Acacia*, *Artemisia*, *Buddleja*, *Choisya ternata*, *Citrus*, *Crataegus*, *Erica*, loquat (*Eriobotrya*), *Escallonia*, avocado pear (*Persea*), sage (*Salvia*), star jasmine (*Trachelospermum*), and wisteria, to name only a few. On a sunny day in midwinter the flowering rosemary buzzes with bees. Bees and wasps are rarely antagonistic and usually become dangerous only when they or their nests are threatened. If you are allergic to bee stings, however, use the above plants with restraint or avoid them altogether.

We have always had dogs, currently a jet-black Labrador, a glorious sight when silhouetted against the sea. There is no such thing as a destructive dog. The moment a puppy comes into our life, we let it know our likes and dislikes with a caress or a scolding—never a thrashing. The pup may pull out a plantlet, as do the hares and rabbits that occasionally chew on new additions to the garden, but it will seldom uproot an established plant. Training (ten minutes a day for a week, aided by morsels of meat) will teach the young dog to accept the fact that we don't want it to take a sunbath or dig a hole in the middle of the flower beds. However, we should remember a dog's need for exercise and match its size to the size of the garden (or vice versa).

There are many advantages to owning a dog. They are unconditional friends and watch over us in uncertain

A meadow can be turned into a grazing ground.

To avoid health hazards, sheep should not graze longer than two hours on lush grass.

times. For the gardener, one advantage is that a dog has to be walked outside the garden. This is when I lay my tools aside and simply observe the surrounding countryside or take a stroll along the path for a rare moment of leisure. It is moments like this when I wonder to myself what happens to the dew and how does it benefit the plants? Why are the cyclamen coming out so early this autumn, and which specific *Merendera* is it whose flowers I find between rubble in rock-hard soil? Within our garden, our creation and its results—for good or for ill—are an overriding concern, but outside the garden things are different. We should count ourselves fortunate if we live near an area where nature has not been tampered with but left to its own devices.

Sheep grazing under olive trees add greatly to the atmosphere of a grove. Their presence is made possible by the person who cares for them during your absence—the shepherd. There is no mystery to shepherding. Years ago, during a cold winter, I helped the shepherd drive the flock every day into a field where they would find good pasture. Then, a few hours later, we would return them for the night to the place they had come from. We walked at great speed over uneven terrain, over fields and hills, driving several hundred sheep, which have a tendency to stop at every blade of grass they find. Speed was of the essence: sheep have to be kept moving before they can disperse. We exchanged few words, as I was supposed to know what had to be done. I loved the job.

My Sheep Park

When we annexed an abandoned olive grove to our garden, I decided to leave it unfenced so that the sheep could go on grazing and keep the grass down. All I had to do, or so I thought, was underplant the trees with our surplus of *Iris germanica* and find

additional plants that sheep would despise, besides the few that already grew there naturally, such as many rock roses (*Cistus*), the rare spurge olive (*Cneorum tricoccon*), the versatile *Euphorbia dendroides*, endemic *Hypericum balearicum*, and rosemary. Mastic (*Pistacia lentiscus*) and buckthorn (*Rhamnus alaternus*) were sufficiently tall to be out of sheep-reach. But, as often happens, modest beginnings will evolve into more complicated results, and so the Sheep Park was born.

Not knowing any better, I planted *Agapanthus*, red-hot poker (*Kniphofia*), and calla lilies (*Zantedeschia*) as ground covers, but the sheep considered them a juicy addition to their daily fare. Potato vine (*Solanum jasminoides*) and sugar bush (*Rhus ovata*), of which I also had a surplus, suffered a similar fate.

Sheep gather around an ancient water well, shaded by an almond tree.

So I started to hunt for thorny plants and planted the tall floss silk tree (*Chorisia speciosa*) and the bulky bitter orange (*Poncirus trifoliate*). Firethorn (*Pyracantha*), the thorny barberry (*Berberis*), *Colletia cruciata*, Kei apple (*Dovyalis caffra*), and *Mimosa lindheimeri* did fine. *Gleditsia triacanthos* was planted too young, while the thorns were still soft, and was thus a failure because sheep consider young thorns a delicacy. I ought to have known better! But now, thanks to temporary fencing, its thorns are hardening, and I am looking for other thorny plants that thrive in our area.

Tip: To transplant an agave with ease, tie its leaves into a tight bundle and wrap sacking around it for added safety before pulling the plant out of the ground. Agaves transplant successfully with only a few roots, but they must be firmly staked.

To add more color, we used tall *Jacaranda mimosifolia* and Jerusalem thorn (*Parkinsonia aculeata*), which is invasive in hot coastal climates, as well as beefwood (*Casuarina*) for its quick growth. The poisonous *Nerium oleander* was another suitable choice; its flowers contrast beautifully with the mass of dark green foliage. In South America, I once saw half-starved cows beside oleander, its lush foliage right next to their mouths, yet not a leaf was missing. Since no animal in its right mind would chew on it, oleander is an excellent ornamental for grazing land where the choice of flowering shrubs is limited.

You can protect trees and other plants by wrapping them in a "box" to a height of 5 feet or so (150cm). We use transparent corrugated roofing material, of which we have a surplus. Tie it at the seam and fasten it securely to a pole. This material is preferable to wire netting, which would provide some animals with a foothold. A few well-placed stones will also protect a plant and mark the site. Allow time for plants to settle before discarding the boxes. If you use wire netting, use a very narrow gauge where sheep graze, so that the lambs do not get their heads caught when they try to investigate the other side of the fence.

My sheep park was in the making when I received a telegram from a friend that read: "Have cleared our hill. Whatever we plant is eaten by sheep. Stop. Any suggestions?" I replied: "Use well-staked plants, tall enough to be out of reach for the sheep, such as *Castanea, Robinia hispida, Schinus, Pinus, Prunus*, and many palms. For color, add oleander and waves of rosemary, lavender, and rock roses." Not having seen the place, it was difficult to do more than suggest a few tough plants. However, within twenty-four hours, a devastating flood washed the scant soil left after our friend had "cleared the hill" straight down into the sea.

From Australia, the sheep continent, I received the following suggestions of sheep-proof plants, although I have not yet tried them out: *Acacia pulchella* var. *glaberrima* and *A. ixiophylla, Banksia candolleana, Dryandra sessilis, Hakea obliqua*, and *Labichea lanceolata*.

Over the months, I have observed that the butterfly bush (*Buddleja davidii*), as well as ivy (*Hedera helix*), germander (*Teucrium fruticans*), and laurustinus (*Viburnum tinus*), were eaten through a fence of wire netting, as were buckthorn (*Rhamnus alaternus*), mirror plant (*Coprosma repens*), rose of Sharon (*Hibiscus syriacus*), and *Brachyglottis greyi*. *Aloe arborescens* was nibbled on while the nearby Hebe was left untouched. *Iris germanica* was sometimes eaten and sometimes not, which shows that a wide range of factors must guide animals in their choice of food. Grazing depends on how hungry the animals are and on how well established the plants. Animals also tend to investigate new plants that have only recently been introduced into the garden and are therefore relatively vulnerable.

When one morning I discovered sheep droppings inside the fenced area, I seized the opportunity to see which plants had not been eaten by the five or six sheep that had managed to jump the fence and remain in the garden for a few days. The choice of food that the garden offered them was so wide that they first selected the plants they liked best. If they had stayed longer, with ample time to sample new fare, they would have grazed on more plants and the list below would have been shorter!

Garden Plants Not Preferred by Sheep

Hungry sheep will eat these plants if they are readily available, but they are not the first plants to go. Try these out with other animals that invade your garden.

Abelia x grandiflora
Acacia covenia
Acokanthera speciosa
Agave americana,
    fully grown
Alyxia ruscifolia
Amarine
Anisodontea
Artemisia
Arthropodium
Asteriscus
Banksia marginata
Berberis
Brugmansia
Buddleja officinalis
Caesalpinia gilliesii
Callistemon, various

Camellia
Campsis radicans
Centranthus
Chorisia speciosa
Cistus palinhai
    and others
Clematis cirrhosa
Coleonema pulchrum
Colletia armata,
    vicious thorns
Corokia
Cneorum tricoccon
Crataegus
Cussonia paniculata
Cussonia spicata
Dovyalis caffra,
    partly erica

Eriocephalus
Erythrina crista-galli
Euphorbia dendroides
Grevillea
    'Wimpara Gem'
    (G. 'Ronda' is eaten)
Hakea laurina
Hakea suaveolens
Hypericum balearicum
Indigofera japonica
Lantana camara
Lavandula spicata
Leonotis leonurus
Leptospermum
    laevigatum
Leucadendron

Leucospermum
    thymifolium
Melaleuca alternifolia
Mimosa lindheimeri
Myoporum parviflorum
Mystroxilon
Nerine
Nerium oleander
Osteospermum
Pelargonium
    pseudoglutinosa
Phlomis fruticosa
    and P. italica
Phygelius aequalis
Pittosporum
    undulatum
Plectranthus variegatus

Plumbago
Puya alpestris and
    P. chilensis, grown-up
Rhamnus
    ludovici-salvatoris
Rosmarinus
Ruta
Salvia aurea
Salvia officinalis
Senecio petasitis
Westringia fruticosa
Widdringtonia
Yucca filamentosa,
    when fully grown

Watch birds feed on the seed of the sunflower (Helianthus annuus).

The tough leaves of loquat (Eriobotrya japonica) are unpalatable to sheep.

Plants Not Eaten by Sheep

This is a list of plants that could be safely planted outside the garden where sheep roam. You can enlarge the list by including woody plants tall enough to be beyond a sheep's reach.

Artemisia absinthium
Buxus balearica
Cistus
Chamaerops humilis
Cneorum tricoccon
Crataegus monogyna
Erica multiflora
Eucalyptus spp.

Euphorbia dendroides
Helichrysum
Hypericum balearicum
Nerium oleander
Phlomis italica
Pistacia lentiscus,
    young shoots are
    eaten

Puya alpestris
Rosmarinus officinalis
Rhamnus
    ludovici-salvatoris
Ruta graveolens
Santolina
    chamaecyparissu

Arbutus unedo is spared by sheep, but who knows what would happen if they were hungry!

A Country Garden
Reviving an Abandoned Farm

This garden, ideal for family life, is aimed at those who seek to make a garden on abandoned farmland. I discuss its restoration and suggest how to cultivate the land, preserving existing plants to great advantage and encouraging the corrective pruning of neglected trees and shrubs. Stonework is carefully repaired once the land has been tidied up. I also pay homage to the stonemason, an important traditional figure in countries around the Mediterranean and often a master craftsman. I also suggest some ideas for plantings that look right with old stonework.

The first question you are likely to ask yourself after buying that derelict farmhouse surrounded by fields is: "What will I find here?"

Careful restoration of this abandoned farm has begun. Notice the cleared access road and the repaired walls.

For more ideas, see:

While exploring the property, cutting through vicious bramble, you might discover some unkempt fruit trees behind the sleepy farmhouse that was the reason you bought the land in the first place. A messy hedge sporting a wilderness of entangled shrubs might also attract your attention. You will wonder how to use various features, such as the carob (*Ceratonia siliqua*) leaning against the house, or the enclosure next to it attached to a ruined pigsty, or the field of sprawling prickly pears—all of it covered in brambles. A centuries-old olive tree on an upper terrace might complete the picture, except for that far-away grove of pine trees reduced to shrub stature by foraging animals.

At first it all looks like a mess that anyone in his right mind would simply clear away before starting anew. "Who in his right mind?" you ask yourself, and hesitate. In your mind's eye gleams a crop of sweet, juicy plums, neither fumigated nor fertilized, of a variety no longer sold in supermarkets. Surely it might be worth trying to help the tree recover from years of neglect? Slowly you start to cut out the dead wood, in the hope that it will respond favorably.

Finding Lost Treasures

When, only a few months later, you sit beneath the tree whose foamy white blossoms stand out brilliantly against a blue spring sky, you start to look more closely at the rest of the "mess" and suddenly comprehend its potential. Encouraged by the speedy recovery of the plum tree, you take on the entangled hedge, bit by bit. Once the dead wood has been removed, you identify flowering hawthorn (*Crataegus monogyna*), the vitamin-rich sloe (*Prunus spinosa*), a lovely, wild scented rose (*Rosa sempervirens*), and sturdy, equally aromatic honeysuckle (*Lonicera*), and you start to appreciate the flowering potential of them all. Working carefully, you preserve the strongest plants, leaving a few questionable ones whose fate will be determined once you have a chance to evaluate their growth performance.

Meanwhile, a healthy bramble (*Rubus fruticosus*) has grown unhindered to a formidable size, its long, vigorous shoots rooting wherever they touch the ground. While you take on the job of tackling this beast, your family picks its sweet and juicy fruits and declares that removing the blackberry is out of the question. And so, outvoted, you confine the plant to an allotted space and in the process uncover a well-set stone wall, a treasured find. In a year or two, liberated from the weight of the brambles, the nearby pomegranate (*Punica granatum*) will grow into a generous, rounded volume that defies any summer drought.

Encouraged by your family, you now turn to the carob tree, whose lower branches block a window of your future home, as the upper branches are in the process of lifting a few roof tiles. In years to come, after judicious pruning, this tree will shade your family gatherings and cool your house during hot mediterranean summers. In spring children will discover scented violets at its feet. Remember that the roots of a tree close to a house may undermine the structure, or already have done so, so be sure to

Artemisias, eriocephalus, lavender, and rosemary brighten up an established section of the sheep park.

check carefully before deciding a tree's fate. In the past, a stately, tall Oriental plane tree (*Platanus*) was usually planted to shade a spring, so if you find one on your land, it may indicate that water is not far away.

Meantime, your ancient olive tree (*Olea europaea*) is growing strong new branches. You decide on its framework and look ahead to the day when home-grown olives will grace your table (see also The Olive Grove, page 78). A single Mediterranean hackberry, or southern nettle tree (*Celtis australis*), is often found near an old Mediterranean farmhouse, and its pliable young wood is still used for animal collars from which to hang bells. Once this tree becomes very old, it is prone to rot and to break in storms, but it is worth your while to "nurse" its impressive trunk. If you cut out dead wood generously, rebalance the branches and selectively prune the suckers, a hackberry may last for many more years, or even earn a new lease on life. Other plantings will come up in its shade to create or improve a wildlife habitat. Even the oldest trunks tend to spring back to life, as the carob, oak, and olive do. Their roots have had hundreds of years to reach way down into the ground and insert themselves into cracks or crevices, which they often pry apart. They have stored an enormous amount of energy, which new plantings will be unable to match in anyone's lifetime.

You may also find a vegetable patch to cultivate.

All olive trees were carefully pruned and some were transplanted.

Tip: In those places where a carob, olive, or oak might be in the way, cut it back gradually to a shrubby size, so that it can fulfill an important function in your future garden in the guise of a large green volume.

The spiny fig cactus (*Opuntia*) was customarily planted near a farmhouse and its pigsty. In difficult conditions, these plants would have given refuge to animals and discouraged even the hardiest soul from venturing near them, not even to harvest the golden-orange fruit (which today most people prefer to buy at the market). Once the workmen begin repairing the tumbledown walls of the sty, you finally turn your attention to the impenetrable thorny thicket. As your saw touches an opuntia "leaf," it breaks off, and once you have cut away a few more downward-growing "leaves," a path will open up and allow you to move around as you would in an orderly orchard. With a minimum of maintenance, the cactus plants will soon resemble moderately sized fruit trees. Take a minute to admire their outline against a whitewashed wall or the sky.

Protected by the opuntias, an almond tree (*Prunus dulcis*) has sprung up from the roots of another that fell as a result of old age. The young plant will soon reach fruiting size and needs to be staked. Take advantage of this discovery, for its roots will already have become established, whereas a newly planted almond tree might dislike the site chosen for it and require replanting. Nearby you will find a few mutilated pine trees, which with the help of your judicious pruning, may eventually be able to do what they have wanted to do all their lives—reach toward the sky. It is here that you may discover the rare *Daphne gnidium*, wild jasmine (*Jasminum fruticans*), or any Jerusalem sage (*Phlomis*).

As you make progress, that rambling grapevine (*Vitis vinifera*), tied back to its pillar, will once again shade the arbor as it did in times past. By now members of your family are competing with each other searching for "what is there" and all of you decide jointly on how to use your discoveries.

In this garden you may be lucky enough to find a complete pharmacy. All parts of the hawthorn (*Crataegus monogyna*) are antispasmodic and sedative and lower both blood pressure and fever. Sloe (*Prunus spinosa*) is astringent, diuretic, and purifying and contains vitamin C. *Rosa sempervirens* acts as a tonic and heals wounds. The bramble (*Rubus fruticosus*), as we have already seen, is an anti-diabetic with multiple other medicinal properties. No doubt you will discover many more plants that can be used as infusions, teas, and dressings. But remember that wild fruiting and medicinal plants should be used with care, and always have on hand reliable field guides and herbals, especially when you are not familiar with the vegetation in an area new to you.

Cornerstones require special attention if a house is to last.

The Stonemason

A well-chosen stone exudes beauty. In the past, a stonemason was a necessary contributor to most Mediterranean gardens; today one is more likely to find a bulldozer instead. Anyone who discovers the traces of a careful stonemason's work is lucky indeed. He put up walls and he terraced the land, laid steps, or built a cistern, where water could be pulled up from the cool depths. With patient hands, he

selected the appropriate stone or cut it into shape with a special hammer. Corner stones, which are usually larger than the rest, need special attention if a wall is to last. Larger stones are laid at the bottom of the wall, their size decreasing as the wall progresses in height. The stonemason laid the stone at the correct site, never to be moved again, let it fall into place, and gave it a slight tap. Nothing was hurried: each stone was patiently selected and added to the preceding one, and by the end of the day another stretch of wall was complete.

One wonders who that stonemason was, whether he worked alone, where he lived, how he dressed, even what he ate. One can imagine him rubbing a clove of garlic over a thick slice of dark bread, sprinkling it with pure olive oil and sea salt, eating it slowly, and giving the odd morsel to his friend the dog, as he contemplates the work already done. He might comment on its future use or discuss the shape of a stone with a passing shepherd.

As you walk around your land, you may come upon the traces of this man's toil. If so, as I have said, you are lucky, for past generations knew how to manage the terrain. Once tumbled walls have been repaired, steps cleared, and the cistern emptied of fallen leaves, the design will emerge—simple and

Protruding slabs were located while the wall was being built, a quicker solution than steps.

This rustic wall, beautified by almond trees, was built with stones cleared from an adjoining field.

to one side and patches of *Euphorbia*, *Cytisus*, *Salvia*, and germander (*Teucrium*). The Mediterranean *Clematis cirrhosa* and *C. flammula* enjoy the cool root run provided by a wall and will climb over it. They also like to clothe a shrub. Honeysuckle (*Lonicera implexa*) or *Rosa sempervirens* will ascend a half-broken tree to disguise its mutilated branches. The result is clean and clear outlines, simplicity, and a feeling of peace.

right. Let it guide you as you consider the layout of your garden; often you will see that the "land-scaping" has already been done.

Depending on the lay of your land, you may also find terracing that will provide the horizontal areas that are convenient for easy walking, for efficient carting around of materials, and for keeping soil in place. It may take time today to find someone to undertake the necessary repair work, but it is certainly worth being patient. After having watched a stonemason at work, a neighbor of ours started to do his own minor repair work and became proficient at it.

Expert stonework demands respect and calls for planting in proportion. Cascades of flowers spilling over a wall or sheets of bloom draping it are super-fluous. These cascades and sheets will be needed elsewhere, perhaps to conceal an unsightly corner, but not to hide well-set stone. Frame it or underline it; place a cypress or a mediterranean fan palm (*Chamaerops humilis*) next to it as an accent if needed, but avoid anything that distracts from the strong, simple beauty of the stone.

To accompany a wall, a carob tree (*Ceratonia siliqua*) or a Judas tree (*Cercis siliquastrum*) would look right, or savin (*Juniperus sabina*), mock privet (*Phillyrea angustifolia*), and buckthorn (*Rhamnus alaternus*). For an evergreen mass, choose mastic (*Pistacia lentiscus*) or myrtle; for color, plant laurustinus (*Viburnum tinus*) or oleander (*Nerium oleander*). For more flowers at the foot of a large wall, add the rounded masses of rosemary, lavender, and rock roses

Rescued Plants

Celtis australis	*Phlomis*
Ceratonia siliqua	*Pinus*
Cercis siliquastrum	*Pistacia lentiscus*
Chamaerops humilis	*Platanus orientalis*
Cistus	*Prunus dulcis*
Clematis cirrhosa	*Prunus x domestica*
Clematis flammula	*Prunus spinosa*
Crataegus monogyna	*Punica granatum*
Cupressus	*Quercus*
Cytisus	*Rhamnus alaternus*
Daphne gnidium	*Rosa sempervirens*
Euphorbia	*Rosmarinus officinalis*
Jasminum fruticans	*Rubus fruticosus*
Juniperus sabina	*Salvia*
Lavandula	*Teucrium*
Lonicera implexa	*Viburnum tinus*
Myrtus communis	*Viola*
Nerium oleander	*Vitis vinifera*
Olea europaea	
Opuntia ficus-indica	
Phillyrea angustifolia	

Renewing an Urban Garden
A Lost Treasure Rediscovered

Gardeners acquiring a city garden in a mediterranean climate often find themselves faced with a neglected, overgrown jungle. In this section, I deal with the renewal of such a garden, stressing the need to let in air and light. I discuss the transplanting of palm trees and propose a range of pollution-tolerant plants. Patience pays off.

Are you the proud owner of an overgrown city garden, perhaps on the Ligurian coast, that came along with the house of your dreams, one of those delightful turn-of-the-century creations left to you by a great aunt? After years of sleepy seclusion, this garden has become a lush jungle that looks best when admired from a balcony on a moonlit night. When you give it a closer look, you will see that many plants have been fighting for the light for decades, the stronger ones elbowing the weaker to the ground. Masses of glorious bougainvillea—their blossom best seen from the nearby church tower or while you are repairing your roof—have nearly smothered the trees. A palm pushes its large fronds against a vigorous araucaria that has long since overtaken it. When you discover the clean lacquered leaves of Southern magnolia (*Magnolia grandiflora*), you have found a treasure that will carry exotic scented bloom in summer, but only if sufficient light reaches it. A few meager pittosporums, denuded of all but the uppermost leaves and surrounded by a crop of equally meager seedlings (usually *P. tobira*),

await an experienced hand. You may also find lanky aloes, spiny agaves, and spindly pelargoniums vegetating in the dark shade. All these survivors are a sure bet if given the right growing conditions, which in this case means full sun. The dense shade has left nothing on the ground but dry leaves to be trampled underfoot. Children will soon discover this dark hideaway to play in.

This process is best done gradually, and letting air in is always a good principle to follow. Once it is possible to make a realistic evaluation of the status quo, take time to contemplate your garden at leisure. Assess the potential of what you see, wait for the right season to transplant things, and ask neighbors or a nursery for advice if you have any doubts. Remember: A large tree is quickly cut down; a young one will take a long time to reach the same stature.

Once you have removed the dead wood from your overgrown plants, cut them back gradually in several stages; the same also goes for exuberant climbers. On the other hand, the wisteria that is often found in old, overgrown city gardens will tolerate a heavy slashing. Give the space it deserves to the drought-tolerant *Magnolia grandiflora*, which takes years to flower. If pittosporums fit the design you have in mind, cut them low so that young growth fills them at medium height, and reserve one or two that display a good framework as small trees. Pull out the seedlings of most of these plants, roots

Ivy and a flowering *Chorisia speciosa* intermingle happily on this handsome balustrade.

Trees with long-lasting needles are sensitive to pollution, such as that caused by chlorine, fluorine, and sulfur fumes, which are most harmful to cedar and the Italian stone pine (*Pinus pinea*). Deciduous plants, on the other hand, will regrow leaves damaged by pollution. Where pollution is a problem, use the horse chestnut (*Aesculus californica*) for its delightful flowers, the London plane (*Platanus acerifolia*) for its height, and the tree of heaven (*Ailanthus altissima*) for its rapid growth, although the invasive roots of the latter will need to be contained. For blossom, consider forsythia and witch hazel (*Hamamelis*), both of which require winter cold and some water. Oleanders (*Nerium oleander*) are a faithful standby. If given weekly water, manzanita (*Arctostaphylos* 'Point Reyes') will cover the ground. For a wider range of plants in a polluted area, be inspired by what grows well in your neighborhood, and choose those that are to your liking. Refrain from planting almond, citrus, and fig, which prefer clean country air.

Those involved with restoration of an overgrown garden will find *Hidden Gardens* by Penny David (2002) a good companion. The book presents a series of case studies in garden restoration in the United Kingdom. The original creators are discussed, together with a history of each site and a chronicle of their progress. Although written for the U.K., the book contains good advice for mediterranean regions.

and all; if you simply cut them back, they will return the following year with renewed vigor. Once light and sun reach the aloes, agaves, and other succulents and once the pelargoniums have been cut back, they will all revive and spread.

Cypresses will not regrow branches from bare wood low down on the trunk, but regular shearing will fill their outward coat and improve their appearance. They can also be reduced to about half their green growth volume for later fattening up. Replace cypresses where they have gone beyond repair; new ones will grow quickly.

Well-grown palms in a garden are precious and costly items. To transplant them, you should probably seek professional help. It is said that the right moment to do so is at the very onset of the warm season (although another dictum favors summer). Once you have transplanted a palm, secure its stem firmly until new roots have anchored it. Wrap the growth tip of older palms in sacking and wait patiently for new fronds to grow.

Remember: There is only one growth tip, and if you lose it, you lose the palm.

Pollution-Tolerant Plants

Aesculus californica	Hamamelis
Ailanthus altissima	Nerium oleander
Arctostaphylos 'Point Reyes'	Petunia
Calendula	Platanus acerifolia
Forsythia	Tipuana tipu
Ginkgo biloba	Zinnia

The Andalusian Courtyard
An Intimate Outdoor Space

Outdoor living has always been a part of Mediterranean life, and the Andalusian-style courtyard is designed to meet this need. An example of the Mediterranean lifestyle, secluded and protective, this garden will enable you to shake off the tyranny of the lawn. Here I will discuss the decorative paving that replaces a lawn, suggest a small water feature, and mention the wide use of containers that are characteristic of a courtyard garden. Courtyards resembling those of the Mediterranean may also be made in more northerly climates. This project has been planned with Mediterranean natives, but you can also use plants from other regions as long as such imports have proved their worth over time (most of them need sun) and their volumes, textures, and scent are right.

S ince ancient times, the Mediterranean environ-ment has been one of outdoor living. Although open land today is annexed to the house, requiring ample planting to cover all the ground, in former times outdoor life centered on a courtyard. Courtyard gardens can be traced back to as early as 1400 B.C. in Egypt. There, in a high official's garden in Thebes, we would have seen many of the elements that make up today's courtyard gardens. Much of the planting would have provided food for the household, such as date palms (*Phoenix dactylifera*), figs (*Ficus carica*), and grapes on a pergola. Ornamental planting for shade would have been included too; around a pavilion, cypress trees would have given much-needed shade. Cisterns provided water for irrigation.

For more ideas, see :
- Going Back in Time, page 16
- The Mediterranean Garden, page 60
- Mediterranean Style, page 74
- Refreshing Shade, Delightful Scent, page 110
- Living under Pines (fire prevention, page 128)

A climbing rose 'Mermaid' spills over a glazed oil jar.

In Roman times, prominent citizens had an atrium or a central open court in which to relax or, during favorable weather, take their meals. The practice was exported throughout Europe as the Roman Empire advanced, and was later adapted and enhanced by the Moorish conquerors in Spain. During the Moorish occupation of southern Spain, most palaces had a shady, enclosed garden that served as a welcome retreat from the midday heat and offered both privacy and protection.

Today, traditional Andalusian courtyards can still be found in Seville and Cordoba. You can see wonderful courtyards simply by asking to enter. Glimpsed through filigree wrought-iron work, these gardens are havens in a tumultuous world. The peace, the exuberant flowering, and the rich greenery are a delight to the eye, without distracting from the beautifully complementary ceramics. Such an enclosed space is a tranquil sanctuary during the ravages of the long, hot Mediterranean summer. The cool effect can be further enhanced by introducing water, either bubbling in a bowl or cascading from a small fountain. The sound of gently splashing (not gushing) water is an important ingredient in courtyard gardens and adds to the restful, relaxing nature of the place.

A useful extension to the house, today's courtyard is the immediate result of Mediterranean climatic conditions that permit its use as an additional living space or outdoor dining room. A square or rectangle of moderate size is all you need. The Andalusian courtyard also makes good use of small spaces surrounded by walls. If you have no walls, plant cypresses. The aim is a restful and tranquil setting.

Paving is your first concern and will be a testimony to your artistic abilities. It eliminates the lawn—the subject of so much contention nowadays—and provides an easily maintained ground cover. This is the place to show creativity, the craftsman's or your own. Any material may be used, from terra-cotta tiles to white marble. If you plan the same colors and tiles

In Seville one may discover countless attractive courtyards.

both inside and outside the house, you will create a sense of unity and make the space seem larger than it actually is. The floor should be even so that furniture can be moved around without difficulty. Paving also ensures a cool root run for neighboring plants and gives children a clean area on which to play. Built-in benches are very Mediterranean in style, as well as being decorative and labor-saving. Plan for one or two and make them an attractive feature of your courtyard.

Add containers. These outdoor spaces are often furnished with a wide array of decorative pots, tubs, and containers, which reflect the gardener's taste, botanical interest, or propagation skills. White candytuft (*Iberis sempervirens*) spilling over a terra-cotta pot will relieve the formal design. But do exercise restraint so that the classical outline of an Andalusian courtyard is not blurred.

You will need a water tap in order to water your pots or quench your own thirst, although it could be present in the guise of a small, decorative fountain. A shallow, rectangular water basin is an attractive feature of enclosed courtyards, originally inspired by the Mogul emperors' gardens. Today, recirculation equipment will help you save on water. This arrangement has many advantages, including style, usefulness, and low maintenance.

Summer cooking is often done alfresco mediterranean-style, and a barbecue will provide the opportunity for you to do likewise. All it needs is a simple roof to protect against the odd rain shower and a table. Grow your mediterranean herbs and spices nearby (marjoram, rosemary, savory, thyme) to enjoy their fragrance as well as keeping them handy for the cook.

As you create your Andalusian courtyard, plan for protection from the wind, which is crucial if you are to trap the sun's warmth in winter. To achieve this, you must pay close attention to the position of the sun throughout the day and throughout the year. A deciduous tree or a climber will let the cherished winter sun through and provide cool shade in summer.

Restrained planting is desirable in courtyard gardens. Plant lavender and thyme near the seating area, where their scent will promote and invoke a sense of well-being and contentment. Most native shrubs and some exotics can be utilized, but brightly colored plants would be ill suited to such a subdued and peaceful area. Masses of bold architectural plants would also look out of place. Once the initial groundwork has been laid, a classic and rather formal planting plan for an Andalusian courtyard might include four or six lemon trees (*Citrus limon*) for their shiny evergreen foliage and reduced size. Their bewitching scent will saturate the air all day long. Lemons are sturdier than orange trees and not demanding of water; if they are well cared for, they will remain healthy. They do not require spraying with chemicals, an advantage in a spot where people will be sitting. Lemons also need less heat than other citrus fruit, but watch out for their spines.

In Seville, the trees that produce the famous bitter Seville oranges are planted in every street, and when the flowers are out on a sunny day, the entire town is pervaded by their scent. Also called bigarade or marmalade orange, *Citrus aurantium* makes a rounded crown and may grow as high as 28 feet (9m). The thick, rough peel and acid pulp of its fruits are what you need to prepare real marmalade. The smaller 'Chinotto' variety has finer leaves and a formal appearance.

At the feet of these shaped trees, **tuck in small bulbs,** such as early spring-flowering *Allium, Anemone, Crocus, Fritillaria, Iris reticulata, Muscari, Scilla, Tulipa clusiana,* and *T. saxatilis*. Consider, too, the autumn-flowering *Sternbergia*. The winter-flowering *Narcissus tazetta* 'Paper White' provides delight in a season poor in flowers. A group of the heady-scented Madonna lilies (*Lilium candidum*), the only native Mediterranean lily, can be shallow-planted and provides a striking display, as do such annuals as bellis or petunias. Laurel and myrtle offer atmosphere, and their fragrance and color endow the warm environment with an added dimension. A perfumed climber such as jasmine—not a Mediterranean native but traditionally used since time past—will fill a corner or tumble over a wall.

A grapevine (*Vitis vinifera*) is essential in the Mediterranean and will quickly cover a sunny pergola, while the drought-tolerant honeysuckle (*Lonicera etrusca* and *L. implexa*) will clothe a trellis with foliage, flowers, and scent. The delicate *Clematis cirrhosa* scrambles through any shrub at hand or can be trained on a wall. Its charming winter flowers may be greenish white or red-spotted cream. Although best suited to coastal gardens, a pink, feathery-flowered tamarisk will hang gracefully over a sunny wall. The golden, widely used "mimosa" (actually an *Acacia*, which is not native but an early introduction) brings spring in winter, as does broom (*Genista*), whose sweet fragrance complements its cheerful blossom. To shade your meals with fragrant white bells, plant the deciduous snowbell (*Styrax officinale*), which grows as either shrub or tree. Clipped box, cypress, or spurge olive (*Cneorum tricoccon*) may frame the entrance door, accompanied on either side by sheared rosemary or lavender. This planting requires sun.

If your courtyard is a shady one, you can replace

the lemon trees with standard laurel, myrtle, or mock privet (*Phillyrea*). Underplanting requires a certain conformity so the classical design is not disrupted. To this end, choose shade-tolerant bulbous plants (aroids, cyclamen, *Leucojum*) or consider an evergreen ground cover of *Liriope* or the Algerian *Iris unguicularis*, whose scented flowers will delight you during many winter months. Or use any herbs that lend themselves to shearing. They suit such a design well. Finally, box is a great standby that fills many needs.

In early times—well before introductions from foreign lands enriched the choice—only the mostly evergreen plants mentioned below were available to those intent on furnishing an Andalusian courtyard. Most lent themselves to creative or formal clipping to prevent them from outgrowing their space. Thus, a traditional Andalusian courtyard has few flowers. The bulbs that are native to the Mediterranean Basin are numerous, but the Mediterranean climbers, for instance, are few. Today, we may make our own selection among the wide range of plants that suit a mediterranean climate, and climbers can always be enriched by those from the Cape of South Africa. Consider *Jacaranda mimosifolia*, an early introduction from the Americas. Many tender house plants will thrive in the protected environment of the courtyard.

An Andalusian courtyard can also be created in milder areas in northern regions. To create the Mediterrean look, use those plants of mediterranean origin that can be grown in mild northern areas and that are available locally. They will all feel at home in a mediterranean setting. Provide as much sun and warmth as you can, and be generous with any earth-moving that contributes to achieving excellent drainage. These plants also cherish good air circulation. What drought-tolerant plants dislike intensely is sodden foliage, which means that they profit from being raised off the ground level, for instance, by hanging over a wall. Their main survival strategies enable them to fend off dehydrating heat, but they are not equipped to withstand cold humidity.

Balconies in Andalusia are always adorned with colorful pots.

Plants for an Andalusian Courtyard

Trees, Shrubs
Acacia, smaller ones (introduced)
Acacia dealbata
Buxus balearica
Buxus microphylla
Buxus sempervirens
Citrus aurantium
Citrus limon, short stiff spines
Cneorum tricoccon
Cupressus
Genista
Laurus nobilis
Lavandula, compact-growing ones
Myrtus communis
Myrtus communis spp. *tarentina*
Phillyrea angustifolia
Phillyrea latifolia
Styrax officinale (introduced)
Teucrium fruticans

Herbs
Artemisia, compact-growing species
Ocimum basilicum
Origanum majorana
Mentha spicata
Petroselinum crispum
Rosmarinus officinalis
Salvia officinalis

Santolina chamaecyparissus
Satureja hortensis
Thymus vulgaris

Climbers
Clematis cirrhosa
Jasminum (introduced)
Lonicera etrusca
Lonicera implexa
Vitis vinifera

Bulbous Plants
Allium
Anemone
Crocus
Cyclamen
Fritillaria
Iris reticulata
Iris unguicularis
Leucojum
Lilium candidum
Liriope, introduced from Asia
Muscari
Narcissus tazetta
Scilla
Sternbergia
Tulipa clusiana
Tulipa saxatilis

Hedges, Screens, and Boundaries
Protecting Your Privacy

Hedges and screens not only find countless uses in a mediterranean-style garden, they also protect your privacy from adverse conditions and screen you from the outside world, yet they put few demands on you. This section discusses their maintenance, considers special requirements, and gives plant lists for different types and sizes of hedges. Those for whom this chapter was written will use their own imagination to explore the full potential of hedges and screens and they will discover many enticing possibilities.

Tall cypresses, clipped or not, traditionally marked borders in formal gardens.

Those who have visited the great Renaissance gardens in Italy or the Moorish palace gardens in southern Spain will invariably have come across the tall, clipped cypress hedges that are such an outstanding feature of classical Mediterranean gardens. Visitors always marvel at the intricate boxwood labyrinths or mazes and are enchanted by

clipped parterres of scented rosemary. They will also have admired golden gravel spaces contained by low box hedges, as well as herb gardens edged with myrtle, all distinctly Mediterranean in style.

With the resurgence of interest in formal gardens, such examples are very inspiring. Whereas one gardener wants the garden to grow at its own rhythm, others envisage a structural framework of tightly clipped greenery. The latter group plans such impressive features as a cypress avenue, or *allée*—slender cypresses grown in a precise row—or a central garden axis flanked on both sides by soaring evergreens. These gardeners may also be drawn to the elegant simplicity of a round, shallow pond ringed by tall cypress trees or to the complex, often amusing plant forms known as topiary. If you fall into this group, try to bridle your imagination with prudent restraint so that your formal garden will be both satisfying and orderly, not overwhelming or fussy.

Enchanting design possibilities are presented by garden spaces designed like rooms, edged with boxwood or closed off by any of the plants listed below. Low walls can be formed of mock privet (*Phillyrea angustifolia*), perhaps embellished with an arcaded gallery (like the Roman peristyle), which would make a delightfully shady walkway—much appreciated in mediterranean summers. A path flanked symmetrically by two large clumps of silk

For more ideas, see:
- A House That Lies Well in Its Land, page 44
- A Coastal Garden, page 86
- A Garden in the Hills, page 138
- The Container Garden, page 198

tassel (*Garrya elliptica*) could lead the way to a charming garden pavilion. A tall yew tree (*Taxus baccata*) might signal the entrance to a shady path whose rigid lines are softened by low, clipped lavender. A stately cypress pine (*Callitris preissii*) might cast mysterious shadows over the paving.

In all places where a wall is needed (a low balustrade or a higher design feature), plants can come to our assistance. By choosing species that take well to clipping, you can give a "green wall" the exact dimensions you desire, and at a lower cost than if you had to call in the stonemason. Straight, undulating, or shaped evergreen walls when seen against the sea

Where space is limited, a cypress hedge can hide what should not be seen.

or the sky will intrigue the passerby, but it is worth remembering that a hedge may also hide an attractive view outside the garden. Mediterranean garden makers of the past found a clever solution to this; they cut "windows" into the foliage of a hedge or wall and thus opened vistas of the world outside or a faraway horizon. Doors, archways, or tunnels can be also cut into or carved out of an evergreen partition of tightly clipped cypress, yew, or arborvitae. Or, if you feel enterprising, you can design a series of arches. A narrow passageway or a small door to one side could lead to another part of the garden, perhaps the vegetable plot or *potager*.

A recess or alcove cut into a dense evergreen wall is the perfect spot for a bench on which strollers can rest. As an attractive diversion, a niche can be carved out of a thick hedge to house a decorative vase or to display a statue—these were standard features of the Mediterranean gardens of the past. Color and aroma can be attractive byproducts of an evergreen hedge. When recently clipped or sheared, such a hedge will put forth an attractive light green foliage that later darkens, in the process releasing a pungent, refreshing scent.

Walls, hedges, and screens are not only decorative features, but they also shield you from adverse conditions. Nowadays, they screen out street noises, unsightly views, and air pollution. Thorny hedges can protect you from invasive dogs or incompatible neighbors. And perhaps best of all, they combat the wind. In other words, a dense hedge, like a stone wall, keeps nature at bay. Even on an exposed site, screens that provide shelter for the gardener will also create microclimates for selected plants. Whether you consider these screens in the form of enclosing walls, hedging, or boundary vegetation, the result will be protection and seclusion. Since hedges take up a fair amount of space in the garden, however, consider carefully before planting whether adverse conditions make a barrier necessary or desirable.

For a symbolic fence in a modern mediterranean garden, three or four wires may suffice, or if you have good neighborly relations, even a single one might do. Where a boundary line cuts across well-kept land, use the least visible wire netting, not an inch higher than necessary.

My tip: When we strung wire netting to keep sheep out of the garden area, posts were placed to coincide (on either side) with a shrub or tree trunk. This made them less visible. A lonely pole in an open space was later turned into an asset when we planted a climber to grow over it.

A combination of a wire fence, hedge, and screen, when carefully designed to match your garden, can give a harmonious overall impression. Where you have enough space, select a group of evergreen shrubs according to their height and width to provide the screening you want. If you select for flowering periods throughout the seasons and for blossom color and leaf texture, a handsomely arranged group of shrubs will often be more pleasing to the eye than a straight line of shorn privet. For "selective hedging," see the illustration on page 46 and make your neighbor's planting your own.

A series of arches can be cut into an evergreen wall, here revealing an antique vase.

Selecting Your Plants

Do not choose your plants until after you have come to a decision about your landscaping ideas. Decide whether you want to achieve a manicured or a more natural look and whether blossom is essential. Reflect on the purpose of a hedge, whether it should be low or high, and on the space allotted to it. There are many evergreen, drought-tolerant plants to choose from. Combine them as needed, using a straight row only where your design or limited space require one. If ugliness is creeping up on you in the form of tall buildings, for example, and if little space is available, consider cypress to block out once and for all what you do not wish to see. The Australian cypress pine (*Callitris*) and the false cypress (*Chamae-cyparis*) are good alternatives in mediterranean climates. Mediterranean in style, they lend themselves to creative inventiveness—such as a backdrop for a bench, a distinctive architectural feature itself, or as a setting for camellias in attractive containers (have them face the morning sun).

Because there is a wide range of plants used in mediterranean-climate regions for edging and for hedges, screens, boundaries, and windbreaks, we may select the appropriate plant for each site without having to compromise or resort to unsuitable or unattractive choices. Traditional Mediterranean plantings would include—after classical boxwood (*Buxus sempervirens* or the lower-

A white-washed wall is a way to achieve privacy and offers many opportunities for adornment.

growing *B. microphylla*)—sweet bay (*Laurus nobilis*), myrtle (*Myrtus communis*), *Lonicera nitida*, mock privet (*Phillyrea angustifolia* and *P. latifolia*), shiny dark-green buckthorn (*Rhamnus alaternus*), and germander (*Teucrium fruticans*). From other continents, the versatile hebes, Pacific wax myrtle (*Myrica californica*), small-leaved *Pittosporum tenuifolium*, and coffeeberry (*Rhamnus californica*) join in. Long-lasting yew (*Taxus baccata*) and somber arborvitae

Garden furniture, a pergola for shade, paving and gravel for easy walking, all contribute to the comfort of this peaceful retreat.

(*Thuja orientalis*) create contrast of color and form, together with the sturdy coast rosemary (*Westringia*). I have already mentioned scented rosemary and silvery-gray santolina, which are easily sheared and satisfy today's need for minimal maintenance.

Arborvitae (*Thuja*) naturally displays an orderly growth that you do not need to fatten up by shearing. The dense, narrow, and erect *Thuja plicata* 'Fastigiata' or the lower-growing *T. p.* 'Striblingii' will stand alone as a neat focal point or make an effective screen when grown in a group. Low evergreen hedges around an area of gravel are an attractive water- and

labor-saving device (try Mediterranean drought-tolerant plants such as box, myrtle, rosemary, or santolina). Equally appealing in summer as in winter, such an evergreen garden will be conducive to outdoor living. You will linger in the protected environment of the enclosing walls as the refreshing scent of the freshly clipped cypress comes your way.

Topiary is found in many mediterranean gardens and invariably adds a charming detail to an otherwise unpretentious setting. Myrtle may be clipped into spheres or mop-headed or grown as standards; dark yews can be sheared with accuracy to form balls or large cones. Shiny laurel, too, suits all the larger shapes you fancy. The most majestic of all, the slender Mediterranean cypress tree, will convey a sense of tranquility and elegance when tightly sheared or bent into arches.

No flowers are needed in this garden to accentuate the various shapes of clipped boxwood or the low rosemary edging. Although you would not want flowers to take the front of the stage, they can, in a subdued manner, accompany a successful scene just as a supporting actor does. Here, evergreen or ever-gray plants will fill your needs. A large pot set in a corner might overflow with white plumbago (*Plumbago auriculata* var. 'Alba'), softening the sharp edges. A bare expanse can be covered, for instance, by a silvery white or light green carpet of santolinas (*Santolina chamaecyparissus* or *S. rosmarinifolia* spp. *rosmarinifolia*).

Maintenance

A mediterranean garden can be easy to take care of once the hedges have been clipped twice yearly to a tidy, even surface and height. All hedges, whether they grow in a traditional or a modern garden, should be sheared to taper at the top in order to let sufficient light reach the bottom, where you want growth to remain bushy. When a hedge has gone bare at the bottom and is beyond repair, unobtrusive wire netting may be needed to keep out dogs from the street or rabbits from the fields. Older plants that have grown out of control can be gradually taken back, but not all plants will resprout from mature wood (see also Renewing an Urban Garden, page 174).

Frequent shearing will result in dense growth, but it also promotes twiggy growth that turns woody after a few years. Stumps will rot, and the lack of ventilation often fosters health problems, a frequent complaint in old gardens. On the inside, hedges should be kept tidy, since pests and diseases are always looking for confined locations. This aspect of hedge-keeping is labor-intensive, and it can be hazardous where thorny material is involved. You might instead consider taking out every second plant or cutting the plants back to the ground from where most will resprout.

Often recommended for a tall hedge are these small trees: the strawberry tree (*Arbutus unedo*), *Euonymus*, *Myoporum*, tobira (*Pittosporum tobira*), buckthorn (*Rhamnus alaternus*), and laurustinus (*Viburnum tinus*). But you will run into maintenance problems when you try to limit their height to 9 or 10 feet (3m), to which their annual growth will add even more. That additional growth may be enough to block a favorite

These cypresses have been chosen for their even growth in order to avoid labor-intensive pruning.

view, and you will either have to cut the trees back severely every few years or balance yearly on a precarious ladder with your hedge cutter in hand. Clipping tall hedges, especially when they are wide and thorny, is a difficult undertaking and sometimes requires the use of scaffolding. You may get tired of fighting the impenetrable thicket of, for instance, kei apple (*Dovyalis caffra*) and leave it to grow as it wishes until one day you decide to replace it with something more manageable.

To reduce maintenance, visualize carefully the ultimate height and width of the plants you want, especially the strong-growing ones. Match their final size with the location they are meant to fill before you buy. You might prefer, for instance, compact-growing cypresses, even if the initial investment is higher. An informal hedge of, say, New Zealand flax (*Phormium tenax*) or *Grevillea rosmarinifolia* (occasionally pruned rather than clipped) will save the gardener from the yearly maintenance work demanded by a clipped hedge. Over the years, all this may mean considerable savings in time.

Plants for Hedges, Screens, and Boundaries

The plants listed below tolerate clipping, shearing, and pruning, as well as drought and wind. The tall ones work well as a windbreak. The size they will ultimately reach depends on the growing conditions.

Evergreen Edging, Dwarf Hedges up to 3 feet (1m)

Buxus sempervirens, much used in Roman times

Buxus microphylla, finer foliage

Coleonema album, clips into neat shapes

Hebe cupressoides, dense

Hebe diosmifolia, dense

Lavandula angustifolia

Lavandula dentata, for warmest corners

Lavandula stoechas

Lonicera nitida

Myrsine africana, dense and neat, use like box

Myrtus communis, dense and for all sizes

Plumbago auriculata, flowers all summer

Rosmarinus officinalis, choose compact form

Santolina chamaecyparissus

Santolina rosmarinifolia spp. *rosmarinifolia*

Ugni molinae, dense growth

Evergreen Hedge up to 10 feet (3m)

Abelia x *grandiflora*, fountainlike growth

Acacia cultriformis

Acacia longifolia

Arbutus unedo

Buddleja salviifolia, smoky lilac plumes in winter

Callistemon

Choisya ternata, rounded shape

Coprosma repens, open growth

Corokia cotoneaster,

C. x *virgata*, stand clipping

Dodonaea viscosa, suitable for a narrow space

Elaeagnus pungens, impenetrable dense hedge

Escallonia, shearing sacrifices flowering

Euonymus japonicus, best as a screen

Garrya elliptica, a screening shrub for the front line

Grevillea rosmarinifolia

Griselinia littoralis, stands repeated clipping

Hebe odora 'Blue Gem'

Hebe parviflora var. *arborea* stands repeated clipping

Heteromeles arbutifolia, maintain at desired height

Laurus nobilis, slow

Leptospermum laevigatum

Leptospermum scoparium

Ligustrum japonicum replaces the invasive *L. vulgare*

Melaleuca armillaris, fine feathery foliage

Metrosideros excelsa tolerates heavy clipping

Myrtus communis, stands much clipping

Nerium oleander, occasionally cut to the ground

Olea africana, turns into an impenetrable thicket

Olearia lineata 'Dartonii', the fastest

Olearia paniculata, popular New Zealand hedge

Osmanthus fragrans

Pittosporum eugenioides

Pittosporum ralphii

Pittosporum tenuifolium

Pittosporum undulatum

Plagianthus divaricatus, tolerates sea wind and clipping

Portulacaria afra

Prunus ilicifolia

Prunus laurocerasus, reliable

Rhus, all species good as sheared hedges

Teucrium fruticans, impenetrable gray hedge

Viburnum suspensum

Viburnum tinus var. *lucidum*

Westringia fruticosa, shears well

Evergreen Trees, as Tall Screens

Callitris preissii

Calocedrus decurrens, windbreak

Ceratonia siliqua

Chamaecyparis lawsoniana

Cupressus

Juniperus, many different sizes

Lagunaria patersonii

Podocarpus, stands repeated clipping

Populus nigra 'Italica'

Rhamnus alaternus

Schinus molle

Taxus baccata

Thuja orientalis

Thorny Evergreen Shrubs, up to 10 feet (3m)

The species listed below make impenetrable thickets if they get ample space.

Acacia armata, needlelike spines, secure hedge nesting opportunities for small birds

Acacia verticillata, prickly rather than spiny, easily sheared

Berberis, spiny, select tall species

Colletia paradoxa, extremely thorny, slow-growing

Dovyalis caffra, the spiny, edible, but acid Kei apple

Hakea suaveolens, prickly, invasive at the Cape of South Africa

Pyracantha angustifolia, white flowers in spring

Deciduous Spiny Shrubs or Small Trees, up to 15 feet (5m)

Maclura pomifera, the inedible Osage orange or bow wood

Poncirus trifoliate, white blossom, small inedible "oranges"

The Lazy Person's Dream Garden
Labor-Saving Methods

Not everyone wants to—or can—spend a lot of time working in the garden. In this section, I propose a wide range of labor-saving approaches, such as lawn replacements and drought-tolerant plants that spare the gardener the chore of watering. I also offer advice on what a "lazy" gardener can afford to avoid. As a special tip, I have added a list of reliable, undemanding plants for beginners. As with all gardens, careful planning at the outset will give even the Lazy Person's Dream Garden the best chance for success.

While you plan your garden, "borrow" your neighbor's garden for a nice view, and perhaps inspiration.

For more ideas, see :

I might as well say it right at the beginning: A garden that does not involve work does not exist, but some gardens involve less work than others, and it is these I have in mind here. Loving my Mediterranean garden to the point of being besotted, I like the enslavement it imposes on me. It delights me to let warm earth run through my fingers as I mix soils or tie raspberry canes on a sunny winter day. Weeding makes me happy. What I dislike is the work that results from lack of design, planning, or order—in other words, work that goes down the drain, time lost. So, the first step is to prepare a good design for your labor-saving garden. Although the initial investment for a well-designed garden may be greater, over the years it will repay you by its easier management.

STEP 1. Labor-saving gardens are well designed.
Decide early on where you need a path. If you do not want to spend money on surfacing it right away, at least mark out its course. It will be much easier to cart materials around if you have easy access to all areas of the garden. Make small ramps connecting different levels for the wheelbarrow and lawn-mower. Think ahead to all future garden activities, such as potting seedlings or preparing mulch and

compost. When your tools are stored in a suitable location, you will not tire yourself searching for the string or the pruning shears.

If you plan to install irrigation, it is best to do so when starting out. It is easier to find plants that fit the available water than planting first and then trying to match the plants with suitable irrigation. An underground pipe and a few faucets (depending on the size of the garden) obviate the need to carry the watering can or drag a hose everywhere. To save time, especially in larger gardens, it will be worth investing in modern equipment, such as a drip irrigation system with electronic controls. You will be very glad later on to have thought of this in time.

If labor is on your mind as you garden under a mediterranean sun, you will **give the lawn careful consideration**. Lawns are labor-intensive and involve more work than most plantings (mowing, watering, feeding, weeding). You have heard this many times. Part of a lawn can easily be replaced by paving, the so-called hardscapes; these are a typical feature of a mediterranean garden and do not need more than an occasional sweeping. Larger expanses of hardscape will heat up in summer, but a surface exposed to the sun can be partly shaded by one or several litter-free palms or other tall plants.

STEP 2. Labor-saving gardens use the right plants.
Plant selection. The choice of plants is crucial if you want to have a labor-saving garden. When you visit the nursery, choose plants carefully, selecting strong individuals, in bloom if possible to indicate their potential and confirm their color. Reject any plants whose roots have been confined in small pots. And when you get the plants home, prepare well-dug holes with proper soil and appropriate plant food. Consider these suggestions:

• **Quick-growing trees** facilitate dappled shade and promote plant growth. Such shade can be achieved by *Acacia*, southern ironwood (*Casuarina*),

A firm path confines the plants on both sides, which facilitates maintenance.

A yearly cutting-back keeps this billowing mass of *Artemisia arborescens* in shape.

carob (*Ceratonia siliqua*), cypress, fig, silky oak (*Grevillea robusta*), *Jacaranda mimosifolia*, *Myoporum*, pine, the pepper tree (*Schinus molle* or *S. terebinthifolius*), and maintenance-free palms.

• **Evergreen foliage** keeps weeds at bay and shades the ground. Hard-leaved (sclerophyllous) mediterranean natives fill this demand. Often long-flowering, they "furnish" the entire garden, sparing you the laborious task of filling in with annuals. Bear in mind, however, that although litter-free evergreens produce far less debris, their fruits—for example, ripe olives—can stain the paving.

• **Drought-tolerant evergreen or gray mediterranean plants** spare you the chore of watering and thus are one of the principal labor-saving devices.

• **Plants whose size fills the space allotted to them** will enable you to avoid the need for time-consuming corrective pruning and shearing. Remember that although quick-growing plants make speedy headway, they may require labor-intensive cutting back.

• **Neat, clean plants** spare you the tasks of grooming and cleaning up. Palms manage with an annual clean-up, which is best done by a professional. Especially avoid putting plants that litter near pools, driveways, or terraces.

• **Grouped shrubs** replace labor-intensive hedges. Try the evergreen strawberry tree (*Arbutus*), rock roses (*Cistus*), the bridal veil broom (*Retama monosperma*), the attractive pomegranate (*Punica*), and the palmito (*Chamaerops*), or opt for California lilac (*Ceanothus*), honey flower (*Melianthus*), all grevilleas, and kapuka (*Griselinia*).

• **Climbers** should match the site for which they are intended. Self-clinging cat's claw (*Macfadyena unguis-cati*), for example, makes labor-intensive staking unnecessary. Or let jasmine spill over a wall.

• **Bulbous plants** will provide color and do not require much more than an initial planting. After dying down in summer, they are restored by the autumn rains.

• **Undemanding plants** require only scant attention. The so-called common plants, unjustly referred to as "vulgar," are an open secret for labor-saving gardens. Place them carefully, surround them suitably, and give them the little care they need. If well groomed, they will turn into attractive specimens.

• **Container plants** normally require slow, careful watering and are thus labor-intensive. However, if you choose succulents for your containers, they can make attractive arrangements that need little watering. The same is true for sword-leaved and accent plants such as yuccas and phormiums.

Note: For covered areas, such as a terrace adjoining a house, consider modern double-bottomed containers. Their water reservoir does not need replenishing more than three times a year.

An even surface of santolinas is a fine substitute for a lawn in an otherwise rather labor-intensive garden. Design by Charles Shoup.

STEP 3. Labor-saving gardens use fewer species, but in larger quantities.

Another secret to creating a labor-saving garden is to use fewer types of plants but in larger quantities. If a wide range of plants is used, each plant needs specific attention and possibly different tools, which results in labor-intensive maintenance. It is better to use a reduced choice of plants but in larger patches, which means that the plants in each patch will have the same cultural requirements (tools, products, timing).

STEP 4. Labor-saving gardens group their plants by their water needs.

Those that require frequent watering should be located near the house and a tap, where they can all be attended to at the same time. Plants that need weekly water make up a second group. Drought-tolerant plants, the third group, do without watering and can be planted together and further away from the house. If you choose well, these plants can virtually be left to themselves. If you add new plants later on, match them with these groups.

STEP 5. Weeding is easy in well-mulched ground.

Mulching will help you make weeding a great deal easier. Place uprooted weeds under a nearby plant where they can serve as a weed-suppressing mulch, thus avoiding the chore of removing them. Cut weedy patches with a string-mower until the desirable plants have taken over. Many gardeners avoid the need for weeding altogether by covering the ground with a sheet of black plastic with holes cut in to accommodate the plants. Drip irrigation installed beneath the plastic will help keep the plants in humid conditions, although too much water can induce rotting, and black plastic isn't as attractive as a natural mulch. Gravel or a similar material would make a more desirable covering. Com-posted bark looks attractive but is not usually sterilized, so that harmful microorganisms could invade at the plants' roots. There are many mulches to choose from—cocoa shells, cedar bark, almond hulls.

A bed of calla lilies (*Zantedeschia*) takes care of itself.

STEP 6. Initial work well done saves on labor.

Good planning and hard work at the beginning will enable you to enjoy the fruit of your toil later. A well-dug planting hole guarantees a healthy plant, and paying attention to plant needs in a timely manner will prevent troublesome health problems later. Working the other way around seldom gives satisfactory results.

When you are at a nursery, choose plants carefully and select strong ones, iin bloom if possible, which will show their later potential and, of course, confirm their flower color. Reject plants with roots that have been confined in small pots. Quick-drying peat moss as a planting medium is a liability.

As you progress with your labor-saving garden, more labor-saving practices will occur to you. The easiest garden of all is the Imaginary Garden. It has flowers everywhere—printed on cloth, painted on porcelain, inlaid on furniture, engraved on glass. When I had no garden in which to raise flowers, I collected embroidered textiles.

What the Lazy Gardener avoids:

- any plant that may become invasive
- plants that require continuous shearing
- plants that grow too exuberantly and require frequent attention
- a lawn
- a maintenance-requiring water feature

A Selection of Labor-Saving Plants

These plants will come to your rescue whenever you are hard-pressed for a solution. Clean and attractive (when reasonably well kept), they will delight you with flowers, fruits and scent. Use them for their sturdiness, drought tolerance, and ease of maintenance and you will spend your summer in the hammock (occasionally snipping off a few spent flowers). More come to my mind, but this list provides a solid core, the plants I chose for you.

Trees, Shrubs, Palms

Abelia x *grandiflora*
Acacia, most
Arbutus unedo
Artemisia arborescens,
    compact one
Bupleurum fruticosum
Buxus balearica and *Buxus*
    sempervirens, both slow
Callistemon, many
Carissa
Casuarina, invasive

Ceratonia siliqua
Ceanothus
Chamaerops humilis
Cistus, most
Coronilla, all
Cupressus, compact one
Cussonia paniculata
Cussonia spicata
Cytisus, the taller ones
Elaeagnus, most
Eriobotrya japonica
Eriocephalus africanus

Escallonia
Euonymus japonicus
Euryops pectinatus
Fatsia japonica, weekly water
Ficus carica, roots invade
Genista hispanica
Grevillea, all
Griselinia
Heteromeles arbutifolia
Jacaranda mimosifolia
Juniperus, most
Koelreuteria, all
Lagerstroemia indica
Lantana camara
Laurus nobilis
Lavandula, all
Magnolia grandiflora
Melianthus
Myoporum, most
Myrsine africana, suckers
Myrtus communis
Nerium oleander
Olea europaea
Palms
Phlomis fruticosa,
    yearly cutting-back
Phormium tenax
Phylica ericoides
Pinus, use the fine-needled
    litter as an asset
Pittosporum tobira
Pittosporum tobira
    'Compactum'
Pittosporum undulatum
Plumbago
Polygala myrtifolia
Punica granatum
Quercus ilex and other oaks
    that suit your region
Retama monosperma
Rhamnus alaternus
Rosmarinus officinalis

Schinus molle
Schinus terebinthifolius
Tamarix, except the
    invasive *T. aphylla*
Teucrium fruticans,
    requires space
Viburnum tinus, requires
    an open stand
Westringia rosmariniformis
Yucca, all

Climbers

Jasminum, the smaller ones
Macfadyena unguis-cati,
    self-clinging
Tecomaria capensis
Trachelospermum jasminoides

Ground Covers

Agapanthus
Aloe arborea
Argyranthemum frutescens
Clivia miniata
Crassula multicava
Gazania
Iris foetidissima
Iris japonica
Iris unguicularis
Osteospermum
Plectranthus arabicus
Ruscus hypoglossum
Salvia officinalis
Sedum telephium
Tropaeolum majus
Vinca difformis

Gray and green lavender need no care.

The Mini-Garden
A Showcase for Collectors' Items

A great deal can be done in a tiny garden. This section offers numerous suggestions for limited areas, such as a sunlit roof terrace or a wheelchair-friendly small space with raised beds. For collectors, I propose rare plants, as well as the so-called summer-rain bulbs that need water in summer, unlike the mediterranean winter-rain plants. These may well become a botanical enthusiast's new hobby.

Size should never be a criterion for the enchantment a garden space can create, or for the lasting enjoyment it can give the gardener. Much can be done with 1 square yard (1m²) of soil. Some of the most charming gardens I have known were tiny, including one that I used to have. It measured little more than 15 x 15 yards (15 x 15m) and was surrounded by high whitewashed walls. The essence of that garden was that it was a secluded world, enclosed and intimate. A great variety of plants flourished in the warm sun and also provided shade for meals. Scented climbers and large-leaved foliage created a junglelike ambience where white lilies (were they *Lilium longiflorum*?) grew to towering heights.

I also remember a botanist friend's enclosed garden, a small square that housed his prized *Daphne* collection. The sides were as high as a pigeon coop, which is what the enclosure probably was at an earlier time. Raised beds had been made with sandstone slabs to a height that permitted comfortable work and also provided excellent drainage. The side walls accommodated choice mini-climbers, such as scented hoyas. Shaded by a trellislike cover, this tiny garden protected small treasures that would have been lost in an open garden space. Such an arrangement would also permit a disabled person to work in the garden without leaving the wheelchair. The height of the raised bed would have to match that of the chair, and its depth would depend on the mobility of the gardener.

Imagine one of those large roof terraces with whitewashed walls. Palms, such as the canary date palm (*Phoenix canariensis*), planted at ground level, encircle the terrace on all sides. Their long, arching fronds reach onto your terrace and also out into the void. A jasmine climbs up from the ground and, once it has reached your terrace, throws its evergreen weight over the railing. When the jasmine is in flower, the scent is dizzying. This sparse planting lets you take in the view—glimpses of the distant blue sea perhaps—and lets you watch the ever-changing sky. Such a simple arrangement may be all you want. The idea is to plant a few well-chosen trees or palms at ground level and enjoy their evergreen (and flowering?) company throughout the year without having to move another finger.

Or imagine your roof terrace again, preferably facing south or west. To the left, for protection from

For more ideas, see :
- Conservation of Mediterranean-Type Plants, page 25
- A House That Lies Well in Its Land, page 44
- Mediterranean Style, page 74
- The Olive Grove (see bulbs, page 80)
- Refreshing Shade, Delightful Scent, page 110
- Hedges, Screens, and Boundaries, page 180
- The Container Garden, page 198

A table on a balcony can display your cherished possessions.

winter winds, you have put up a wall or a trellis, covered by the evergreen bignonia or bower plant (*Pandorea jasminoides*), which flowers pink or white all through the summer. Such a terrace may be the ideal place to house a valued collection of succulents, for they need little space and most are water-conserving. Their main requirements—a dry bed to rest their heads on and protection from excessive rain or frost—could be met to perfection on the terrace. As a matter of fact, any terrace or balcony has the potential to suit plant collections (rare bulbs, herbs, and more).

There is no end to what can be done with a reduced space. If you have tried it all and are looking for new horizons, there is always enough plant material to keep you busy until the end of your life.

The suggestions in this section focus on plants for the botanical enthusiast, and a container collection on your terrace can hold many treasures. Not all of the plants I enumerate below are widely known, nor do they thrive without care, like so many of the other plants I have proposed to you. Some rarities are difficult to obtain and easy to raise, others easy to obtain and difficult to raise. Some are neither, but apparently no one thought of growing them. With the right soil, the appropriate exposure, and the proverbial green thumb, your chance for success is excellent.

A frame of neat, shiny leaves is the best way to feature your selection of flowering plants. Many unusual plants are particular about water and will not do with a weekly hosing. They abhor summer baking and wind and require a rich, plentiful soil. To succeed, they may involve a bit of research into their heat requirements, and it may also take time to find their particular niche. But when your first giant lily (*Cardiocrinum giganteum*) opens its fragrant flowers, you will know that all your care has been well worth it and that you are on your way. Choose from among these flowering plants:

• The Mexican **Bouvardia longiflora** reaches out with slender arching branches covered by scant leaves and perfectly shaped waxy white stars in terminal clusters. As if that were not enough, its scent is memorable. It favors a warm, protected corner with summer water and should be cut back after flowering.

• **Brunfelsia pauciflora** ultimately grows into a 6-foot (2m) bush, covered with bloom in changing colors (lavender to white). Keep this in a container if your garden does not provide enough warmth and move indoors in winter.

• **Camellia**, often considered difficult, is really for the beginner—if it is grown in acidic soil in a correctly sized pot with morning sun. Failure is more often caused by faulty drainage and untimely transplanting than by overexposure to the sun. Still, the camellia's roots should be kept cool with a thick layer of mulch; just barely cover the root crown, never the stem!

• **Clerodendrum thomsoniae**, the climbing glory bower, and the dainty shrub *C. ugandense* could be excellent additions to a plant collection. Their flowers are delightful. They require rich soil in dappled shade, weekly summer water, and yearly cutting back.

• **Dais cotinifolia**, the South African pompon tree, is difficult to obtain but worth growing for its pink flowers. It requires average soil and weekly water. Trained into a single stem or left to grow as a shrub and planted in dappled shade, it will always reach toward the sun.

What nobody has: the beautiful *Canarina canariensis* grows in laurel woods in Tenerife from a tuberous root. Fruits are edible.

• **Dombeya x cayeuxii** is easy to grow if you can give it South African heat, sufficient shelter from the wind, and twice-weekly summer watering. Your greatest problem may be obtaining the plant, even a cutting. Once you have grown the sweetly scented dombeya from summer rain regions, however, you will never want to be without it.

• **Gardenia jasminoides** is a plant to which I am addicted. I had admired them in a shaded, secret courtyard at the Chèvre d'Or in the south of France, where they were grown in containers and were covered in flowers. The arrangement looked easy—perfection always does—but for years I tried to grow them without success. Gardenias seem to demand shade, although in California I had seen them flourish in hot sun. After heavy losses, I have now found a way to make my last two plants thrive (it may be the application of Osmocote, a well-composed but, alas, expensive plant food, every three months). Our garden is not accustomed to chemicals, but who wouldn't make an exception for the lovely gardenias?

• **Hoya carnosa**, semi-succulent and shade-loving, would suit your Mini-Garden to perfection. It likes rich, well drained soils, mulch, and weekly watering in hottest months. The wax plant's fragrant bloom is worth the trouble you take, especially patience. Consider also the dainty *Hoya bella* for its riveting scent.

Clerodendrum ugandense (Verbenaceae) likes to live in the sun.

• **Lapageria**, an exquisite climber of reduced size, is the Chilean national plant. Look for plants from central Chile, one of the regions with a mediterranean climate. All barberries (*Berberis*) and most fuchsias come from that region.

Evergreen *Brunfelsia pauciflora* is a useful but tender spreading shrub.

• **Spathiphyllum**, the peace lily, is mostly used as a houseplant but can be grown in a warm, frost-free garden in dappled shade. The white spathes, not unlike small callas, stand out against the new apple-green leaves and the older dark foliage. It requires rich soil and summer water.

Dais cotinifolia tolerates hot, dry summers, but its roots should be kept well mulched.

• **Streptocarpus** is widely used as a houseplant but it too can be planted outdoors. It likes a rich, friable soil in shade. Contrary to common belief, streptocarpus is not demanding of water, but it does better with regular watering. Augment your stock by leaf cuttings.

• **Cardiocrinum giganteum** is a giant, long-stalked, and lilylike bulbous herb with glossy leaves. Native from the Himalayas to southwest China, the plant has fragrant white flowers with maroon stripes. Plant in part shade in deep, humus-rich soil that never dries out. You will need patience, but the first bloom will be worth the wait.

• **Cymbidium**, easy to grow and obtain, mostly at reasonable prices. Leave the plant out in the open year round under the shade of an oak tree. Take it indoors, however, if you expect heavy rains, because these will play havoc with the waxlike blooms.

Tip: If you put the cymbidium container on top of a turned-over pot, the plant will not drag its long leaves in the mud.

• **Eucharis grandiflora**, the Amazon lily, is grown in a frost-free region and taken indoors over winter. Its scented, waxy, white bloom is so beautiful that the trouble taken to grow it is worthwhile many times over.

Tip: I grow the Amazon lily in a double-bottomed container in a well-lit room and leave it indoors through the year.

• **Leucocoryne ixioides** from Chile and the Aztec lily (*Sprekelia*) from Mexico both have exquisite blooms and are not difficult to grow.

• **Rare bulbs** are often delightfully scented. Try the spider lily (*Hymenocallis*) from Peru or *Ixiolirion* from

Asia. Both will attract the attention (and envy) of other bulb collectors. For shade, experiment with bulbous plants in the Araceae family, such as *Arisaema*, *Arisarum*, or *Arum pictum*. *Calochortus albus*, native in California, is a drought-tolerant but delicate plant that may be best left to the enthusiast who can shower loving care on it.

• **Summer-rain (SR) bulbs** are not native to the mediterranean climate and will require a different regime, but you may want to experiment with them for the sake of their attractive flowers. They are not more difficult to grow than the mediterranean winter-rain (WR) bulbs we cultivate in all our gardens. However, while gardeners in a mediterranean climate can let nature take care of their mediterranean bulbs, summer-rain bulbs need special attention. This involves watering them in summer (to replace the summer rain of their native regions) and to keep the bulbs dry in winter (to imitate their native dry winters). Summer-rain bulbs also require excellent drainage to prevent root rot. They are planted in spring, when the winter cold is over; preferably in pots so that they can be brought under cover for a simulacrum of a dry winter before the mediterranean winter rains start.

Some SR bulbs, however, will adapt to a summer drought and winter rain. The evergreen *Agapanthus* and *Clivia*, for instance, adapt well to the mediterranean summer-dry climate. *Zantedeschia aethiopica* dies down in summer (as do the WR bulbs) and is a good example for an SR plant that can be grown in a Mediterranean-climate garden without additional attention.

Dietes robinsoniana, of Australian origin, propagates well by seed.

A Few Collectors' Items

Nowadays, the Internet is a perfect tool for locating rare plants. *An asterisk indicates a summer-rain bulb.

Shrubs, Ground Covers
Bouvardia longiflora
Brunfelsia pauciflora
Camellia
Clerodendrum thomsoniae
Clerodendrum ugandense
Dais cotinifolia
Dombeya x cayeuxii
Gardenia jasminoides
Hoya bella
Hoya carnosa
Lapageria rosea
Spathiphyllum
Streptocarpus

Bulbous Plants
*Cardiocrinum giganteum**
Chlidanthus puniceus
*Crinum bulbispermum**
*Crinum campanulatum**
*Crinum moorei**
*Cyrtanthus mackenii**

Dietes bicolor
Dietes grandiflora
*Eucomis autumnalis**
*Eucomis undulata**
*Galtonia candicans**
Gladiolus callianthus
    (formerly *Acidanthera*) *
*Gladiolus dalenii**
*Gloriosa superba**
Haemanthus albiflos
    and other species
*Hymenocallis**
*Hypoxis setosa**
*Littonia modesta**
*Nerine filifolia**
Nerine sarniensis
Scadoxus puniceus
*Schizostylis coccinea**
Sprekelia formosissima
*Veltheimia bracteata**
Veltheimia capensis
*Zantedeschia rehmannii**

Galaxia fugacissima grows from a corm, photographed in the wild in South Africa.

The Container Garden
A Moveable Feast

Containers for balcony, courtyard, patio, or rooftop offer a special opportunity for some creative attention. A common feature throughout the Mediterranean, containers on balconies and terraces overflow with flowers. Terra-cotta pots that have been filled to the brim convey rich mediterranean luxuriance, and they are full of romantic suggestion. In this section I discuss growing plants in containers, offer a selection of containers to choose, and draw special attention to the condition of the soil. A wide range of plants is suited to cultivation in containers; some even prefer crowded container conditions.

For centuries olive oil was transported up and down the Mediterranean Sea in amphoras, urns, and barrels. Water was kept cool in large earthenware jugs. Huge clay jars, called *pithária*, were used to store grain for times of need, like the Minoan jars at Knossos. Amphoras that once held wine are still being raised today from the depths of the sea where ships sank hundreds of years ago. Many ancient containers were decorated with lavish designs and often outdid the plant they were meant to house. In those days, good soil and water were reserved for the orchard and the vegetable garden; the flower garden developed later. But a cherished plant could always be kept in a pot in the courtyard and be given a rare drink. I remember a lovely raised bed on a terrace of the Queluz Palace in Portugal, which was originally intended for rare plants from distant lands This morning I found a smooth, red shard in the dark soil beneath a giant oak tree.

Today containers continue to serve multiple purposes, and they are still prominent where there is no space for a garden, where planting in the ground is limited, or where soil is scarce. On a windowsill, hung on a railing, or framing an entrance door, containers make the most of the smallest areas. They furnish or decorate balconies and terraces and bring gardening to those who do not own a garden. Larger tubs holding a small tree or a bulky shrub can shade an area that heats up under the midday sun and provide a refreshing breeze. On a roof garden, plants in containers bring with them aesthetic and climatic advantages, such as improved winter and summer insulation, not to mention reduced pollution. Near a pool, containers hold the soil and thus keep the surroundings clean. Pots can harbor small plants that would get lost if planted out; they also keep together (for easier surveillance) rare bulbs or cuttings on their way to establishment. Tubs can also confine invasive roots. This works well for mint (*Mentha*), the invasive tree of heaven (*Ailanthus*), or the equally invasive bamboo.

Containers let you cater to a plant's requirements. They suit plants that need conditions different from

For more ideas, see :

- Going Back in Time, page 16
- The Simple Methods Rule, page 47
- The Mediterranean Garden, page 60
- Mediterranean Style, page 74
- The Swimming Pool Garden, page 98
- Refreshing Shade, Delightful Scent, page 110
- The Andalusian Courtyard, page 176
- The Mini-Garden, page 192

Where the outside of a jar is exposed to the sun, water needs should be closely watched

The Container Garden

doubt, keep the new plant in its pot in the spot you have chosen for it for a while before the final planting. The roots will be protected and you'll have a chance to assess the site in advance of planting.

Container Selection

Which containers to choose? Decorative pots, oil jars, wine barrels, and even enormous terra-cotta jugs adorn Mediterranean courtyards, hang on Andalusian walls, and furnish outdoor patios. They reflect the gardener's taste, his or her botanical interest and propagation skills, and economic means. Although there is no limit to your imagination, select a simple design and use it in different sizes. **Containers that bring out the beauty of the plant are often best.** Group pots carefully and avoid dotting them about. Greater harmony often results from taking away rather than adding.

Tip: So that wooden containers won't rot, raise them an inch off the ground.

The size of a container will have an impact on growth performance, so select pots that correspond appropriately to the plant's root volume. Roots should not touch the bottom of the container, but if a container is too large, the nonfunctional roots of a plant that has recently been divided or of a young cutting will be unable to absorb the available humidity and will start to rot, especially in a cold winter. Remember that terra-cotta pots dry out more quickly than plastic ones.

Not many plants like to be pot-bound, but a few qualify, making do with small containers or putting up with very little soil. *Clivia* actually prefers having its roots crowded, although after a while its roots

those your garden offers (for instance, different soil pH). Containers are useful for holding plants that require water in a water-conserving garden. Plants in containers may also be moved into the shade when summer heat is excessive, or indoors when winters are harsh. You can even use intermediary steps in moving plants from one exposure to another.

Tip: It is often difficult to match a plant and its best site. If you are in

■ 199

tend to crack the pot (beware if you have them in valuable containers).

Soil and the Roots

The minute microorganisms that make nutrients available to plants demand as much from the soil in which they live as a plant's root system. Some of the demands are the same, such as well-aerated soil and good drainage, and like plants, microorganisms asphyxiate in caked soil. Plant roots work hard to absorb both water and nutrients, using the energy they derive from taking in oxygen. Oxygen abounds in humid soil, but the warmer soil becomes, the less oxygen it contains. Without oxygen, a plant's ability to "breathe" is impaired and its growth is limited. When a container is exposed to sun, soil life is impaired, humidity loss accelerated, and vital oxygen reduced. If the soil remains cool, the oxygen and moisture will last longer, ensuring better soil life and a slower breakdown of nutrients. **Cool roots induce growth, while hot roots lead to dormancy.** To assist container plants, therefore, it is desirable to add moisture-retaining elements (such as water-absorbing polymers) and to lighten the soil porosity. Also consider the pH factor and remember to provide adequate drainage.

Remember: Mediterranean drought-tolerant plants go dormant when the season, in this case summer, turns unfavorable. They do this not only above but also below ground, which means that their roots go dormant, too. If they are watered throughout the summer and drainage is poor, most of the roots will rot and the plant will die.

To protect roots from overheating, place pots in groups or put several plants together in a large pot. Stuff the spaces between the plants with insulating paper, vermiculite, or gravel. Plants that trail and overhang the pot will shade its sides. In full sun, containers may accommodate succulents and many drought-tolerant plants, such as South African plumbago. On the other hand, most plants from northern regions prefer cool roots. The filtered light under a pergola suits a wide range of climbers, such as clematis, which like cool feet with their heads in the sun.

Nursery-bought plants mostly come in black or red plastic pots, having been grown in quick-drying peat. If you cannot transplant your purchase right away, these plastic pots will heat up in a very short period of time, even over a weekend, sending your treasured acquisition on its way to the compost heap. This is particularly true in summer, when the soil dries out quickly (and in peat moss it will dry in no time at all). Whenever immediate planting is not possible, transfer your plants into larger pots and move them very gradually out into the sun. I had to learn this through bitter experience, and now I rush my plants into the shade, closely grouped, as soon as I get them home.

Colorful containers greet visitors who descend the steps.

Water

Slow, patient watering is what most container-grown plants require. While the soil in the first container absorbs its first dose of water, go on to the next pot and the next. Repeat the process several times until the soil in each pot is evenly moist. Stop before water runs out at the bottom, however! For easier watering, fill the pot with soil to an inch below the rim and top the soil with fine gravel. This will help prevent the soil from caking and also from being washed over the edge.

Dry soil as it shrinks will create a gap at the sides of the pot through which water rushes and comes out at the bottom. This gives the impression that the container has been well watered, but if you knock the plant out of the container, you will see that the opposite is true: the caked soil has absorbed virtually no water and needs to be changed.

The quantity of water needed will depend on such factors as the size and material of the container, the quality and quantity of the soil, the number of plants sharing the container, and, above all, the container's location. More water will be needed in a sunny exposure. In summer, the midday and afternoon sun is particularly stressing, but good ventilation, as on an airy balcony, cools the plant. Your own observation will be your guide.

Keep in mind that **prolonged watering washes out valuable nutrients** and that after a certain time, the soil in a container will need to be changed. Carefully remove some soil and top up the pot with compost and mulch, or re-pot as required. Use a slow-release fertilizer that keeps the plant fed for a certain period of time (not necessary for ferns and succulents).

My tip: Double-bottomed containers, ideal on a covered terrace or indoors, are indispensable for holiday gardeners or lazy ones. Their water is replenished not more than three times a year and the roots draw on it at will, finding water where they ought to look for it, way down. Fertilizers can be given in liquid form in the water.

In this courtyard in southern France, potted pelargoniums are grouped along the stairway.

Maintenance

Container plants must be maintained attentively, but they will repay the attention you give them. Because they need frequent grooming and watering, they tend to be more time-consuming than garden vegetation. If you have only a little time, give preference to undemanding plants that will withstand drought and poor soil. You can achieve excellent results with well-chosen succulents and sword-leaved plants, but give them a year, or sometimes two years, to become well established and to reach their full potential. Plants that tolerate crowded roots need less repotting and thus save on labor.

Clivias do not object to crowded roots.

Plant Selection

Traditional courtyard containers in full sun accommodated lemon, orange, and myrtle; today, we may also enjoy the abundant fruit (and flowering) of pineapple guava (*Acca sellowiana*), kumquat (*Fortuella margarita*), or calamondin (x *Citrofortunella microcarpa*), the latter with hundreds of small acid fruits hanging from a tall, columnar plant. Ask your nursery for advice as to which variety to choose, for the selection is extensive. Most readers are undoubtedly familiar with the wide range of evergreen houseplants that are eligible for a shaded terrace, balcony, or patio.

Tall plants in larger containers will help you shade wide-open spaces, especially paved surfaces, or the so-called hardscapes. Consider using a litter-free cycad and a few palms such as the mediterranean palmito (*Chamaerops humilis*) and the rare

Trachycarpus fortunei, or any *Phoenix*. Evergreen pine with time grows into a sizeable, trouble-free specimen. It takes kindly to judicious pruning or shearing, but when it becomes too large, transplant it into the garden.

Tip: An unused water tank can house very large plants. Before filling it with soil, position the tank an inch above the ground; which will make it easier to move around later. Trailing plants will hide its unsightly exterior and will also keep it cool. Its shallow cover, upside down, will provide a container in which succulents feel at home.

Shade-giving bulk, screens, or space dividers are found among *Abelia floribunda*, *A.* x *grandiflora*, *Ceanothus*, *Cotoneaster* (red berries in winter), *Cytisus*, *Elaeagnus*, *Eriobotrya*, *Euonymus*, *Ilex*, *Metrosideros excelsa*, *Nerium oleander*, *Pittosporum*, *Sophora japonica*, *Styrax officinale*, and many more. Change to increasingly larger pots as the plants grow. Camellia tubs are best smaller and can be left unchanged for years. Appealing branch patterns and spectacular flowers can shade a sunny terrace or break up paved expanses: graceful *Abutilon*, exquisite *Dombeya*, colorful *Hibiscus*, *Lagerstroemia*, *Punica granatum*, and *Sparrmannia*, judiciously shaped, will reach ten feet (2–3m).

For **formal evergreen accents** in beautiful containers, the following small-leaved plants can be

Although spines are a liability near a pool, agaves look wonderful in these containers. (Cut the tips of the spines.)

Where there is no soil for planting, containers provide a comfortable home for drought-tolerant oleanders.

sheared or shaped to great effect: *Acca sellowiana*, *Buxus*, *Citrus*, *Hebe*, *Lonicera nitida*, *Myrsine africana*, *Myrtus*, *Olea europaea*, *Rosmarinus*, *Taxus*, *Teucrium chamaedrys*, *Westringia*, also compact privet (*Ligustrum japonicum* 'Rotundifolium'). These smaller (not screening) plants do well in full sun: *Convolvulus mauritanicus*, *Dimorphotheca*, *Lantana camara* (many colors), *Osteospermum fruticosum*, *Pelargonium hortorum*, *P. peltatum* or scented-leaved species, many *Salvia*; also trailing *Lantana montevidensis*, and *Lotus berthelotii*.

For **prostrate growth**, try the arching, spreading branches of several *Ceanothus* and *Cotoneaster* species, of *Convolvulus cneorum*, and *Juniperus chinensis*, *J. conferta*, and *J. horizontalis*, together with

shiny-leaved *Coprosma repens*.

Most annuals give a quick return. Single-color splashes are preferable to garish color mixes and will instantly brighten up a dull corner. Pansies grouped in a wide, flat cachepot will flower throughout the spring. A low terra-cotta container may hold marigold (*Calendula officinalis*), California poppy (*Eschscholzia californica*), or *Tagetes*, all with bright, long-lasting flowers. Petunias, in a deeper pot, cool their own roots as they spill over the rim.

Shade-loving flowering plants include *Hebe speciosa*, many *Plectranthus* (excellent), *Spathiphyllum*, and *Trachelospermum jasminoides* (scent!). *Bletilla striata* and *Cymbidium*, and, as a matter of fact, many orchids, are container-friendly.

Sculptural *Cordyline*, *Dasylirion*, *Phormium*, and *Yucca* waterwise and sun-loving, add contrast, and look dramatic against an evening sky. They thrive in warm, lean container soil, preferring perfect drainage and a restricted root-run; they also tolerate neglect for weeks at a time. Plan for increasingly large containers as age enhances their beauty. In shade and for a well-defined outline, use striking leaf patterns (evergreen *Alocasia*, *Fatsia japonica* and *Schefflera*) and water in summer.

This large stone trough makes an excellent bed for succulents.

Tip: The invasive roots of yucca require control, which a container will provide. But beware of its formidable thorns. Either place it well away from foot traffic, or cut off the tips, preserving its looks and at the same time protecting passersby.

At midday, a spacious summer terrace requires shade that will provide a gentle breeze. **Climbers** supported on simple structures include *Campsis radicans* and *Macfadyena unguis-cati* or evergreen *Pyrostegia venusta* and *Tecomaria capensis*, all with brilliant orange or yellow flowers and in the Bignoniaceae family. The evergreen *Pandorea jasminoides* hurries up a wall and sports exquisite white bloom. *Solandra* reaches into space with its evergreen shoots; cut it back for a bulky, shiny-leaved mass, but refrain from doing so before flowering. Evergreen, heat-demanding *Jasminum azoricum*, *J. officinale*, and *J. sambac* will cover a wall with scented white bloom. So does *Trachelospermum*; often slow to start, it needs positioning and if pruned heavily performs as a spilling shrub. For rarer climbers, try *Mandevilla*, *Passiflora violacea*, *Sollya heterophylla*, or *Thunbergia*. If you would rather not have to bother too much, rely on *Lonicera* or *Plumbago*. Reduced container space in full sun suits the colorful bougainvillea. *Ampelopsis*, *Cissus*, and *Parthenocissus* favor shade and will cover anything unsightly.

Herbs suit containers to perfection. The narrowest balcony in sun accommodates lemon grass, marjoram, oregano, rosemary, rue, sage, tarragon, and thyme. Group them according to their water needs and devise a decorative display scheme. Most can be clipped into formal shapes. Laurel will eventually grow into an impressive mass that will suit a large container in a wide-open space. Mint requires some water and is best plant-ed separately to confine its runners.

Bulbous plants are easy to grow. Once well established, most fill up larger containers. Low-growing spring bulbs suit window boxes. Where roots heat up at the edge of a container, for instance, use cape bulbs (*Babiana*, *Ferraria crispa*, *Freesia*, *Gladiolus carneus* and *G. tristis*, *Ixia*, *Moraea*, *Sparax*is, and *Tulbaghia simmleri*).

Plants That Grow Well in Containers

Trees, Shrubs, Palms

Abelia floribunda
Abelia x grandiflora
Abutilon, all
Acca sellowiana, fruit
Agonis flexuosa
Alocasia odora, fragrant
Brugmansia, part shade
Buxus, shaped
Camellia
Ceanothus
Chamaecyparis lawsoniana
Chamaerops humilis
Choisya ternata, scent
Citrus, traditional
Coprosma repens
Cotoneaster, many
Cupressus
Cycas
Cytisus
Daphne odora, fragrant
Dombeya, heat
Elaeagnus
Eriobotrya, large, quick
Euonymus, shaped
Fatsia japonica
Ficus carica, fruit
Fortunella, fruit
Griselinia littoralis
Griselinia lucida
Hebe albicans
Hebe propinqua
Hebe speciosa
Hibiscus
Hydrangea, water, shade
Ilex
Juniperus chinensis
Juniperus conferta
Juniperus horizontalis
Lagerstroemia indica
Lantana montevidensis
Laurus nobilis
Lavandula
Libocedrus plumosa
Ligustrum japonicum
Lonicera nitida
Metrosideros excelsa
Myrsine africana
Myrtus
Nerium oleander

Olea europaea
Pittosporum crassifolium
Pittosporum eugenioides
Pittosporum tenuifolium
Prunus laurocerasus, large
Punica granatum, easy
Rosmarinus officinalis
Schefflera
Sophora japonica
Sparrmannia, large, quick
Styrax officinale
Taxus
Thuja occidentalis
Trachycarpus fortunei
Viburnum tinus
Westringia

Sword-leaved Plants

Beschorneria
Cordyline australis
Dasylirion
Furcraea
Phormium tenax
Yucca gloriosa

Succulents

Aeonium
Aloe
Aptenia cordifolia, trailing
Cotyledon
Crassula
Kalanchoe uniflora
Lampranthus spectabilis
Portulacaria afra
Sedum

Annuals, Ground Covers, Herbs

Aloysia triphylla
Calendula
Convolvulus cneorum
Convolvulus mauritanicus
Cymbopogon citratus
Dimorphotheca
Eschscholzia californica
Lotus berthelotii, trailing
Mentha
Origanum
Osteospermum fruticosum
Pelargonium, scented-leaved

Petunia
Plectranthus, shade
Ruta graveolens
Salvia officinalis
Santolina chamaecyparissus
Spathiphyllum, shade
Tagetes
Thymus
Verbena

Bulbous Plants

Agapanthus
Amaryllis belladonna
Babiana, many
Bletilla striata
Canna indica
Clivia, evergreen
Crinum moorei
Cyclamen, many
Cymbidium, orchid
Cyrtanthus elatus
Cyrtanthus mackenii
Ferraria crispa
Freesia
Gladiolus
Haemanthus albiflos
Haemanthus coccineus
Hippeastrum, slug-prone
Hedychium
Ixia
Kniphofia
Lilium regale and others
Moraea
Nerine sarniensis
Scadoxus puniceus
Sparaxis
Sternbergia
Strelitzia reginae
Tritonia crocata
Tulbaghia simmleri
Veltheimia bracteata
Zantedeschia aethiopica
Zantedeschia elliottiana
Zantedeschia rehmannii
Zephyranthes

Climbers

Ampelopsis
Antigonon leptopus, heat
Bougainvillea

Campsis radicans, deciduous
Cissus, for shade, cut back
Clematis paniculata
Ficus pumila, wallcover
Hedera
Hoya carnosa, twining
Jasminum azoricum
Jasminum officinale
Jasminum sambac, heat
Macfadyena, warm wall
Pandorea jasminoides
Parthenocissus
Passiflora, many
Pelargonium peltatum
Plumbago
Polygonum, deciduous
Pyrostegia venusta, heat
Solandra, warm wall
Solanum jasminoides
Solanum wendlandii, heat
Sollya heterophylla
Tecoma capensis
Thunbergia, windshelter
Trachelospermum, shelter

Plants That Tolerate Crowded Roots

Many succulents can be added to this list.

Agapanthus
Aloe
Clivia, prefers crowded roots
Haemanthus
Hippeastrum
Kniphofia
Nerine
Palms
Pelargonium
Scadoxus
Sternbergia
Yucca

Glossary

acid soil Soil with a pH factor in solution of less than 7

alkaline soil Soil with a pH factor in solution of more than 7

annual An annual plant completes its life cycle in one growing season.

bulbous plants Herbaceous perennials that have swollen food-storage organs at or below ground level. The technically correct categories are: bulb, which stores food in scales; corm, a thickened underground stem with food stored in the center, from which it produces a whole plant each year (*Gladiolus* and *Crocus*); rhizome, a creeping stem above or just below ground in which food is stored (*Iris germanica*); tuber a thickened, fleshy underground stem that does not extend as rhizomes do (potato); tuberous root, a thickened, food-storing root (not stem).

chlorophyll Green pigment of plant cells that is the receptor of light energy in photosynthesis

chlorosis Reduced development of chlorophyll

corm See bulbous plants.

deciduous Plants that shed their leaves yearly (summer- or winter-deciduous)

drainage The passage of water and air through the soil. Sandy soils with larger granules let water drain through quickly, when it is replaced by air, which is vital for roots. Heavy clay soils with small granules allow water to drain away much more slowly.

drip line A plant's outer perimeter, usually indicating the horizontal extent of its roots

ecology The study of relationships between living things and the environment

endemic Referring to plant or animal species confined to a certain region

evaporation Loss of water from the soil

evergreen An evergreen plant seems to keep its leaves year round, but it actually sheds some of them at a time (though never all at once) while new leaves grow.

garrigue A type of landscape found in the Mediterranean Basin consisting of low, evergreen, man-modified, fire-prone scrubland, with an herbal undergrowth and occasional flowering bulbs. Usually somewhat more deteriorated than *maquis*, *garrigue* is useful ony as pasture, particularly for goats, and for beekeeping.

geophyte Any plant that copes with summer drought by shedding its aboveground body and survives by its underground storage organs (bulb, corm, rhizome, tuber)

glabrous Smooth, hairless

glaucous Coated with a fine bloom, whitish, blue-green, or gray, easily rubbed off

halophyte A plant tolerant of or adapted to saline soils

herbaceous plants Plants that die down to the ground annually to grow again the following season

humus A decomposing, water-retentive, dark-brown, organic matter in the soil, an ideal medium for an active soil life and congenial to roots

life cycle The development and dying down of plants, occurring at fixed seasons

maquis Shrubby, mostly evergreen vegetation found in coastal regions of the Mediterranean

mycorrhiza A symbiotic association between certain fungi and plant roots

organic matter Material that derives from a once-living organism

perennial plants Plants that live for more than two years (biennials are two-season plants)

pH A factor that indicates the concentration of hydrogen ions in a (soil) solution. Below 7 is acidic, 7 is neutral, and above 7 is alkaline.

photosynthesis The conversion of carbon dioxide and water into carbohydrates, taking energy from light (helped by chlorophyll)

rhizome See bulbous plants

sclerophyllous Hard-leaved

soil life See H. Gildemeister, *Mediterranean Gardening* (1995), chapter 1, The Soil

stolon Stem that creeps along the ground, taking root at intervals and forming new plants

stoma, stomata (pl) Minute openings mostly on the underside of leaves

stratification A process by which seeds are exposed for a certain time to cold (to simulate a cold winter period) so that the ensuing warm period will induce seeds to germinate

stress Any situation that goes against a plant's growing needs

sucker A growth that arises from the plant's roots, sometimes distant from the mother plant, and that with time will develop into an identical plant. Severed from the root with sufficient fine roots, it will continue to grow.

summer dormancy One of the survival strategies by which plants cope with long, hot, and dry summers

taproot A primary root that grows straight down into the ground from the embryonic root

tender Refers to a plant that is sensitive to frost, as opposed to hardy

transpiration Loss of water vapor through the pores (stomata) on the leaves of plants

tuber See bulbous plants

Addresses

The following list, arranged by continent and country, offers first the names of public gardens that are of interest to mediterranean-climate gardeners and then addresses for suppliers of plants or seeds. Note that importing plants or plant materials may require a phytosanitary certificate. Every effort has been made to ensure that factual details were accurate at the time this book went to press. Also listed are a few periodicals or associations that publish useful newsletters or bulletins.

The Mediterranean Garden Society is an international group with branches in thirty-seven countries. Visit the web site for information. The site *http:/MediterraneanGardenSociety.org/* also has a chat room, where gardeners from all mediterranean-climate regions discuss plants. To participate with this group and to avoid spam, register at no cost, simply giving your name.

EUROPE

England

The Good Gardens Guide
(ISBN 0-09-185246-3)
1,000 of the best gardens in the British Isles and Europe

Royal Horticultural Society (RHS)
80 Vincent Square, London, SW1P 2PE.
www.rhs.org.uk, advisory@rhs.org.uk
Members receive a monthly journal, *The Garden*; an annual seed list, and free entry to the RHS Gardens Wisley, Surrey. Visit the plant sale, the largest botanical bookstore in Europe, and the Mediterranean Bank.

The Royal Botanic Gardens Kew
Richmond, Surrey TW9 3AB
Visit the Mediterranean area.

Beth Chatto
White Barn House, Elmstead Market,
Colchester CO7 7DB
She sells mediterranean plants.

Henry Doubleday Research Association
Ryton Gardens, Ryton-on-Dunsmore,
Coventry CV8 3LG
tel +44 203 303517
Organic gardening advice,
also a branch in Australia.

RHS Plant Finder (ISBN 0-7513-3705-6)
Where to buy 70,000 plants online
www.rhs.org.uk/

Thompson & Morgan Seeds
London Rd., Ipswich IP2 0BA

France

Clos du Peyronnet (William Waterfield)
Avenue Aristide Briand, 06500 Menton
tel +33 4 93 35 72 15

Foire du Château de Bellecoste
(spring fair)
Caissargues, 30230 Bouillargues (between Arles and Nîmes)

Jardin Exotique de Monaco (succulents)

Jardin des Plantes (Botanic Garden)
163, rue Auguste Broussonnet,
Montpellier

Jardin de Provence
BP 9, Route d'Avignon
13210 Saint-Rémy-de-Provence

Jardin Villa Thuret (Botanic Garden)
Chemin G. Raymond, Antibes

Journées des Plantes de Courson
Courson-Monteloup, 91680
Bruyères-le-Châtel
coursondom@aol.com; www.courson-dom.com
Visit May and October.

Bonaut Elie
566, chemin des Maures, 06600
Antibes
Rare Mediterranean climate plants

B & T World Seeds
Paguignan, 34210 Olonzac
www.b-and-t-world-seeds.com

Addresses

Bulb Argence (species)
Mas d'Argence, 30300 Fourques
tel +33 466 01 65 19
www.bulbargence.com

Pépinières de Kerisnel
29250 Saint-Pol-de-Léon

Pépinières La Mayrale
Route de Marcorignan, 11100 Narbonne
Wide plant choice

Pépinière Jean Rey
Route de Carpentras, 84150 Jonquières

Villa Val Rahmeh
Avenue Saint-Jacques,
Menton-Garavan

Germany

Insel Mainau, Bodensee
Mediterranean vegetation in summer

Flora Mediterranea
Königsgütler 5, D-84072 Au/Hallertau
www.floramediterranea.de

Horst Gewiehs
P.O. Box 1270, 2720
Rotenburg/Wuemme
Bulbs

Greece

Kaisariani Forest
Near Athens
Visit the eleventh-century monastery.

Sparoza
Box 14, Peania, 19002 Greece
Seat of the Mediterranean Garden
Society, a not-for-profit association,
which acts as a forum for everyone
with a special interest in the plants
and gardens of the mediterranean-
climate regions of the world. It
organizes garden tours for members;
contact the MGS secretary at the
above address.

Italy

Giardini in fiera, Villa Le Corti
San Casciano in Val di Pesa, Firenze
lecorti@ftbcc.it
www.principecorsini.com
Visit the plant fair.

Hanbury Gardens
La Mortola, 18030 Latte

Istituto Botanico
Via Lincoln 2, 90133 Palermo

La Landriana Plant Fair, near Rome
Via Campo de Carne 51,
00040 Tor San Lorenzo Ardea
tel +39 06 910 14140

Orto Botanico
35123 Padua (founded 1545)

Il Cercapiante (Plant Finder for Italy)
(ISBN 88-374-1366-1)
Order via tel +39 02 43 31 33 67
or gardenia@edgm.it

Patrucco
Via Privata delle Rose 1,
18010 Diano S. Pietro
Roses for Mediterranean gardens

Spain

Alcazar, Seville
Moorish gardens

Cap Roig Garden
Calella de Palafrugell, Costa Brava

Generalife Gardens, Granada
Moorish gardens on the grounds of
the Alhambra

Jardines de Mar y Murta, Blanes
Costa Brava

Parque de Ruben Dario, Barcelona
A garden above the port

Real Jardin Botanico, Madrid
(founded 1755)

Adena Forestal
Calle Sol 7, 02270 Villamalea/Albacete
Native trees for reforestation

Viveros Orero
Apartado 9, Segorbe/Castellón
Fruit trees

Viveros Vallgorguina
Carretera de San Celoni a Arenys,
near Barcelona

Switzerland

Isola di Brissago Botanic Garden
Ticino, Switzerland
Mediterranean plants

AUSTRALIA

Australia and New Zealand
(mediterranean regions)

Australian Plant Society (APS)
South Australia Region Inc.
P.O. Box 304, Unley S.A. 5061
www.iweb.net.au/aps

Australian Plant Society, Victoria Inc.
P.O. Box 357, Hawthorn, Vic. 3122
www.vicnet.net.au/

Burrendong Arboretum,
near Wellington, NZ

King's Park and Botanic Garden
West Perth WA 6005
tel 618 94 80 36 05
www.kpbg.wa.gov.au

The National Botanic Gardens,
Canberra
Features the plant world of the
Australian heathland.

Waite Arboretum,
University of Adelaide
Glen Osmond, SA 5065
tel/fax +61 8 83 03 74 05

Wildflower Society of
Western Australia Inc.
P.O. Box 64, Nedlands, 6009, WA
Sells seed together with "Hints on
Growing Native Plants."

The Digger's Club Heronswood
105 La Trobe Parade, Dromana Vic 3936
tel 03 59 87 18 77
www.diggers.com.au
Plants and seed by mail order

St. Kilda Indigenous Nursery
525 Williamstown Road,
Port Melbourne
Coastal plants in tubes

Nindethana Seed Service
939 Woogenilup, 6324, WA
Native trees, shrubs, books

Republic of South Africa (mediterranean-climate region)

Kirstenbosch National Botanical Garden (South African native plants)
Rhodes Drive, Newlands
Private Bag X7, Claremont, RSA
Tel: +27 21 799 88 99
www.kirstenbosch.co.za
Wander for hours through expertly landscaped gardens; members receive quarterly *Veld & Flora* and annual seed list.

African Bulbs
P.O. Box 26, Napier 7270,
Western Cape, RSA
tel +27 28 423 36 51
africanbulbs@haznet.co.za

Cape Seed & Bulbs
PO Box 6363, Uniedal 7612, RSA

The Indigenous Bulb Association of South Africa
PO Box 12265, N1 City 7463, RSA
Members receive annual seed list, newsletter.

Rust-en-Vrede Nursery
PO Box 231, Constantia 7848, RSA
indigenous bulbous plants, seed

Silverhill Seeds & Books
P.O. Box 53108, Kenilworth 7745 RSA
tel +27 21 762 42 45
www.silverhillseeds.co.za

Simply Indigenous Nursery
Box 292, Skeerpoort 0232, RSA
tel +27 12 207 10 77
leigh@simplyindigenous.co.za
Export, mail order

NORTH AMERICA

United States of America (California mediterranean-climate region)

Look for the symposium "Gardening Under Mediterranean Skies," which takes place every other year in September/October. It is organized by the Strybing Arboretum (County Fair Building) in San Francisco, the Los Angeles Botanical Garden, and *Pacific Horticulture*, together with the Mediterranean Garden Society. For information, visit www.pacifichorticulture.org.

Huntington Botanical Gardens
1151 Oxford Road, San Marino, CA 91108
tel. 626 405 2100
www.huntington.org

Leaning Pine Arboretum,
Environmental Horticulture Science
California Polytechnic Institute
San Luis Obispo, CA

Los Angeles Botanical Garden
301 N. Baldwin Ave., Los Angeles, CA
tel 626 821 3222

Rancho Santa Ana Botanic Garden
1500 North College Avenue,
Claremont CA 91711
tel 909 625 8767
Native plants

Regional Parks Botanic Garden
Tilden Regional Park, Berkeley, CA 94708-2396
Native plants

Santa Barbara Botanic Garden
1212 Mission Canyon Road,
Santa Barbara, CA 93105
tel 805 563 2521
Native plants, bookshop

Strybing Arboretum and
Botanical Gardens
Ninth Avenue at Lincoln Way,
San Francisco, CA 94122
tel 415 564 3239
www.strybing.org
Native plants

Theodore Payne Foundation
for Native Plants
10459 Tuxford St., Sun Valley, CA 91352
tel 818 768 1802
www.theodorepayne.org
Publishes a newsletter, *The Poppy Print*

International Bulb Society
P.O. Box 336
Sanger, CA 93657-0336
amaryllis@bulbnrose.com

Native Sons Nursery
379 West El Campo Road,
Arroyo Grande, neat Pismo Beach, CA
tel 805 481 5996
www.nativeson.com

San Marcos Growers
Santa Barbara, CA
www.smgrowers.com
Plants from around the world

Yerba Buena Nursery
19500 Skyline Blvd.,
Woodside, CA 94062

California Horticultural Society
California Academy of Sciences
Golden Gate Park,
San Francisco, CA 94118
Publishes a bulletin.

The Gardener's Companion
(Southern California)
PO Box 3549, Van Nuys, CA 91407-3549
tel 818 780 5072
thegardeners@earthlink.net

Pacific Horticulture (quarterly)
P.O. Box 485, Berkeley, CA 94701

Southern California
Horticultural Society
P.O. Box 41080, Los Angeles, CA 90041-0080
tel 818 567 1496

Bibliography

Books on Waterwise Gardening

CHATTO, B. (1988) reprint
The Dry Garden
London: Dent

DUFFIELD, M.R., AND JONES, W.D. (1981)
Plants for Dry Climate
Tucson, AZ: HP Books

ELLEFSON, C., et al. (1992)
Xeriscape Gardening: Water Conservation for the American Landscape
New York/London: Macmillan

GILDEMEISTER, H. (1995)
Mediterranean Gardening, A Waterwise Approach
Palma de Mallorca: Editorial Moll/Los Angeles, CA: University of California Press (2002)

JOHNSON, E., et al. (1993)
The Low-Water Flower Gardener
Tucson, AZ: Millard Publishing

PERRY, B. (1992)
Landscape Plants for Western Regions: An illustrated guide to plants for water conservation
Claremont, CA: Land Design Publishing

PERRY, B. (1989 reprint)
Trees and Shrubs for Dry California Landscapes
Claremont, CA: Land Design Publishing

RAINES WARD, D. (2002)
Water Wars: Drought, Flood, Folly, and the Politics of Thirst
New York: Riverhead Books

SUNSET, eds. (1989)
Waterwise Gardening.
Menlo Park, CA: Lane Publishing

Mediterranean-Climate Flora

BECKETT, E. (1993)
Illustrated Flora of Mallorca
Palma de Mallorca: Editorial Moll

BLAMEY, M., AND GREY-WILSON, C. (1993)
Mediterranean Wild Flowers
London: Harper Collins

BRICKELL, C., ed. (2002, revised ed.)
The RHS New Encyclopedia of Plants and Flowers
London: Dorling Kindersley

CHALK, D. (1988)
Hebes and Parahebes
London: Christopher Helm

HUXLEY, A., AND TAYLOR, W. (1984)
Flowers of Greece and the Aegean
London: Chatto and Windus

INNES, C. (1985)
The World of Iridaceae
Ashington, UK: Holly Gate International

JOHNSON, H. (1973)
The International Book of Trees
London: Mitchell Beazley

LENZ, L. & DOURLEY, J. (1981)
California Native Trees & Shrubs
Claremont, CA: Rancho Santa Ana Botanical Garden

LOPEZ GONZALEZ, G. (1982)
La Guia de INCAFO de los Arboles y Arbustos de la Peninsula Ibérica
Madrid: Incafo

MULLER, K. (1974)
Trees of Santa Barbara
Santa Barbara, CA: Santa Barbara Botanic Garden

MUNZ, P.A. (1974)
A Flora of Southern California
Berkeley, CA: University of California Press

NOAILLES, V. DE & LANCASTER, R. (1977)
Plantes des Jardins Mediterranéens
Antony : Editions Floraisse

PHILLIPS, R, AND RIX, M. (2002)
The Botanical Garden: Trees & Shrubs, vol. 1;
Perennials & Annuals, vol 2
London/Macmillan/Toronto, ON: Firefly Books

POLUNIN, O., AND HUXLEY, A. (1972)
Flowers of the Mediterranean
London: Chatto and Windus

RIKLI, M. (1943)
Das Pflanzenkleid der Mittelmeerlaender
Berne: Verlag Hans Huber

SCHOENFELDER, I. AND P. (1984)
Wild Flowers of the Mediterranean
London: Collins

STEARN, W., AND DAVIS, P. (1984)
Peonies of Greece
Kifissis, Greece: Goulandris Natural History Museum

STRID, A. (1980)
Wild Flowers of Mount Olympus
Kifissis, Green: Goulandris Natural History Museum

VANDERPLANK, J. (1991)
Passion Flowers
London: Cassell

Northern Hemisphere
BAUMAN, H., et al. (1993)
Greek Wildflowers and Plant Lore in Ancient Greece
London: Herbert Press

CORRECHER, C. (1993)
The Gardens of Spain
New York: Abrams

DALLMAN, P. (1998)
Plant Life in the World's Mediterranean Climates
Oxford: Oxford University Press; Berkeley, CA: University
of California Press

HUXLEY, A , ed. (1992)
The New RHS Dictionary of Gardening
London: Macmillan

JONES, L. (1992)
Gardens in Provence
Paris: Flammarion

LATYMER, H. (1990)
The Mediterranean Gardener
London: Windward

MATVEJEVIC, P. (1999)
Mediterranean, A Cultural Landscape
Berkeley, CA/London: University of California Press

NOTTLE, T. (1996)
Gardens of the Sun
Portland, OR: Timber Press

ORIGO, B., et al (2001)
La Foce: A Garden and Landscape in Tuscany
Philadelphia, PA: University of Pennsylvania Press

QUEST-RITSON, C. (1992)
The English Garden Abroad
New York/London: Viking

RACINE, M., BOURSIER, E., AND BINET, F. (1987)
Jardins de Provence, Jardins de la Cote d'Azur
Aix-en-Provence

SMITHEN, J. (2002)
Sun-drenched Gardens
New York: Abrams

SUNSET, eds. (1988)
New Western Garden Book.
Menlo Park, CA: Lane Publishing

TYRWHITT, M. (1998)
Making a Garden on a Greek Hillside
Evis, Greece: Denise Harvey

Bibliography

WALTON, S.
La Mortella: An Italian Garden Paradise
London: New Holland Publishers

WATERS, G., AND HARLOW, N. (1990)
The Pacific Horticulture Book of Western Gardening.
Boston, MA: David Godine

WELSH, P. (2000)
Southern California Gardening
San Francisco: Chronicle Books

Southern Hemisphere
CAVE, Y., AND PADDISON, V.
New Zealand Native Plants
Auckland, NZ: Godwit Publishing

COATES PALGRAVE, K. (2002, revised ed.)
Trees of Southern Africa
Cape Town, RSA: Struik

CROSBY, D. (1996)
Bush Plants for Perth Gardens
National Trust for Australia (WA)

GLEN, H. (2002)
Cultivated Plants of Southern Africa
Jacana, RSA: High Branching & National Botanical
Institute

GRACE, J., ed. (1983)
Climbers and Trailers
Wellington, NZ: Reed

GRACE, J., ed. (1984)
Handbook of Trees and Shrubs (Southern Hemisphere)
Wellington, NZ: Reed

HOFFMANN, A. (1979)
Flora Silvestre de Chile, Zona Central
Santiago, CH: Ediciones Fundación Claudio Gay

JEPPE, B. (1989)
Spring and Winter Flowering Bulbs of the Cape
Cape Town, RSA: Oxford University Press

JOFFE, P. (2002)
Creative Gardening with Indigenous Plants
Pretoria, RSA: Briza Publications

LORD, E., AND WILLIS, J. (1984)
Shrubs and Trees for Australian Gardens
Melbourne: Lothian

MANNING, J. ,et al. (2002)
The Colour Encyclopedia of Cape Bulbs
Portland, OR: Timber Press

MARCHANT, N.G., et al. (1987)
Flora of the Perth Region
Western Australian Herbarium, Dept. of Agriculture

PIENAAR, K. (1999)
Gardening with Indigenous Plants
Cape Town: Struik

PLESSIS, N. DU, AND DUNCAN G. (1989)
Bulbous Plants of Southern Africa
Cape Town: Tafelberg

SALMON, J.T. (1982 reprint)
New Zealand Flowers and Plants
Wellington, NZ: Reed

SNAPE, D. (2002)
The Australian Garden
Melbourne: Bloomings Books

General Books
BERRY, S. (2002)
Container Topiary
San Diego, CA: Laurel Glen; London: New Holland

BRADLEY, S. AND V. (2002)
Fragrant Gardening
San Diego, CA: Laurel Glen; London: Murdoch Books

CAPE PROVINCIAL ADMINISTRATION (1985)
Plant Invaders, Beautiful but Dangerous
Cape Town, RSA: Cape Provincial Administration

CAPON, B. (1994)
Plant Survival
Portland, OR: Timber Press

CASTRI DI, F. (1981)
Ecosystems of the World, vol. 11,
Mediterranean Type Shrublands
Amsterdam: Elsevier

COLES, C. (1997)
Gardens and Deer, a Guide to Damage Limitation
Shropshire, UK: Quiller Publishing

DAVID, P. AND BEARDSHAW, C. (2002)
Hidden Gardens
London: Cassell Illustrated

DAVIS, S. et al. (1986)
Plants in Danger, What Do We Know?
Gland, Chile: International Union for Conservation

EMERY, D. (1988)
Seed Propagation of Native California Plants
Santa Barbara, CA: Santa Barbara Botanic Garden

FARRAR, L. (1998)
Ancient Roman Gardens
Phoenix Mill, Gloucestershire, UK: Sutton Publishing

GOMEZ-CAMPO, C., ed. (1985)
Geobotany 7, Plant Conservation in the Mediterranean Area
Dordrecht: Dr. W. Junk Publishers

GROVES, R., AND DI CASTRI, F., eds. (1991)
Biogeography of Mediterranean Invasions
Cambridge/NY/Melbourne: Cambridge University Press

HARDESTY, N. (1984)
Oak Woodland Preservation and Land Planning
Palo Alto, CA: Hardesty Associates

HOBHOUSE, P. (1989)
Garden Lovers' Guide to Italy
Princeton, NJ: Princeton Architectural Press

IUCN (1986)
Plants in Danger; What Do We Know?
Gland, Switzerland: IUCN

KEATOR, G. (1998)
The Life of an Oak
Berkeley, CA: Heyday Books

KHANSARI, M., et al. (1998)
The Persian Garden, Echoes of Paradise
Washington, DC: Mage Publishers

KING, P., ed.
The Good Gardens Guide 2004
London: Frances Lincoln

LARNER, J. (1999)
Gardening with a Wild Heart, Restoring California's Native Landscapes at Home
Berkeley, CA: University of California Press

OGREN, T. (2000)
Allergy-free Gardening
Berkeley, CA: Ten Speed Press

OVERY, A. (1997)
Sex in Your Garden
Golden, CO: Fulcrum Pub

RAVEN, P. (1986 reprint)
Biology of Plants
New York: Worth Publishers

READMAN, J. (1991)
Soil Care and Management and Weeds: How to Control and Love Them
Tunbridge Wells: HDRA/Search Press

SEALE, A. (1999)
New Life for Old Gardens
London: New Holland; New York: Sterling (paperback)

STURTEVANT, E. (1919)
ed. by U. Hedrick
Sturtevant's Edible Plants of the World
New York: Dover Publications
London: Constable & Co.

TODD, K. (2001)
Tinkering with Eden: A Natural History of Exotic Species in America
New York: W. W. Norton

WYK, B. VAN, et al. (2002)
Poisonous Plants of South Africa
Pretoria: Briza Publications

Index

Page numbers in *italic* refer to illustrations, roman type to references in the text.

Index

Index

Index

Index

TEMPERATURE CONVERSION

$$°C = 5/9 \, (°F − 32) \qquad °F = 9/5 \, (°C + 32)$$

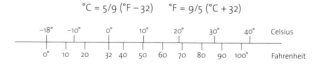

MEASUREMENT CONVERSION

1 cm = 0.39 in.   100 cm = 1 m   1 in. = 2.54 cm   1 ft = 30.5 cm

Acknowledgments

My gratitude goes to the owners of all gardens where I could photograph in peace, exploring the spirit of the place, and to garden friends who sent slides from their regions. South Africa: Liesl v.d. Walt p. 5, 91, Ernst van Jaarsveld p. 92 top and J. Loedolff p. 25. Australia: Daniel Burke p. 94-96, Tim North p. 37. California: David Fross p. 28. The Mediterranean Basin: Louisa Jones p. 4, 80, 124, 139, 148, 156, Eduardo Mencos p. 107, Evan Parker p. 62 and Helen Schreiner p 147. Charles Mann photographed p. 80 top, 83, 85, 86, 98, 129. Much admiration goes to Charles Shoup whose garden in southern Greece shows many elements inherent in a mediterranean garden, and to Thalia Fani who sent photographs taken there: p. 6, 16, 52, 58, 59, 112, 142, 143, 189. Much gratitude goes to the garden help and to the garden itself that was, and still is, my teacher.

My gratitude goes to Caroline Harbouri for her initial linguistic advice, to Derrick Donnison-Morgan for his suggestions on plant life, and to Cyrus Farmanfarmaïan for having checked text on Persian gardens. I am grateful to Anne Serroy, Isabelle Parent, and their *équipe* at La Martinière who, faced with a tight deadline, carried out the French translation and the shaping of this book, and to Barbara Burn, who saw to the original English text with unfailing good humor.

My husband's encouragement contributed clearly to making this book possible—to him I dedicate it.

First published in the United Kingdom in 2004 by
Thames & Hudson Ltd,
181A High Holborn,
London WC1V 7QX

www.thamesandhudson.com

Original Edition © 2004 Aubanel, Geneva
Text and photographs © 2004 Heidi Gildemeister

Design: Anne-Danielle Naname

British Library Cataloguing-in-Publication Data
A catalogue record for this book is available from the British Library

ISBN 0-500-511837

Printed and bound in Italy